THE ROAD TO MONETARY UNION
IN EUROPE

THE ROAD TO MONETARY UNION IN EUROPE

The Emperor, the Kings, and the Genies

TOMMASO PADOA-SCHIOPPA

CLARENDON PRESS · OXFORD

1994

Oxford University Press, Walton Street, Oxford OX2 6DP

Oxford New York
Athens Auckland Bangkok Bombay
Calcutta Cape Town Dar es Salaam Delhi
Florence Hong Kong Istanbul Karachi
Kuala Lumpur Madras Madrid Melbourne
Mexico City Nairobi Paris Singapore
Taipei Tokyo Toronto
and associated companies in
Berlin Ibadan

Oxford is a trade mark of Oxford University Press

Published in the United States
by Oxford University Press Inc., New York

British Library Cataloguing in Publication Data
Data available
ISBN 0-19-828843-3

Library of Congress Cataloging in Publication Data
Padoa-Schioppa, Tommaso.
The road to monetary union in Europe : the emperor, the kings, and
the genies / Tommaso Padoa-Schioppa.
p. cm.
Includes bibliographical references and index.
1. Monetary policy—European Economic Community countries.
2. European Monetary System (Organization) I. Title.
HG930.5.P34 1994 332.4′566′094—dc20 94–1878
ISBN 0-19-828843-3

1 3 5 7 9 10 8 6 4 2

Set by Hope Services (Abingdon) Ltd.
Printed in Great Britain by
Bookcraft (Bath) Ltd
Midsomer Norton, Avon

ACKNOWLEDGEMENTS

The ideas expressed in these writings were developed in continuous dialogue with many friends, colleagues, and companions of different nationalities, professions, and backgrounds who shared, often without knowing one another personally, convictions and hopes that I recognized as my own. The exchange of views and values that I enjoyed with them was full and disinterested, its sole aim being to further the common search for ways to improve both monetary arrangements and European relations. Without naming them individually, I wish to offer heartfelt thanks to each one of them for the priceless intellectual and moral benefits that I have received.

The bibliographic note at the end of the volume gives the original titles and places of publication of the writings that appear in this collection. Some minor changes were made in the original texts, with ceremonial phrases addressed to the audiences deleted, a number of repetitions eliminated and the terminology made uniform. A few notes to the texts provide the reader with supplementary information or bring the discussion up to date.

A largely similar collection of writings was published in 1992 in Italy by Giulio Einaudi Editore. I am grateful to the Italian publisher for assistance in the preparation of that collection and for waiving all its rights. For their assistance in preparing some of the writings, I am indebted to Lorenzo Bini Smaghi (Chapters 4, 8, and 10), Giampaolo Galli (Chapter 9), Wolfgang Gebauer (Chapter 3), Francesco Papadia, Fabrizio Saccomanni, and Alfred Steinherr (Chapter 1). In selecting the texts for inclusion and in editing the book, Maria Teresa Pandolfi and Francesco Papadia gave me valuable advice. Valeria Sannucci provided thoughtful and attentive co-operation throughout, from the choice of texts to the final revision, and prepared the index. Silvia Vori helped to draw up the chronology. John Smith used his computer-aided indexing program to compile the index, translated chapters from the original Italian version, improved my limping English, and contributed to editing the book. He and Maria Grazia Ciorra worked on the manuscript with care and patience. To all of them I express my gratitude.

CONTENTS

viii   *Contents*

Introduction

1. INTRODUCTION

The chapters of this book were written over a span of ten years as separate contributions to the debate on monetary issues in the European Community. Though not conceived as a unified work, they address the same general theme and reflect some deep convictions of the author: that the task of setting the sovereignty of Europe's nation-states within a common, legally constituted order is the legacy of two world wars; that this order cannot be achieved without institutions empowered to address and solve common problems; that, in the economic sphere, a single market requires monetary union and both require firm institutional foundations. These ideas are not new, but rooted in a secular tradition of economic and political thought.

Even those who had long argued the necessity and possibility of monetary union were surprised when the Heads of Government gave approval, at Maastricht, to a Treaty setting precise procedures and a timetable for achieving it. In less than four years, beginning in June 1988, the key issues concerning the management of money and the principles of economic policy had been reviewed, discussed, negotiated, and codified. Under strong political pressure a technical and organizational *tour de force* had been accomplished, involving hundreds of officials, each with the potential to influence the final outcome, and an even larger number of persons working in research, in the media, in industry and trade unions, in government offices and parliaments. The product of this complex endeavour was widely recognized to be consistent with well-established economic and constitutional precepts, although marked by the compromise solutions that are inevitable in a negotiated text.

The regions of Europe whose leaders signed the Treaty of Maastricht had ceased to have an institutionalized monetary

This introductory essay was concluded in January 1994.

union around the seventh century, when the 'local' kings began to strike coins bearing their own images rather than that of the Emperor in whose name they ruled. The Emperor's likeness was the symbol that power was indivisible, and it disappeared from coins with the disintegration of a unified authority in Europe. At the same juncture in European history an attenuation of the clash between diverse peoples, customs, and laws was sought through the adoption of *jus sanguinis*, which sanctioned the coexistence of a plurality of legislative systems in a single territory. It is noteworthy that, with the creation of a union founded on the mutual recognition of national laws and the project of a single currency, Europe seems to be turning back along the road that many centuries ago led from unity under the Empire to a multitude of kingdoms, legal systems, and currencies.

The banknote—the only industrial product that passes through everyone's hands and whose purchasing power is enormously greater than its production cost, but which is none the less universally accepted 'on sight' from complete strangers after only a cursory check—is the most effective symbol of the power of the state and the sense of security that the state must convey. Politicians and citizens grasp far more than economists and even central bankers that it would be senseless to unify the currency in Europe except with a view to political union. That awareness of this has grown as a consequence of Maastricht is hardly strange, for the perception of historical change is slow even under democracy.

When the Treaty was signed, in February 1992, criticism of EMU had virtually disappeared from the media. Ratification was seen as entailing little risk (see, however, Chapter 11, written in October 1991) and exchange markets were calmly discounting an orderly advance towards EMU. The Danish 'no' of 2 June 1992 came as a bolt from the blue. Since then two developments have marked the Community scene: the difficulties encountered in ratifying the Treaty and the prolonged storm in the European Monetary System. The relationship between the two is complex: on the one hand they have fed each other, while on the other the monetary storm was a striking confirmation of the fragility of the EMS that inspired the EMU proposal. Because of these two developments the lenses through which we now view the Treaty and EMU are not the same as those of early 1992.

This introductory essay, concluded in January 1994, starts by summarizing the factors and events that led to the signing of the Maastricht Treaty (Section 2). It then gives the author's interpretation of the events between the late spring of 1992 and early 1994, when the process of ratification and the crisis of the EMS interacted so powerfully (Sections 3 and 4), followed by some reflections on the problems of implementing the Treaty (Section 5), and a few words of explanation about the book (Section 6).

2. WHAT LED TO THE TREATY?

It is still too early to write the history of the making of the Treaty of Maastricht. A detailed analysis of the documents that marked the stages of its technical and political preparation from Hanover (June 1988) to Maastricht (December 1991) has yet to be made. The conclusions of the successive European Councils, the Delors and Guigou Reports, the reports of the Commission, the Committee of Governors, and the Monetary Committee, and successive drafts of the Treaty itself have still to be compared. The archives of the persons and institutions involved are not yet accessible to the public. Moreover, each participant in the negotiations has only a partial view of the process, based on his or her own first-hand experience. Finally, future historical accounts will be decisively influenced by the outcome of developments following the signing of the Treaty. Of such developments we have had a sharp foretaste in the past eighteen months.

Rather than a history of the making of the EMU Treaty, this book constitutes an analysis of the technical and policy issues that arose and were tackled in the course of the ten-year process that produced it. The analyses were conducted as the process unfolded and unavoidably bear the stamp of subjectivity deriving from the author's intellectual and practical involvement. As a result of both the difficulties encountered in ratification and the crisis of the EMS in 1992, leading to the virtual suspension of the ERM in August 1993, the chorus of the critics of the 'Maastricht Utopia' has now come centre stage and drowned out the voice of those who argued in favour of the Treaty, to the point of making it difficult to understand today how it was possible, over a period of several years, to build a consensus on the basic approach to EMU embodied in the Treaty. Very briefly, my own answer to the question of 'What led to the Treaty?' is as follows.

There was, in the first place, the rather compelling logic of two economic propositions, which, consciously or not, strongly influenced decision-makers in the 1980s. The first can be stated as a theorem that is well-known in economic doctrine and history and with which few disagree: free trade, complete freedom of capital movements, fixed exchange rates, and autonomous national monetary policies cannot coexist in the long term. These four elements constitute an 'inconsistent quartet' that can be reconciled only by transforming the fourth element into monetary union or by eroding the first three in varying degrees. This proposition is the principal leitmotiv of the book and is first invoked in Chapter 2 (written in 1982) to account for the failure to implement the freedom of capital movements sanctioned by the Treaty of Rome. The inconsistent quartet is not always presented in the same terms throughout the book: for instance, the question whether the fourth element should comprise fiscal policy as well as monetary policy is not elaborated in the early chapters, while it becomes important in Parts II and III, reflecting the comparatively recent debate on whether monetary union needs to be accompanied by fiscal policy rules.

It would, of course, be possible to analyse the inconsistent quartet in greater depth than is done in this book. It is my deep-seated conviction that any solution radically different from the one embodied in the Treaty of Maastricht would have left the edifice envisaged in the Treaty of Rome with a structural weakness that would have inexorably reduced the Community to no more than a precarious agreement for international co-operation. But I also believe that no ultimate 'analytical proof' of this conviction can be provided through economic reasoning. For in this sphere analysis goes no further than stating the problem and defining the boundaries within which economically sensible solutions are to be found, leaving the choice of this or that solution as a matter of judgement. What must be brought in to support the decisions is the theory of monetary systems and institutions, rather than the theory of exchange rate regimes. In recent years it has become increasingly evident in continental Europe (Chapter 11, 1991) that a monetary union is *not* an exchange rate regime. In the debate on the

European Monetary System illustrious and influential proponents of flexible exchange rates, such as Milton Friedman and Alan Walters, were in fact far more critical of fixed exchange rate regimes than of a monetary reform leading to a single currency. The true alternative to a single currency lies in the proposals for the organization of *domestic* monetary regimes, not for *international* relations between sovereign currencies. The alternative is the monetary competition advocated by Friedrich Hayek, rather than the flexible exchange rate regime proposed by monetarists. Along the lines of currency competition the British Treasury sought an alternative to the Delors Report—without, however, finding a convincing one. Currency competition was discussed in 1990 (Chapter 8), when the British proposal was on the agenda.

The second, related, proposition that influenced decision-makers is based on Richard Musgrave's presentation of economic policy as a triad of functions—allocation, stabilization, and distribution—corresponding to the three objectives of efficiency, stability, and equity. A balance between these three functions must be maintained in each economy and at each level of government, including the international level. The Single European Act, its effects, and the problems that arose in its implementation (Chapter 5, 1987) had to be analysed in the light of this Musgravian triad. The movement towards the single market created an imbalance between the allocation function of economic policy and the other two and this imbalance required correction.

Whereas during the 1970s the logic of the two foregoing propositions had caused intra-EC co-operation to stall and regress, in the 1980s, and until early 1992, their influence was both positive and profound, spreading from the economic field to that of policy-making, generating first the success of the EMS, then the decision to create the single market, and later giving new life to the issue of monetary union. We can say that 1988 marked the start of moves to correct the double imbalance. As regards equity, or redistribution policies, the doubling of the so-called structural funds in February of that year created a new basis for the Community's policies to develop the economically weaker regions, now known as 'cohesion'. As regards stability, or monetary policy, the establishment of the Delors Committee in June of the same year initiated the process of monetary union. The dynamic forces set in motion by these two factors combined with several other decisions and circumstances in creating the long, favourable train of events that led to Maastricht.

In the 1980s Western Europe enjoyed the longest period of economic expansion since the Second World War and the cultural inheritance and background of the leaders of the major continental countries bred them to the ideal of European unity. Their power base was solid, they maintained regular and friendly personal contacts, and they were assisted by a favourable social climate. Throughout the history of the EC, and perhaps also in the wider domain of world co-operation, the twin factors of well-established political leaderships and economic expansion have been necessary and often sufficient conditions for progress. These factors were at work with unusual duration and intensity up to the end of 1991.

Other political factors also contributed: first, the weakening of the anti-EC bias that De Gaulle had bequeathed; second, the loyalty of the German political establishment, and of Helmut Kohl and Hans-Dietrich Genscher in particular, to the European commitment that Germany had entered into after the war, an undertaking maintained even when the project of constructing a united Europe extended to the currency, which was the most important symbol of Germany's growing influence in Europe; and third, the presence of a personality of the stature of Jacques Delors at the helm of the Commission. Finally, there was the decisive *political* influence of an external and totally unforeseen event, German reunification, whose *economic* and monetary consequences were later to have a destructive effect on the EMS. Between the end of 1989 and the end of 1990 the winds of historical change blew strongly and the leaders of the key countries were capable of exploiting them. From the fall of the Berlin Wall (November 1989) to the first free elections in East Germany (March 1990) and the European Council meeting in Rome (October 1990), the settlement of the German question and the development of the Community interacted closely and provided the final thrust for the EMU project (1991, Chapter 10). The crucial element in all this was the determination with which, even in the face of strong domestic opposition, Chancellor Kohl pursued simultaneously—as though they were two sides of the same coin—the historic twofold objective of reunifying Germany and setting it within the Community framework.

Turning to the narrower fields of economic and monetary policy, an important element behind the developments that led to the Treaty was the success in the 1980s of ideas that allowed the construction of a united Europe to go forward with only a modest transfer of sovereign powers. In the economic sphere, the rise of a political philosophy based on 'minimum government' provided the key that unlocked the door to the full implementation of the single market, the original objective of the Treaty of Rome: the combination of minimum harmonization and mutual recognition. In Western Europe the powerful world-wide movement towards supply-side or so-called positive adjustment policies largely took the form of a co-operative project to create a single market primarily through a process of economic deregulation.

Similarly, in the monetary sphere, the growing convictions that monetary policy should concentrate on the primary objective of price stability and that central-bank independence was a prerequisite for a stability-oriented monetary policy implied the notion of limited scope for central-bank discretion and thus provided a fertile terrain for the idea of creating an independent European Central Bank even before attempting complete political union. Acceptance of this idea would have been much more difficult in the intellectual climate of the 1960s, when the task of monetary policy was largely considered to be that of striking a balance between inflation and unemployment, a political decision that could not be easily entrusted to an independent institution or placed outside the framework of a fully fledged political constitution.

It is one of history's ironies that the advance towards EMU in the late 1980s and early 1990s should also have been assisted by those who opposed it or viewed it with concern. Thus, the market-oriented convictions of as resolute an adversary of European integration as Margaret Thatcher helped point the way to the single market and, in line with the doctrine of minimum government, served to deflect proposals to complement monetary union with fiscal union, which would have overloaded and perhaps sunk the project for economic and monetary union. In turn, the Bundesbank, through the success of its approach and institutional model, contributed to monetary union not only by providing, in the Deutschmark, an anchor for stability in the first half of the 1980s, but also by contributing to the acceptance of a central-bank model based on a dominant objective and institutional independence, a model much more compatible with the Community's institutional system than those prevailing in other member countries (1991, Chapter 10). Also, it was both fortuitous and helpful that in Germany, the key nation for monetary union, the dress rehearsal for combining political and monetary union and for defining the fields of responsibility of the government and central bank in this realm was held on an all-German stage rather than in the Community theatre.

Some important tactical choices also need to be mentioned. Had the Commission not taken the sudden and far-sighted decision, in 1986, to set a new target date for liberalizing capital movements well in advance of the 1992 date set for inaugurating the single market, the two issues of a single market and monetary union would probably not have become parallel strands, strengthening each other and forming a logical bond. Had the central banks been excluded from the Committee set up at Hanover, they might have taken a more negative view of the prospect of monetary union and it would have been more difficult for that Committee to draw on the competence and authority needed to produce the document that played, both technically and politically, a role comparable to that of the Spaak Report on the Common Market.

Within the Committee, a number of crucial policy choices were made that profoundly influenced the whole subsequent process. One of these was to adopt the principle of subsidiarity as the overall criterion for assigning new responsibilities to the Community. This principle, which originates from the Christian tradition of political philosophy, had been proposed for the EC by the European Parliament in the 1984 Draft Treaty on European Union prepared at the initiative of Altiero Spinelli. Its adoption by the Delors Committee helped make it a key element of the EC constitution. Another crucial policy choice, to which I shall return, was the decision to espouse a 'fundamentalist' approach that conceived monetary union not as a rule for international co-operation, but as a 'national' monetary system. With this approach, the logic of international agreements gave way to that of monetary constitutions. It may even be that this approach was preferred by some who considered it not only conceptually orthodox, but also too radical to be workable in practice. The fact is that in the first few months of the Delors Committee's work the choice of a fundamentalist approach inspired a number of decisions that were held unchanged right through to Maastricht: the decision, from the outset, to concentrate on the final goal rather than on intermediate stages (Chapter 7); an approach based on institutions rather than on policy co-ordination (Chapter 1); and the notion of the indivisibility of monetary policy.

To attempt to comprehend how the Treaty of Maastricht came about is not to assume that Maastricht was the only possible outcome of all the above factors. Even those of us who laboured to complement the single market with a monetary union and to embody this transformation in a treaty held only that such a transformation was desirable and feasible, not that it was probable or, much less, inevitable. There were many, indeed very many, occasions during the ten years of its preparation when events could have taken quite a different course: the decisions of individuals, the political environment in which they operated, the economic situation, and the background historical events could have combined to give a different turn to the whole process. Thus we might speak of a benevolent historical conspiracy, but certainly not of inevitability. Or, as Francesco Guicciardini wrote in 1525, we might say that 'faith breeds obstinacy', and that 'since the things of this world are subject to a thousand random chances and accidents, unexpected help may appear in many forms in the course of time for those who have obstinately persevered.'

3. THE RATIFICATION STORM

The storm that began to blow up soon after the Treaty was signed in February 1992 has completely changed the European scene and will profoundly influence the state of European affairs in the years to come. In the fourteen months between the 'no' vote in the first Danish referendum in June 1992 and the virtual suspension of the European Exchange Rate Mechanism on 2 August 1993, two related storms developed: a monetary storm within the EMS and a political one concerning treaty ratification. In the background, helping the tempest gather force, was the ebbing of the twin forces that had for so long helped to drive the

EC project forward, namely economic expansion and political stability. The arrival of the recession that had hit the US economy in mid-1990 was delayed in continental Europe by the impact of German unification on aggregate demand. By mid-1992, however, the slow-down in economic activity had become evident and was aggravated by the policy of high interest rates that the Bundesbank felt compelled to pursue in order to curb inflation, running above 4 per cent, and defend its credibility. As to political stability, the long period of strong public support enjoyed by governments in virtually all the EC countries came to an end. The search for co-operative counter-measures accordingly proved difficult and was generally unsuccessful. The dynamics of the EC shifted from a virtuous to a vicious circle.

A monetary storm had been predicted for years, although its timing and violence were unforeseen. The intrinsic fragility of the European Monetary System was a recurrent theme of many analyses over the years and the 'inconsistent quartet' I recalled above is the name I gave to it. This fragility was well known even to the System's founders, who in 1978 had set a period of only two years for the transition to a 'final system'. In this collection the need to look beyond the EMS is indicated in a chapter written in 1982 (Chapter 2). It is true that, partly for the reasons given in subsequent chapters (Chapter 3, 1985; Chapter 6, 1987), the EMS turned out to be more robust than expected and was able to mould economic policies and modify the attitudes of both employers and employees. However, the fear that the latent fragility of the EMS would sooner or later manifest itself was the main reason for proposing to move in the direction of monetary union. 'The System is fragile; . . . a fragility that could lead to a sudden collapse' (Chapter 3, December 1985); 'We must be aware that it would be a big mistake to interpret the fact that we are currently living in a relatively quiet and peaceful monetary environment as proof that we can do without monetary union' (Chapter 7, November 1989).

From 1989 to 1991 the markets took the negotiation of an EMU treaty, the further liberalization of capital movements, the adhesion of new currencies to the ERM, and the entry of the lira into the narrow band as signs of the System's strength. By failing to signal the building up of divergences, markets played a stabilizing role that was consistent only with a rapid move towards

EMU. With the benefit of hindsight we can say that, in reality, they sowed the seeds of the troubles that erupted later and much more violently. Until June 1992, the view that the EMS was developing into a monetary union, sustained by the unbroken and surprisingly smooth political, technical, and diplomatic process that in less than four years had turned EMU from a vague statement of intention into a signed treaty, acted as a stabilizer of financial markets by providing a remedy of sorts to the basic inconsistency of the four elements of the quartet. The EMS had come, erroneously, to be seen by economic agents in both real and financial markets and by policy-makers as a quasi-fixed exchange rate system, a *de facto* monetary union. When the outcome of the Danish referendum was announced, the stabilizer was removed and the fragility of the EMS became apparent.

The political storm concerning ratification preceded and to an extent caused the monetary storm. The lack of democracy in the EC legislative and constitution-making process, long deplored only by a handful of convinced pro-Europeans and ignored by supposedly more practical politicians, suddenly became a trap for the ratification process. It is now clear to everyone that reaching an agreement on the terms of the Treaty was in itself such a technically and politically demanding task that governments did not pay sufficient heed to the fact that public opinion in each country would at some point play a crucial role in approving the Treaty. A sign of this insufficient attention is the esoteric language in which the Treaty was written, often reflecting the difficulty of reaching an agreement. There was a general belief that once the Treaty was signed the difficult part of the job would be over: the countries most willing to go forward had a strong basis on which to build the union, while those with reservations had obtained special clauses allowing a less stringent mode and pace of integration. The Heads of State and Government, who had set 'the objective of ratification by Member States before the end of 1992' as early as April 1990, failed to see that a careful strategy of ratification was needed to avoid the risks and pitfalls of the entirely new game of referenda and parliamentary votes. Had these risks been foreseen, no one would have recommended starting the process with a referendum in a country where European sentiment was known to be cool. The 'no' in the Danish referendum caught both the political establishment and financial markets by surprise and the uncertainty it injected into the EMU process was the proximate cause of the crisis of the EMS.

It would be wrong, however, to think of ratification only in terms of the constitutional formalities of referenda or parliamentary approvals. Formal ratification can be seen as just one of four 'ratifications' that were under way. In each member state these involved: the people, the convergence process, the markets, and the central bank. And although the storm involved the whole system and not just one country or currency, systemic and country-specific factors were closely intertwined: one country was critical in each of the four 'ratifications'.

1. French ratification by means of a referendum was, *par excellence*, ratification by the people. Among the founding members, France is both the country in which the idea of the Community originated in 1949 and, from the rejection of the Treaty providing for a European Defence Community to the crisis of the mid-1960s, that most averse to supranationalism. It was perhaps only right to turn directly to the people to resolve the long-standing ambiguity of presenting the Community as not impinging on the supposedly indisputable and indivisible sovereignty of the nation-state. The referendum debate and its uncertainty showed that an enormous risk was taken in putting the issue to a popular vote. This makes the value of the outcome all the greater.

2. Neither the lira nor the market for Italian government securities had come under serious strain before the Danish referendum, although Italian price and fiscal developments in the previous years should have made the lira a natural candidate for market pressures. Of the countries that had played a central role in the Community's political and economic history, Italy was the only one to be in a seriously divergent position. There the crucial test of the Treaty was not parliamentary ratification, which actually went without a hitch and almost unnoticed, but the link between convergence requirements and participation in EMU. The painful launching of a long overdue structural adjustment policy in Italy and the way this interacted, through market expectations, with the referenda in Denmark and France tested one of the most controversial aspects of the Treaty, the setting of strict and quantified convergence criteria as a prerequisite for participation in EMU.

3. In the UK it was almost as if, after years of subjugation to the idea that EMU had become inevitable, the plethora of dealing-room professionals earning their living from exchange rate movements rebelled against the prospect of seeing their shops closed, 'irrevocably locked' by a decree that would cancel a whole set of rows and columns from the matrix of world exchange rates. The epicentre of this rebellion was London, where it interacted with the unresolved reservations of British political circles and public opinion about relinquishing the exchange rate as a policy variable and the Queen's head on the pound as a sign of national identity. When sterling came under pressure, floating was preferred to any new parity.

4. In Germany the issue was to distinguish between the national and the functional-institutional aspects of central-bank independence, a theme that had emerged as early as 1985 (Chapter 3). EMU means preserving the latter while—or rather, by—forgoing the former. Not surprisingly, the distinction proved particularly hard to make for the central bank that was acting as a *de facto* European central bank: it is more difficult to lead than to follow. As in the process of German monetary reunification, so over the Maastricht Treaty the Bundesbank was confronted with political decisions and constitutional changes that would alter the context within which it performed its special task of preserving price stability. Dealing with this change involved an intensified dialectic between the central bank and the government. The risk for the Bundesbank was, and still is, that of undermining its function by identifying institutional independence too closely with national independence.

In the summer of 1992 these four ratification processes reached a climax, generating huge tensions that lasted over the subsequent months. The sequence of events is well known. The pound sterling and the lira were floated in September 1992. Five realignments took place in eight months, involving the peseta three times and the escudo twice. The markets exerted tremendous pressure on currencies such as the Danish krone and, most of all, the French franc, despite the underlying economies being sounder than those of Germany, Belgium, and the Netherlands on the basis of the convergence standards established by the Maastricht Treaty. Markets forced a devaluation of the Irish pound, even though that country had achieved an enviable configuration of fundamentals. In the end, they imposed a virtual suspension of the ERM rules.

In Chapter 11, written in October 1991, I stressed that there were three fundamental hurdles that had to be cleared for EMU to be achieved: the Treaty had to be *signed, ratified,* and finally *implemented.* While noting that these steps involved very different lengths of time—weeks for signing, months for ratifying, years for implementing—I emphasized that each passage was crucial, in the sense that each could prove fatal. By October 1993 the hurdle of ratification had at last been cleared, though at a tremendous twofold cost: the suspension of the ERM and an almost complete loss of the political momentum that had led to the signing of the Treaty.

4. A CO-ORDINATION FAILURE

The difficulties encountered by the ratification process precipi-tated the crisis of the ERM but were not its underlying cause, which was plainly traceable to what in academic jargon is called a 'co-ordination failure'. It should be stressed at the outset that such a co-ordination failure does not necessarily imply a viola-tion of a system's rules by one or more of its participants. More often it derives from the participants' failure to reach a co-operative agreement in the space reserved to discretionary deci-sions. A co-ordination failure thus reveals a flaw in institutions rather than an infringement of the rules—the central proposition of the book's opening chapter.

The episodes and examples of the co-ordination failure are numerous and need not be reviewed here in detail. There were the unprecedented monetary policy discrepancies between Germany and the USA. There was the precarious situation of the countries that had used exchange rate stability to achieve conver-gence but had failed to complete it and to persuade markets that they were on a course of stabilization. There was the refusal to accept a general realignment and even to call a meeting of the Monetary Committee or of the ministers and central-bank gover-nors when, in September 1992, a general realignment might have calmed the markets. The realignment procedure, once embarked on, did not produce a credible new grid. At various times, and in various ways, through unhelpful declarations that excited markets as well as through policy decisions that caused unnecessary friction, the system was destabilized by its very custodians. A detailed and reasoned chronology of the words and deeds of the System's participants in the face of market developments from August 1992 to August 1993 would provide ample evidence of the deficiency of co-ordination. Such an analysis goes beyond the scope of this introduction. Instead, I shall briefly discuss what can well be considered the crucial aspect of the co-ordination failure that destabilized the ERM: the crisis of the anchor role of the Deutschmark.

The monetary history of Western Europe between 1973 and 1993 can be seen as the history of the rise and decline of a Deutschmark system. This had begun to emerge with the Snake after the collapse of the dollar system. It was extended and consolidated in 1978 with the creation of the EMS. The peseta, the pound sterling, and the escudo joined the System between 1989 and 1992. Since 2 August, only the Dutch guilder has conserved a narrow-band link with the Deutschmark. The special role, problems, and positions of Germany and its currency in European monetary affairs are a leitmotiv of the book (see, in particular, Chapters 3, 7, and 8). Few today would dispute that the new monetary order brought about by the EMS with the help of the German currency contributed greatly to the extraordinary results achieved in the years that followed: the fall in inflation, the prolonged economic expansion, the development of intra-Community trade, and the completion of the internal market.

When the EMS was created, the German Government insisted that the largest possible number of countries should join. Against the backdrop of the 1970s, this position reflected Germany's concern that fresh competitive devaluations would undermine the wide export market on which the Federal Republic had based its post-war prosperity. For many years there was a close coincidence between the German and the European interest in the management of the Deutschmark. At different times in the 1980s the EMS was a key factor for Italy, Belgium, France, and Spain in undertaking stability-oriented policies. An academic literature flourished on the question of borrowing credibility from the Bundesbank in order to buttress domestic disinflation. As for

Germany, throughout the post-war period up to the end of the 1980s it could systematically use currency revaluation as a key instrument to fight inflation, not only because of the low price elasticity of the international demand for most of Germany's exports, but also because German inflation, even when high by German standards, was always lower than that of Germany's EC partners. The Federal Republic could thus import price stability through currency revaluations, at a low cost to its balance of payments and with little opposition from its partners, thereby preserving and consolidating the anchor role of the Deutschmark.

In the late 1980s inflation differentials continued to narrow between member countries. Payments imbalances did not give rise to significant tensions in foreign exchange markets, thanks to the credibility accumulated by fixed parities. Market expectations, however, were not strong enough to produce a significant reduction in nominal interest-rate differentials: in January 1990 French interest rates were more than 3 percentage points above the German level while the inflation differential had been virtually eliminated. The System seemed to be stalled, with participating economies paying the price of convergence towards monetary union but receiving few of the benefits. The EMS, like every other policy arrangement, was subject to a process of erosion and started to suffer from its own success.

Signs of a decline in the Deutschmark's anchor role could be seen in the late 1980s. To quote from Chapter 7, originally addressed to a German audience in November 1989:

a national currency cannot perform the role of international currency for long without being caught in a dilemma that will undermine one or perhaps both of its roles. In my view, the German currency and the monetary policy of the Bundesbank are approaching this situation and the period in which the DM was most successful in this context is probably drawing to an end or may even have ended already.

Two important factors were behind this decline: the success of France's endeavour to match or outperform Germany in terms of price stability, and the emergence, for the first time since the war, of a specifically German domestic inflationary shock arising from national reunification. These two factors prevented the engine of German disinflation, i.e. the revaluation of the Deutschmark, from being used once again. Understandably, France, with lower inflation than Germany, repeatedly refused between 1990 and 1993 to accede to the German monetary authorities and devalue the franc *vis-à-vis* the Deutschmark. The prediction of Otmar Emminger, who in the early 1980s had foretold the advent of an era of competitive *re*valuations among currencies seeking to import stability, was coming true.

For a fixed but adjustable exchange rate regime a satisfactory solution to the problem of policy co-ordination, the n-th currency problem, is a condition for survival, made more stringent by high mobility of capital. The solution is either hegemony or joint decision, there is no alternative. Hegemony was rejected by France, joint decision by Germany. That the route of currency, or policy, competition, advocated by the United Kingdom in the early stages of the preparation of the Maastricht Treaty and backed at one point by the Bundesbank, was not a solution was made plain to everyone between August 1992 and August 1993. Over that crucial period the co-operative spirit of the system should have been dramatically enhanced, whereas it actually grew weaker, with conflicting public statements, no co-ordination in interest rate movements, parity changes inconsistent with economic fundamentals, abandonment of unlimited interventions, and uncompromising priority given to domestic objectives. In these conditions the survival of the ERM would have been a miracle.

Similarities as well as differences can be seen between the rise and decline of the dollar and Deutschmark areas. Common to both cases is a long period of coincidence between national and international interests, followed by the emergence of a conflict. In both experiences a domestic price and fiscal shock linked to a major political event (the Vietnam war, the reunification of Germany) marked the passage from harmony to conflict. Capital movements, albeit of a different size and speed, exacerbated the conflict in both cases. As to the differences, in addition to the economic and political ones described in Chapter 7, it should be noted that the policy conflict that accelerated the decline of the Bretton Woods system arose from the accommodating policy stance of the anchor currency, whereas in the case of the ERM the policy of the anchor currency was restrictive. In both cases the problems caused by the attribution of international status to a national currency and responsibility for running a monetary policy for a group of countries to a national central bank proved to be insurmountable. Small countries may have structural reasons to follow the leadership of a large country. However, when larger countries are involved, markets cannot be led to believe that there is always a coincidence between domestic monetary needs and those of the leading economy.

The intellectual effort now required is to draw the correct lessons from what has happened. In a period of confusion and change this is no easy task. Two quotations from leaders in *The Economist* nicely illustrate how dramatically opinions have shifted in this year of crisis. On 19 September 1992: 'The near breakdown of the ERM makes a strong case not for abandoning the system, still less for making it more flexible, but for striving all the more urgently to create a single European currency'. On 31 July 1993: 'The trick is allowing more flexibility.' Indeed, so strong has been the force of events and so burning the disillusionment of those who, without much reflection, had come to believe that EMU was a sure bet, that a number of analysts and observers are rapidly swinging into an anti-Maastricht mood. The new wisdom preaches that the storm was due to an attempt to force the pace of EMU, and that calm will return by keeping everyone's house in order (convergence) and letting markets do their work (flexibility).

For the author of this book, however, the events of 1992–3 provide a striking confirmation of a quite different analysis and the lessons to be drawn are almost opposite to the anti-Maastricht mood. The first and fundamental lesson is that stable exchange rates, autonomous monetary policies, freedom of capital movements, and free trade do indeed constitute an inconsistent quartet. The crisis was of the EMS, not of its remedy, EMU. This has been driven home in an extreme and highly painful way and requires no further elaboration.

The second lesson is that convergence is not sufficient to overcome the inconsistency of the quartet and ensure exchange rate stability when monetary policies are not co-ordinated. Looking at the fundamentals, the French franc, the Danish krone, and the Irish pound should not have come under heavy pressure and been devalued *vis-à-vis* the Deutschmark. Another way to formulate this lesson is to say that the experience of the crisis confirms the fallacy of the dictum that 'markets are always right'. To argue that exchange rates reflect economic fundamentals and entrust the markets with the task of ensuring exchange rate stability is simply to ignore historical experience.

The third lesson concerns the relationship between markets and central banks, which is similar to that between tigers and their tamer. The latter can bend the former to his will if he uses superior skill, great care, and intelligence. If, instead, the tamer excites and irritates the tigers, they will win. The spectacular growth in the size of markets of the last ten years has widened the gap between the strength of the tigers and that of the tamers, and having more than one tamer in the cage does not help: it may lead to quarrels and in any case creates a problem of co-ordination, such as has been encountered during the last year.

To sum up, a fixed but adjustable exchange rate system is bound to face an insurmountable problem of policy co-ordination. Monetary union is the systemic solution to this problem. The expectation that this solution was around the corner held the system together. The weakening of this expectation destabilized the system. The response to this destabilization was a further weakening of co-ordination. The insurmountable problem was not in fact surmounted.

5. IMPLEMENTATION: WHAT LIES AHEAD?

In October 1993 the Maastricht Treaty cleared the hurdle of ratification while the EMS seems to have ended its fourteen-year life. In January 1994, as scheduled, the European Monetary Institute started its life, chaired by Alexander Lamfalussy and based in Frankfurt.

This outcome may appear the very opposite of what most would have expected: the modest, practical arrangement breaking down in the end and the utopian grand design ratified. However, the message repeated throughout this book suggests that there is a certain rationality in the choice made by the invisible hand of history. Indeed, it would have been utopian to consider an EMS-type system as being indefinitely sustainable. Still, the 'Treaty without ERM' situation that emerged at the end of 1993 is undeniably new, unforeseen by the Treaty, and very difficult to manage, both technically and politically. It requires a fresh analysis. The following are no more than preliminary reflections.

Just as it took several years for markets, business, organized labour, and policy-makers to 'learn' to live with the EMS in the early 1980s, it will take some time for economic agents to react to the new situation. Since August 1993 EC monetary relationships have been in a situation similar to the one that followed August 1971, when the dollar broke its link to gold. The relatively calm monetary situation in the months immediately following the suspension of the ERM tells little about its consequences and the possible outcomes. In theory, a reconstitution of the System would not be too difficult a task if we consider that the 2.25 per cent band was maintained in periods in which inflation differentials between participating currencies reached 16 per cent and that we now have a 15 per cent band with inflation differentials of 5 per cent. However, attempts to restore a binding Exchange Rate Mechanism would be successful only if they were accompanied by a much higher degree of policy co-ordination than would have sufficed to prevent the crisis of the System in the past year. The capital of credibility accumulated over the years has been seriously depleted and can only be rebuilt with a major and more solidly institutionalized co-operative effort by monetary authorities and with strong political leadership by governments.

Although several quarters express their best intentions to work for an early reconstitution of the System, it seems that the genies energized in months of unco-ordinated management of the System and eventually released on 2 August are now too excited to be willing to obey an order by their master to return to the bottle. At least for a while, they are more likely to stay out. The big question is what they will do. Will they behave in a calm and orderly manner? This would mean monetary policies continuing to pursue the primary objective of price stability, convergence remaining the top priority of policy-makers, no unco-ordinated fiscal stimulus being adopted to combat the present recession, and markets not shaking exchange rate relationships. In a word, it would mean that the genies would refrain from using their regained freedom. This highly desirable and unprecedented course of events would build on the fourteen years of experience with the ERM and reveal a degree of understanding by policy institutions of the potentially disruptive effects of letting the System be submerged by the waves of the 1992–3 crisis. In an alternative and unfortunately more likely course of events the liberated genies will continue to sow disorder in markets and discord among policy-makers. Some signs are visible in the conflicts about the implications of exchange rate changes for agricultural prices, in the proposals for limiting capital mobility, and in the complaints that currency depreciation has given country A undue advantages over country B, etc.

That those who fail to learn from history are condemned to repeat it is certainly true. It seems unlikely that a repetition of the competitive devaluations and trade frictions of the 1970s, not to mention the 1930s, will be completely avoided. I am still convinced that the first part of the scenario outlined in October 1987 (Chapter 6: 'if nothing is done, the process of restoring consistency among the four elements of the quartet could develop in an uncontrolled and destructive way . . . possibly leading to the return to floating exchange rates') is going to

be only the first step towards a *remise en question* of the whole *acquis communautaire*. Sooner or later, the existing degree of trade integration and the painful problem of unemployment in most European countries would inevitably cause today's Community arrangements to unravel. Breaches of Community law, failures to adopt the national legislation necessary to implement Community directives, congestion in the presentation and examination of cases before the Court of Justice, a weakening of the policing action of the Commission for infringements of the law and growing recourse to safeguard clauses and retaliatory measures against foreign producers would all be part of this unravelling scenario. The process would not necessarily be obviously dramatic; it could advance in a creeping way and take the form of a historical decline.

Only if the right lessons are learnt from the latest developments will monetary union and the single currency be back on the EC agenda. This brings us to the problem of implementing the Treaty.

In the forty years since the rejection of the Treaty for a European Defence Community by the French Parliament in 1954, European countries have never retried the route of common defence. This would have been the fate of monetary union had the Maastricht Treaty failed to pass the hurdle of ratification. Now that it has been finally approved, the Treaty will instead become the terrain on which the future of the Community will be built, whether this means taking further steps towards unity, or stalling, or sliding back towards disaggregation.

What is meant here by the term 'Treaty' is the EC Constitution after Maastricht, a very complex legal construction covering, with different institutional arrangements and decision-making procedures, not only the economic field (the single market, EMU and other economic policies, coal and steel, and atomic energy), but also foreign and security policy, and justice and home affairs.

A discussion of the way the EC may build on the Treaty goes far beyond the scope of this introductory essay. I shall mention just three points. The first concerns the need to clarify the very nature of the Community. The small body of missing 'aye' voters in the first Danish referendum made it clear that a pronouncement on the ultimate shape of Europe cannot be delayed much longer. Since 1949 Europe has developed according to a composite formula, moving with some ambiguity between different points of reference: between a purely economic project and a political project, between confederation and federation, between a free-trade area and a single market, between technocracy and democracy, between Jean Monnet's functionalism and Altiero Spinelli's constitutionalism. This composite formula has made it possible to gather wider support, to go forward with the help of government officers and experts, and to build a major body of laws and technical provisions. But in the process a 'democratic deficit' has been accumulated that is incompatible with the constitutional heritage of Western democracies.

Bringing the major decisions concerning the Community into the spheres in which public opinion and political forces are involved has necessarily simplified the issues. Citizens were well aware that, beyond the articles of the Treaty, the decision to be made was a choice for or against a united Europe, with the ensuing consequences. During the ratification debate, it was hard in France to maintain the equivocal position that monetary union would leave national sovereignty intact, or in Germany to accept monetary union without political union, or for Italy to proclaim itself European without behaving accordingly on national issues. The cost of ambiguity about the nature of the EC has become less and less sustainable.

I recall Jacques Delors, disconcerted by the fundamentalist positions upheld by some members of the Committee that he chaired, pondering whether history could still 'avancer le visage masqué' and concluding that, at least on the monetary question,

it was better to risk calling a spade a spade, to conceive and propose European monetary union in the same terms as are used for
national monetary systems. There is even less room for ambiguity
and uncertainty today, not only on monetary union but more
fundamentally on the nature of the EC constitution. Postponed
for years, long perceived by the politically aware as necessary to
give the union of Europe solidity and legitimacy, anticipated as
an ineluctable encounter between principles of democracy and the
quest for a supranational order, the time for clarifying the EC
constitutional model has perhaps arrived.

That model will have to be created anew, not borrowed from
earlier historical experiences in Europe or North America. It was
only with the Single European Act that the Community clearly
abandoned the model of the centralized state, forged by the great
monarchies of Europe, and thus laid the basis for rapid progress
towards the single market. Still more recent is the Community's
recognition of the fact that not even the US federal system can
be taken as the model, for it was created by states sharing the
same language and culture and without a long history of their
own, and has not fully succeeded in preserving the nation from a
tendency for power to be centralized. If political union is
achieved by the EC, it will give birth to a new state, even if this
means rebuilding part of what has already been built. The debate
on subsidiarity, which the struggle for ratification has so signally
intensified, is perhaps the first true debate about the constitutional order of Europe.

The second point concerns the final stage of EMU. I remain
convinced that 'in the long term, the only solution to the inconsistency is to complement the internal market with a monetary
union' (Chapter 6). And I am equally convinced that the monetary constitution inscribed in the Treaty is still to be regarded as
the right one, that it takes the best from existing national systems, as well as from post-war history and academic research.
The troubles of the last year may, however, lead to a reconsider-
ation of two important aspects of the Treaty approach that concern the final stage. One is the relationship between monetary
and political union. After the long ratification storm and its
August 1993 denouement, the monetary front is unlikely to
remain the advanced and moving front of European integration,
as it was between 1988 and 1992. The impetus will have to come

from elsewhere and the claim that monetary union must go hand in hand with political union (discussed in Chapter 10) may well lead to initiatives in the political field playing the driving role. This may displease the United Kingdom, and perhaps France, but it may be the only acceptable strategy for Germany.

The other aspect on which a debate may be reopened is the scope and purpose of the independence to be granted to the central bank, in EMU and perhaps even at the national level. One should not forget that the degree of independence foreseen by the Maastricht Treaty has no precedent in national legislation. And we cannot rule out the possibility of growing criticism about the way monetary matters have been managed in this year of crisis; central banks may be criticized for not having used their independence in the general interest and some may be accused of having overstepped their bounds by taking or forcing major political decisions affecting a much wider domain than that of money alone. Those of us who consider central-bank independence a necessary element of a sound monetary constitution can only be concerned by the signs of a backlash.

A more thorough rethinking needs also to focus on the transition. This is the third and final point about Treaty implementation that calls for comment in this introduction. The problems of the transition are analysed in detail in several chapters of the book. They show that the fundamentalist approach and the notion of indivisibility of monetary policy helped to produce a clear and solid solution for the final stage, but made it correspondingly more difficult to define a meaningful second stage.

The transition designed by the Treaty was based on three main elements: the good functioning of the ERM, compliance with severe convergence criteria (including a 'no devaluation for two years' clause), a majority requirement to move to stage three before 1999, the year set as a final and fixed date. The complex task of preparing what Chapter 12 calls the operational and regulatory 'platform' for effectively conducting a single monetary policy from day one of the final stage was entrusted to the European Monetary Institute. This set up is the result of a difficult compromise. If interpreted in a forward-looking manner it allows substantial progress compared with phase one, both in the coordination of current policy and in the preparation of the third phase. If, on the contrary, a static and negative interpretation prevails, it may be used virtually to block both policy co-ordination and the preparatory work. The crucial question is whether the EMI will be given the instruments and the opportunity to accomplish its tasks in full or restricted to being little more than the present Committee of Governors.

After the storm, some of the elements considered by the Treaty for the transition are drifting further away from the conditions set for reaching stage three; above all, the Treaty presupposes a strong and stable ERM, which no longer exists. It is therefore legitimate to wonder whether the provisions of the Treaty concerning the transition will be used as a vehicle for reaching EMU or as a means of preventing this. In this respect there is an analogy with the Treaty of Rome, where the wide application of the rule of unanimity, further strengthened by the so-called Luxemburg compromise, became a crucial impediment to the fulfilment of an otherwise well-identified and sound final objective. And only when an amendment to that Treaty removed the impediment was the way cleared to the single market. To reach the final stage of EMU, the Maastricht Treaty may require its own Single Act at some point.

Three routes are conceivable. The first, which could be called 'soft' gradualism, consists in approaching EMU through a gradual confluence of both economic performance and monetary policy instruments, relying mostly on voluntary co-operation. The second, which could be called the route of 'armed' gradualism, would follow the same path but would be based on strong decision-making procedures both in the field of policy co-ordination and in preparing the platform. The third route would consist in a jump to EMU, possibly by a limited number of countries. A rapid move to the final stage was considered at a certain moment of the negotiations in early 1991. This move, which would have involved a very short stage two, resembled the jump option. The hypothesis was abandoned, largely for political reasons. During the 1992–3 storm the idea of a small group of countries moving immediately to stage three as a response to the mounting tensions was periodically aired but has not gained much ground so far. In fact, the jump option is probably the most rational one, although it is hardly compatible with the present form of the Treaty and would be difficult to envisage in the absence of a strong political initiative.

If no jump is made, the choice offered by the present Treaty approach is between soft and armed gradualism. The experience of the last eighteen months seems to confirm the view of those who always doubted whether soft gradualism could lead to EMU. What Chapter 1 calls voluntary co-operation is bound to fail, as it has in 1992–3. In Jean Monnet's words: 'All too often I have come up against the limits of mere coordination: it makes for discussion, but not decision. In circumstances where union is necessary, it fails to change relations between men and between countries.'

Armed gradualism, in turn, could lead to the single currency. It is clear, however, that this route would imply a definite and institutionalized stepping up of the co-operation between central banks in at least three fields. First, central rates should become the object of a truly common decision and be defended jointly. Secondly, national monetary policy decisions should effectively take account of systemic as well as domestic considerations. Thirdly, efficient decision-making procedures should apply in the preparation of the platform. Taking this route would mean a significant change in attitudes and in the decision-making procedures of monetary and exchange rate policies. It would have profound implications, especially for the position and role of the currency and central bank that have played the anchor role over many years. How far this route will be deemed to be compatible with the Treaty and with the attitudes of the national authorities is the question hanging over us.

The future will answer the question. It would be unwise to improvise an answer at this time or try to chart an exact course for events that are still to come. In truth, reaching the goal defined in Maastricht cannot be taken for granted. The reconstruction offered above of the confluence of factors in the 1980s that led to the signing of the Treaty suggests how complex, imponderable, and unforeseeable is the combination needed to produce certain results, even when those results conform with reason or are sanctioned by law. Nor should it be forgotten that the implementation of the Treaty of Rome came to a virtual standstill for about fifteen years and only a new treaty (the Single European Act of 1986) restored its impetus. If the union is built, this will happen amidst problems, dangers, and opportunities different from those that marked the past decade. We cannot count on the helping hand of economic expansion spreading optimism and attenuating distributive conflicts. There are signs of discouragement and weariness in many countries. For the new generations the memory of the war in Europe, which was such a powerful source of constructive resolve, will no longer be a guide. Monetary union will become a reality only if the two fundamental factors that led to the Treaty continue to operate— namely, the economic factor, which impelled the member states to resolve the contradiction between the elements of the inconsistent quartet, and the political factor, which impelled them to create a supranational rule of law in order to ensure peace among them and manage problems that transcend them individually. In the years to come, the political factor will be decisive. If an economic contradiction was the motor of Community development in the 1980s, a political and institutional contradiction will have to be the motor in the 1990s. The European project would not be complete even with monetary union, and the latter is unlikely to remain a fixed point on the European agenda if the Community is unable to pursue goals beyond it, by fully implementing the political and institutional design of the Maastricht Treaty and supplementing it where it is incomplete and unfinished. On the other hand, monetary union is in itself a fact of such innovative import that the political and constitutional developments to come in the Community, not only in the economic and monetary sphere, will be influenced by the process set in motion in Maastricht.

6. ABOUT THIS BOOK

The years spanned by the articles collected in this book can be divided into three periods, corresponding to the three parts of the volume. The first period began with the inception of the European Monetary System (in 1979) and was marked by the anti-inflationary policies that enabled its members, by hitching themselves to Germany's monetary policy through their participation in the System, to emerge from the long period of inflation that had begun in the early 1970s. The second period followed the adoption of the Single European Act (1985); it saw the preparation of the single market, with the early liberalization of foreign exchange transactions and capital movements. The third period, inaugurated by the European Council meeting in Hanover and the establishment of the Delors Committee (1988), was dominated first by the technical and later by the diplomatic and legal preparation of the Treaty of Maastricht. The Community's focus shifted from macro-economic stabilization to resource allocation, economic and social cohesion, and institutional reforms.

In presenting these writings I have followed their chronological order, which also reflects an evolution of ideas as events unfolded. The final destination was clearly visible, but the course had to be set in the midst of the contingencies and circumstances of each moment. The events of the decade are known and are generally recalled in the literature; a chronological table (Appendix 2), from the origins of the Community to the completion of the ratification process, offers an overall, albeit subjective, picture of the most significant events from the point of view of monetary union. The only exception to chronological order is Chapter 1, which dates from 1983 and is a reflection on the four years I spent with the Commission in Brussels: it is placed first because it offers a methodological key to the whole volume.

A comment on a few issues that are recurrent or else neglected in the book may be helpful. One recurrent issue is the ECU, its essence, and its potential to evolve spontaneously and become the driving force of monetary union. In 1983 (Chapter 4) and 1987 (Chapter 6) I saw it as a possible lever for monetary union, based on a three-tiered monetary system in which the two components of national currencies (bank deposits and monetary base) would continue to exist, but would be anchored to a supranational and jointly managed monetary base. A solution of this kind was implicit in the plans to reform the international monetary system drawn up in the 1960s, which culminated in the creation of Special Drawing Rights. The same approach was developed by the Committee for European monetary union established at the end of 1986 by Valéry Giscard d'Estaing and Helmut Schmidt, which set it at the centre of their proposal for monetary union in February 1988.

The three-tiered solution was discarded at once by the Delors Committee, since the Bundesbank rejected any idea of a parallel currency, and the 'fundamentalist' approach based on the creation of a single central bank and a single currency took hold in the Committee. The ECU approach formed, however, the basis for the British 'counter-proposal' for a hard ECU (November 1989). This was in some ways similar to an idea that I had advanced in 1987 (Chapter 6) and to which the British Treasury referred in support of its own plan. The considerable success of the ECU in the market and an analysis of its technical features had convinced me in 1983 (Chapter 4) that, even within the EMS arrangements, the ECU 'could become a currency to all effects, with its own supply and demand'; and that a central bank was thus more necessary to manage the ECU than to promote its development. The following years brought empirical confirmation of this hypothesis, as the ECU increasingly overcame the constraints of its definition as a basket currency.

There are aspects of the ECU that still need clarifying: chief among them is the course it should follow before becoming the single currency of the union. In general, the issue of the ECU is more complex than that of the central bank, perhaps because it involves the attitudes of individuals, or because the currency has a stronger symbolic and emotional pull than does the institution.

Another recurrent issue is the actual concept of monetary union, what it involves, and how it can be achieved. This concept undergoes changes in the chapters of the book, reflecting both new thinking and an 'exercise in persuasion' in which the opinions of my interlocutors could not be ignored. Historical experience has shown that substantially similar monetary regimes and central-bank systems have been arrived at by different routes. Although I was convinced in 1982 (Chapter 2) that 'the twin objectives of free capital movements and fixed exchange rates (whether explicitly or implicitly expressed in the Treaty) imply the formation of a single area and a single monetary authority', it was only in 1987 (Chapter 6) that I ventured to voice my position that the time had come to firmly inscribe monetary union on the EC agenda. Even then I imagined a broad range of formulae and itineraries, leaving much more room for compromise than later emerged during the Delors Committee's internal discussions and in other fora. To give but two examples: neither fixed exchange rates nor a treaty seemed to me indispensable. For me, '*one* monetary policy and, therefore, a single monetary authority with full decision-making powers and operational means' was a necessary and sufficient prerequisite.

So long as the idea of monetary union seemed not to enjoy much credence in the official, technical, or political arenas, its supporters naturally kept an eye on the dynamic potential of the markets, particularly the ECU market. Convinced as I was that monetary union was a necessary complement to the Treaty of Rome, I believed it *possible* to achieve, if not the actual goal of monetary union, then at least the penalty area, 'from below', through the market; because 'money was not created by the law, but was originally a social, rather than a state institution' (K. Menger, quoted in Chapter 4). However, this approach did not seem *preferable* to the more institutional route, 'from above'.

This dilemma, too, was resolved in the Delors Committee, where, as underlined above, the fundamentalist approach led quickly to the adoption of the 'high road', which in 1987 seemed to me technically simple but not politically feasible. It is not possible today either to exclude or to affirm that, without government guidance, the Community would have taken the 'low road' to monetary union. Nor can we say how much the anticipation or, as some might say, the danger of market pressure persuaded the monetary authorities and governments to follow the path that led to Hanover and Maastricht. It is none the less worth reflecting on the fact that a common currency was publicly advocated by such practically minded individuals as the officials of leading banks and industries—Deutsche Bank, Philips, Fiat, Total. I returned to the subject of the respective functions of institutions and markets in 1990 (Chapter 8), when the concepts and terminology concerning the ECU were much further advanced than at the start of the 1980s.

Some of the issues pertaining to the nature of monetary union remained open right up to the last hours of the Maastricht negotiations and will probably be reconsidered in the years to come: principal among these are the institutional position of the central bank, exchange rate policy and the *quantum* of tax harmonization that should accompany monetary union. The writings in the book neglect the world-wide implications of EMU. Indeed, this collection looks at the themes of European monetary union in a 'domestic', intra-EC perspective. The creation of a monetary union in Europe would, however, profoundly change what we improperly continue to call the international monetary system. Suffice it to mention some of the salient aspects of the outward-looking perspective by formulating some of the questions it raises: would the establishment of a European Central Bank modify traditional ideas about the transfer of monetary powers to an institution standing above states? Would the birth of a single currency in Europe lead to a truly multi-currency system in which the various (probably three) reserve currencies play an equal or comparable role in monetary relations? And would this system breed greater monetary stability or be dangerously unstable? Would only one currency continue to be used in pricing the main primary goods? How would the demand for international reserves and their composition change as a result of the move to monetary union among countries that today hold more than one-third of world-wide reserves and account for nearly half of world trade? What policies should be used to govern these changes? How should monetary policy co-ordination be organized in a genuinely tripolar system? These issues are likely to fuel discussion in the years to come.

I

THE EMS AND ECONOMIC STABILIZATION

1

Rules and Institutions in Multi-Country Economies

1. MULTI-COUNTRY ECONOMIES AT THE CROSSROADS

If we abstract from the presence of actual governments and states, and define an economy as 'a set of economic agents who are engaged in various forms of exchange and interdependencies among themselves, and share a certain number of common interests', it is clear that many economies are multi-country, in the sense that their geographic area falls under the jurisdiction of more than one sovereign state.

The world itself is a multi-country economy, as common interests are embodied in the existence of world trade and world-wide financial relationships. 'Tighter' multi-country economies can be identified at lower levels, by considering factors such as geographical proximity, similarity of political and economic institutions, complementarity of natural endowments, common history etc. Canada and the USA, Luxemburg and Belgium, OPEC, and Scandinavia are thus more integrated multi-country economies than the world, or the American and European continents. Economically unintegrated areas may gradually become a single 'economy' following political and institutional developments, as happened for Sicily and Piedmont after the unification of Italy. Alternatively, an economy may exist and function, albeit in a precarious way, without the benefit of political institutions, as happened for Alsace-Lorraine-Saar-Luxemburg-Wallonia. Indeed, the relationship between economic and political-institutional integration is a two-way one. International arrangements and rules (IMF, GATT, etc.) are both the cause and the effect of the development of closer economic relations between states. The best

April 1983, Brussels. Paper. The ideas in this chapter reflect the author's experience in the field of economic co-operation during the four years he spent in the EC Commission.

example of a multi-country economy with an organization developed almost to the point of giving rise to a fully fledged institutional system is represented by the European Community.

The rules, arrangements, and institutions for multi-country economic co-operation that were created in the 1940s and 1950s at both the world and regional levels have developed the cross-border movement of raw materials, manufactured goods, capital, and labour to a degree never reached before, thus enormously contributing to the increase in welfare and the preservation of peace in the past few decades. They have brought the process of integration to such an advanced stage that nowadays not only economic well-being but also economic disturbances and potential crises are often international by nature.

In the 1930s, the system of fixed exchange rates also acted as a powerful mechanism for the transmission of crises from one country to another. When it collapsed, competitive devaluations and trade restrictions aggravated the world depression. The fundamental problem, however, was one of domestic economic management, while international economic integration was still virtually negligible. In contrast, in the 1970s and 1980s, an important part of the problem has not just been reflected in the international economy but has had its roots there. This is the case as regards natural resources, borrowing and lending, exchange rates, trade, and even unemployment. This evolution has profound consequences for the conduct of economic policy. As long as policy-makers concentrate on the national economy, a growing proportion of problems appear to escape their control because they are determined by exogenous events: changes in oil prices, world interest rates, imported inflation, payments crises, etc. However, what is given at the national level becomes a variable in the wider context, and if the focus shifts all the way to the world economy, then very little is exogenous.

In a rational decision-making process, the international repercussions of national decisions should not be neglected. First, the instrument–target approach of Meade and Tinbergen shows that it is necessary to have at least as many independent policy instruments as targets in order to ensure that the latter are met. However, since what appears to be an independent instrument in a national setting may cease to be so in an international context, co-ordination is necessary. Second, the impact of a national instrument may in some cases be stronger on a partner country than on the domestic economy. The only way to match domestic instruments with foreign objectives is again via co-operation. Third, unco-ordinated policies, even when they are capable of achieving their targets, may entail longer adjustments and sometimes oscillatory paths.[1] Co-ordination can help in shortening the adjustment period and can dampen oscillations. In short, a multi-country economy can hardly operate efficiently if the range of policy actions does not encompass all the sovereign nations of which it is made up. In fact, no government can keep the economic promises for which it has been elected in the absence of a favourable international environment, i.e. unless compatible and, if possible, complementary promises have been made by other governments in other countries, and there is willingness to play the game co-operatively.

The trouble is that international economic co-operation is not only more necessary today, it is also more difficult to achieve. As interdependence has increased, the existing instruments of co-operation have become less and less able to avoid or resolve the conflicts between countries' different policies. In the monetary field, there was a time when fixed exchange rates were universally accepted as the norm and the dollar as the international currency; both these key elements have been abandoned, and nothing has really taken their place. In the commercial field, the geographical area which is significant for GATT has grown wider than that institution's geographical sphere of influence; in addition, it is almost powerless to deal with a number of trade conflicts. In the area of macro-policies, even the weak infrastructure represented by the common acceptance of the Keynesian paradigm as a basis for co-operative efforts has been lost and not replaced, so that today not only policy objectives but also doctrines and ideologies tend to conflict. In a fourth important area, that of capital movements, a fully fledged, largely uncontrolled, international financial system has superseded segmented national markets.

Multi-country economies have thus reached a state of contradiction: on the one side, national sovereignty is formally indisputable and undisputed, and is even 'aggravated' by the deeper

[1] See Cooper 1969.

involvement of both governments and public opinion in economic matters; on the other, national sovereignty is increasingly eroded by growing economic interdependence. Such a contradiction cannot, and will not, last for very long. Either the necessary improvements and adjustments are made in the system of international economic co-operation, or there will be a severe deterioration of commercial and financial relations. Of course, neither the strengthening nor the disintegration of the existing system of multi-country co-operation need occur in a dramatic way. Historic dates such as 9 May 1950 (the proposal to set up the European Coal and Steel Community) or 15 August 1971 (the uncoupling of the dollar from gold) are the exception rather than the rule.

The search for paths along which international economic relationships could evolve towards a better order usually takes one of two approaches. Either specific problems, such as LDC debt or the exchange rate regime, are singled out in order to identify appropriate solutions, or an effort is made to devise comprehensive new arrangements (a 'new Bretton Woods', global negotiations, etc.). Neither of these approaches is followed here. Instead, the methods of international co-operation are analysed and attention focused on two limited but general issues that are rarely discussed explicitly, but which are nevertheless at the heart of the problem of international co-operation: the role to be played by rules and the importance to be attached to the evolution of institutions. More often than is said or even thought, failures in international co-operation depend not so much on conflicts of interests as on conceptions and misconceptions concerning the two key policy ingredients of rules and institutions.

2. RULES

2.1. *Opposite trends nationally and internationally*

It may be useful to start by commenting briefly on the concepts of rules and discretion. In economic policy, whenever a choice has to be made between conflicting objectives, judgement is necessary; economic analysis and logic cannot suffice. In this sense, all policies are discretionary, and what is called a preference for rules simply reflects a belief that conflicts between objectives are apparent but not real (for example, that there is no trade-off between inflation and unemployment) and that, even when such conflicts do exist, frequent twists and turns in preferences entail more costs, in terms of uncertainty and the risk of mistakes, than benefits in terms of the achievement of final objectives. From the operational standpoint, a rule-based approach involves following a predetermined path and giving intermediate targets priority over final policy objectives. It is not true that rules have a stronger legal basis than discretion: not only are rules often self-imposed but, more importantly, discretion exercised within the law is as lawful as the mere execution of a stringent norm. On the other hand, it is obvious that a rule-based approach is only meaningful if the interpretation of the rule is unambiguous, since in practice the grey area requiring interpretation is left to discretion.

In the last fifteen years the place of rules in economic policy has undergone an evolution which seems at first sight surprising. In domestic policies the view has gained ground that the area of discretion has grown too wide and that more rules are needed. In monetary matters, this change has taken the form of at least partial abandonment of fine-tuning accompanied by the adoption of quantitative targets. In budgetary matters, the drift away from discretion has emerged in a revival, as a constitutional requirement, of the classic prescription of a balanced budget (such legislation has been proposed in the USA and Italy). In both monetary and budgetary policy matters, the replacement of discretionary power by rules has been deemed necessary to limit actual and potential mismanagement by the executive power.

In the international sphere both opinions and actions have, on the contrary, moved from rules to discretion. This is one of the most significant aspects of the abandonment of fixed exchange rates in 1973. In the early 1970s, under the joint influence of theoretical thinking and difficulties in macro-economic management, policy-makers came to see flexible exchange rates as a way to free domestic choices from international constraints. Since it was recognized from the start that pure floating was an academic abstraction and that some management would always be necessary, a co-operative effort was undertaken to establish the rules of a new international monetary system. However, in the

Committee of Twenty,[2] formed expressly for this purpose, it soon became apparent that no simple set of rules could be defined for a system between the extremes of freely floating and fixed exchange rates. Eventually, the only feasible solution was to forgo the establishment of rules and to ask the IMF to carry out surveillance of each country's policies and their impact on exchange markets. Earlier attempts at defining statistical indicators and precise rules to govern intervention in exchange markets had to be abandoned. As stated in the 1980 Annual Report of the IMF: 'Surveillance must be judgmental'.

Several explanations can be suggested for the paradox of these opposite trends in the 'rules versus discretion' issue. First, while in the national sphere the need may be felt to protect policy decisions from the pressures of political constituencies, and a reduction in discretion can be seen as a means to this end, in the international sphere such a need does not arise or at least is not apparent. Thus, it could be argued that the reduced involvement of national interest groups in the international sphere is both an advantage and a disadvantage: it facilitates efficient and rational decision-making in the pursuit of global welfare, but it may be seen as an element of weakness in the process of democratic control. Second, in the early 1970s, the situations in the domestic and international spheres were almost exactly opposite, with considerable discretion in the former, many rules in the latter. It was natural, and perhaps appropriate, to interpret the increasing problems of the time as the combined result of misuse of domestic discretion and excessive rigidity of international rules.

Finally, the complexity reached in the international economy, the decline of American leadership, the notable increase in the number of leading players, and the development of a highly integrated international capital market all contributed to the demise of the fixed parity system. The same factors also made it exceedingly difficult, both technically and politically, to formulate a new alternative rule. *Ad hoc* arrangements and largely discretionary interpretation of loose policy prescriptions came to be regarded as the

---

[2] Set up in summer 1972, this comprised representatives from the IMF, the Group of Ten countries (Belgium, Canada, France, Germany, Japan, Italy, the Netherlands, Sweden, the UK, and the USA, plus Switzerland as an honorary member), Argentina, Brazil, Ethiopia, India, Indonesia, Iraq, Morocco, Mexico, and Zaire.

road to wisdom. Beyond these special circumstances, there is also the more general fact that the government function is perceived in very different ways in a national and in an international framework. In the former, a shift from discretion to rules appears to be a way to less government; in the latter, a way to more of it.

2.2. Why more discretion is needed

Various arguments suggest that nowadays the management of multi-country economies requires a widening of the scope for discretionary decisions and a more efficient method of taking such decisions, in some instances replacing rules, but more generally as a means of complementing them. The first consideration refers to the crucial area of exchange rates. It is widely agreed that neither fixed nor perfectly floating rates are viable solutions for the future. These, however, are the only two regimes that can be defined with simple and unambiguous rules. What lies between them is an interplay between private, profit-orientated agents and public, policy-orientated institutions, with discretionary management as the critical factor. The essential point is that, in an interdependent world, floating must be managed jointly and discretion has therefore to be joint discretion. There is no practical possibility of framing and disciplining managed floating in such a way that, by complying with a certain number of simple rules, careful and judgemental consideration of the interests of the partners on a case-by-case basis becomes unnecessary.

A second, related point concerns the co-ordination of macro-economic policies. In its heyday, the rule of fixed rates was largely sufficient, with the help of a stable, dominant, and scarcely open US economy, to enforce an acceptable degree of *de facto* policy co-ordination. In a polycentric world of managed floating, the process is much more complex and requires the discussion of a wide range of instruments and policies, including the balance of payments, interest rates, and budgetary and incomes policies. Each of these variables has a place in the deliberations of national policy-makers; each has a direct or indirect influence on other countries. In a multi-country economy they form a matrix which is much too complex to be governed by a simple rule. Setting priorities, weighing the relative importance of different variables, making intertemporal choices, and deciding which countries should act, are problems that only judgement can solve.

The increased probability of unforeseen events and disturbances of world-wide magnitude requiring a prompt policy reaction is a third factor. Here economic actions are often foreign policy instruments, when they are not substitutes for military intervention: oil embargoes, freezings of assets, economic sanctions, and so on. In a world that is more divided politically and strategically than it is economically, this is perhaps inevitable. And since the opposing camps are themselves conglomerates of sovereign countries, often without clearly established internal leadership (the Arab League, the NATO countries, the non-aligned countries, etc.), the possibility of taking discretionary decisions at a national level does not automatically produce consistent action by any group of countries.

A fourth and final consideration is that in certain areas an integral part of a policy may consist in leaving economic agents in uncertainty as to whether the authorities will intervene or not. A major example, one that international conditions today and in the foreseeable future make particularly important, concerns the function of lender of last resort. There must be one, but its interventions should not be taken for granted; that is, they must be discretionary.

To sum up, a movement from rules to discretion in the management of multi-country economies is in many ways necessary, because it corresponds to the nature of the problems which have to be dealt with in the present situation. Seen from this perspective, developments that have taken place in more recent years point in the right direction. But greater reliance on discretion does not mean that the management function in a multi-country economy has to be weakened or softened. On the contrary, it means that it has to be made stronger, more effective, and more adaptable to complex and unforeseen situations. In this sense, there are good reasons for questioning whether the evolution that we have witnessed has really entailed a sharpening of multi-country management actions or, on the contrary, a loosening of the already too loose arrangements we used to have. This leads us to the problem of institutions.

3. INSTITUTIONS

3.1. Institutions and co-operation

The *Concise Oxford Dictionary* defines an institution as follows: 'established law, custom, or practice; organization for promotion of some public object; buildings used by this'. This suggests the possibility of a great variety of organizational forms, with the solemnity of a comprehensive and written constitution not being absolutely essential. To be sure, the 'promotion of a public object' can occur in an efficient and systematic way through uncodified co-operation, and this 'practice' may become sufficiently 'established' to deserve the name of institution. In the international sphere, such an informal approach was the pre-1914 gold standard; whereas the Bretton Woods system is an example of a formal institution, based on an international treaty. It is the difference between these two approaches to monetary organization that Keynes was implicitly stressing at the end of the Bretton Woods conference, in his wry remarks about the American habit of always negotiating with the help of an army of lawyers.

True, institutions are instruments of organized co-operation; and firmly established co-operation can be seen as a kind of institution. However, such common elements should not generate misunderstandings. Indeed, it is essential to be fully aware of the sharp border between the institutional and *ad hoc* approaches to co-operation. *Ad hoc* co-operation is a method by which partners meet, discuss, and, if they agree, act together. If they do not agree, they will skilfully draft a press communiqué to give the public the impression of a joint commitment to general values and goals, and then return to their respective capitals to conduct, within the limits of their national autonomy and strength, mutually inconsistent and possibly conflicting policies. The history of the last ten years provides numerous examples of both these possible outcomes, perhaps more of the latter than of the former.[3]

---

[3] Dam 1976. Dam argues strongly in favour of what he calls the co-operative approach based on an analysis of the reform of the international monetary system after the disintegration of the Bretton Woods system. In his view 'co-operation' (our *ad hoc* co-operation) was the only feasible approach and had flexibility, unlike the constitution-drafting approach (our 'rule'). 'Discretion plus institutions' is not considered. Dam is the outstanding example of the common

Institutionalized co-operation starts where the *ad hoc* approach ends. It ensures that decisions and actions will be taken at the system level, even if the parties fail to agree. In other words, it guarantees that decisions will be taken at the right level, which in our case means the level of the multi-country economy, though it naturally cannot guarantee that the right decisions will be taken. The distinction between institutional and *ad hoc* co-operation is particularly important in the international sphere, where failure to agree on a common course of action means unilateral, unco-ordinated, and probably conflicting actions by the individual parties. The danger of confusion is specially great today, now that the practice of international consultations (in committees, councils, conferences, summits, etc.) has been given an 'institutional veneer', so that the public has the impression that a form of international management does exist.

It is worth noting that the institutional approach is superior not only to unsuccessful but also to successful *ad hoc* co-operation, because it is more permanent and more certain in character. The institutional approach is defined by the rules on which it is based, for example allowing decisions to be taken by majority voting rather than requiring unanimity. With co-operation, the existence of a public good has to be acknowledged anew every time, so that its fulfilment is difficult. With an institution this existence is assumed.

To be effective, an international institution requires the transfer of some powers from the national to the international level. However, this does not mean that nations have to surrender control of the area of competence concerned. They will continue to exercise this control at a different level, that is, within the multi-country institutions. Nor does it imply that control is a zero-sum game—that what is gained at one level is lost at another. On the contrary, establishing management at the lowest possible level (the so-called principle of subsidiarity) means that the very purpose of an international institution is to regain control over phenomena which, due to increasing interdependence, would otherwise tend to escape control completely.

---

failure to distinguish between the two issues of 'rules versus discretion' and '*ad hoc* versus institutional co-operation': a single line of reasoning produces what seems to us a desirable conclusion on the first issue and an undesirable conclusion on the second.

3.2. Why institutions should be strengthened

At the present stage of the evolution of multi-country economies, satisfactory performance of the decision-making function requires a strengthening of institutions because the alternative method, namely, *ad hoc* co-operation, is bound to fail in too high a proportion of cases. This is due to many causes.

In the first place, the areas involving a genuine common interest of the multi-country economy which require discretionary acts of policy, rather than the mechanical application of rules, have become wider. Even at their best, co-operative methods are in general too slow to produce the necessary decisions at the right time. Notwithstanding the good intentions of the partners, the process of defining a course of collective action rarely meets the deadlines set by the pace of economic reality. As a consequence, action is taken at the lower, suboptimal level of the nation-state, thus creating welfare losses and unnecessary frictions. Co-operation fails because the machinery of high-level diplomacy between nation-states is congested.

Furthermore, co-operative methods rarely operate at their best. Their performance lies in the hands of officials and politicians, who are severely constrained by their local constituencies, even when, as individuals, they are perfectly willing to co-operate. The electorate, particularly in periods of recession, is generally more in favour of inward-looking measures than either ministers or officials. Top officials are usually engaged in domestic affairs, and sometimes regard activity on the international front as a waste of time and those in charge of it as too prone to compromise and grant concessions.

The process of educating officials involved in international negotiation takes time. The success of a co-operative approach depends to a considerable extent on the personal relationships between those involved in the process and on their familiarity with the values and traditions of this particular branch of government. Today, however, political instability has so accelerated the turnover of governments and high-ranking officials, that the training process often fails even to maintain the existing degree of know-how and willingness to co-operate. The result is an erosion of the capital of international goodwill that is necessary for efficient *ad hoc* co-operation.

Reaching agreement within the framework of *ad hoc* co-operation is also becoming more difficult because the number of negotiating parties grows with the number of nation-states and the wider participation in international bodies. It has been said that the Bretton Woods conference was a meeting of one and a half countries; the IMF now gathers together close on 150 nations. The difficulty of large group negotiation is compounded by the increasing divergence between the interests of different countries, particularly during periods of economic recession. Economic summit meetings between the heads of governments of the Group of Seven countries (Canada, France, Germany, Japan, Italy, the United Kingdom, and the United States) illustrate the difficulty of reaching decisions even among a small number of countries. Moreover, when such decisions are announced, their interpretation immediately becomes controversial and their acceptance by those excluded remains a problem.

In addition, the information base for decision-making is becoming so complex and controversial that co-operation is increasingly suffering from a well-known dilemma: those who have the authority and vision to judge and decide do not sufficiently master the details of the problem, while those who have studied the dossier often have too weak and narrow a perception of the necessity and urgency of reaching agreement. This is particularly so when economic problems are closely interconnected. Recent years provide examples both of the virtual impossibility of arriving at a synthesis of issues in meetings where specialists assemble and of summits where heads of state willing to compromise get lost in the details.

Finally, policy-makers increasingly have to face international problems arising at the intersection of different fields rather than in just one field: trade and exchange rates, exchange rates and financing, financing and aid. Yet both *ad hoc* co-operation and the existing system of international institutions are highly specialized and offer very few possibilities of negotiating packages involving different areas. The summits of the seven Western industrial countries are a notable exception, promoting interdepartmental co-operation nationally as well as internationally. Unfortunately, however, they suffer from other drawbacks: the congestion of problems relative to the time available for dealing with them, the lack of a central independent body entitled to speak for the common interest, the absence of essential partners such as the developing countries and OPEC, and a tendency to prefer publicity to substance.

Even if the above seem quite compelling arguments, it is nevertheless worth considering the popular objections to the main contention that international institutions should be strengthened. Though phrased in many different ways, they all boil down to questioning either the need for or the possibility of building stronger institutions.

As to the need, the argument is usually formulated by saying that if every country kept its own house in order, international order would automatically follow. In a weaker form, the priority of domestic order is advocated. In either form, these objections ignore not only interdependence, but also the fact that 'order', far from having just one value, is the very object of political choice in a democratic society. The flaw in the own-house-in-order argument is that it presents a necessary condition as a sufficient one. In practice, its strength lies in the fact that it is generally used by large strong economies to justify a certain disregard for the potential consequences of their policies on other countries.

As to the possibility, it is of course an open question whether it is realistic to pursue the objective of strengthening international institutions at a time when so much wisdom has relegated supranationalism to the attic of post-war dreams. One should not forget, however, that institutions can change without requiring dramatic moves or even new legislation. In many instances institutions are simply reshaped by the changing nature of the problems confronting them. Some claim that a recent example of such a change is the new role played by the BIS in arranging bridging operations for debtor countries with liquidity difficulties. Since such systemic changes can take place independently of each nation's will, it would certainly be preferable to control them rationally than to accept the force of events. Nor should it be feared that changing an institution takes too long. If that were the case, late would still be better than never, but it is *not* the case. What takes time is the negotiation of details. Historical experience shows that systemic changes are implemented rapidly because what makes them possible are special political, or crisis, circumstances that do not usually obtain for very long. The

Bretton Woods conference lasted a few weeks. The EMS was set up in about six months. In contrast, an EC negotiation to harmonize technical norms on the rear reflectors of cars may take years.

One final word is perhaps in order to counter a common criticism regarding the performance of existing international institutions, namely, that they are not, after all, either better or more efficient than the gatherings of national leaders practising *ad hoc* co-operation. The answer to this criticism is simply that it is true. Indeed, present-day institutions, inasmuch as they are not really given the charters, the powers, and the instruments to follow a genuinely institutional approach, are bound to fall back on the *ad hoc* pattern and to act as an 'additional partner' in the exercise of *ad hoc* co-operation. Thus, strengthening international institutions must serve to create the conditions permitting them to play their role more effectively.

4. CONCLUSIONS

For more than twenty years, multi-country economies, as measured by world trade and international financial intermediation, have grown at about twice the speed of national economies, as measured by GDP and domestic financial assets. This extraordinary dynamism has enabled these economies to evolve out of the systemic problems arising from the coexistence of sovereign powers. The growth of world trade has reduced conflicts, increased the number of economic agents with an interest in maintaining open trade, fully developed the potential of the arrangements and institutions created in the 1940s and 1950s, and even filled the gaps left by the shortcomings in the arrangements and institutions themselves. It has also concealed the weaknesses and the lacunae of the instruments available for the management of multi-country economies.

The wide divergence between these two speeds of growth is bound to be a transitory phenomenon, lasting until the gaps due to pre-existing trade and financial barriers are filled. As long as it is under way, the process of removing these barriers, which was initiated at some point in the past, will continue to act as a 'policy', performing an active role in the management of the multi-country economies. When this function is exhausted and the growth of these economies slows down to that of national economies, it will become clear that, while the latter often have an excess of government, multi-country economies have too little. In difficult times, when risks, uncertainties, and conflicts are experienced in trade and financial relationships, it is the economic agents that benefited most from the removal of barriers and international economic integration who tend to turn to governmental powers for support and protection. Today, governmental powers are only national. With the exception of the European Community, there is no multi-country economic power to which an individual economic agent can turn directly. The almost inevitable consequence is that government interventions in support of the economy tend to have a protectionist character and to erode the capital of international co-operation and goodwill. Here is where the process of multi-country economic integration could easily go into reverse; in the 1930s it took only four years for world trade to shrink from three to one million gold dollars.

In this chapter I have argued that the movement from rules to discretion that has characterized the evolution of international economic relationships in the last decade will not be sufficient to avoid the danger of disintegration. It will be equally necessary to accept the exercise of this discretion at the level of the multi-country economy concerned and not allow it to fall to the level of national economies.

Clear awareness of the enormous, almost insurmountable difficulty of progressing in the direction suggested here is indispensable if action is to be successful. However, caution and realism must not be allowed to obscure the sense of what is the necessary direction.

2

Capital Mobility: Why is the Treaty Not Implemented?

1. THE EARLY 1960S

1.1. The legal framework

Article 67 of the Treaty of Rome provides that 'Member States shall progressively abolish between themselves all restrictions on the movement of capital . . . to the extent necessary to ensure the proper functioning of the common market'. And the EC Council was called upon, in Article 69, to 'issue the necessary directives for the progressive implementation' of this provision. The Council was remarkably rapid in its response: it adopted a first directive in 1960 and a second in 1962, graduating the freedom of capital movements according to the nature of the flows concerned, ranging from direct investments to financial placements of various maturities and to purely short-term and potentially speculative flows. Under the directives member states were unconditionally obliged to liberalize movements of capital directly connected with the flow of goods and services (e.g. for direct investments, investments in real estate, and commercial credits), of personal capital, and of securities quoted on the stock exchange. In another category, 'conditional' liberalization was envisaged for the issuing of bonds and for capital flows of a purely financing nature such as longer term financing loans. Liberalization remained non-compulsory for short-term financing loans and new foreign bank accounts.[1]

June 1982, Milan. Address to the 'Second Symposium of European Banks'. The EC Council had just rejected some Commission proposals for a strengthening of the EMS. The drive towards exchange liberalization had not started at the time.

[1] In recent years the problem of short-term capital movements and their control has become of primary importance for the international economy and has been widely debated in the literature. The key distinction is between controls on long- and short-term capital flows and is reflected in the different treatments they receive in the first two EEC directives, as well as in the IMF Articles of Agreement, and the OECD Code of Liberalization of Capital Movements.

The basic philosophy underlying these initial successes on the road to liberalization was clear enough. The most comprehensive description is to be found in the well-known report on the formation of a European capital market, drawn up in 1966 by a group of experts chaired by Professor Claudio Segré.[2] This study, which has become a Community classic in its own right, argued that a European-wide capital market would become increasingly necessary, not only to finance economic growth but also to stimulate the implementation of Community policies in other areas. In particular, a European capital market was considered a necessary precondition of economic and monetary union within the Community, since it would contribute to the smooth functioning of an international monetary system based on fixed exchange rates and completely liberalized foreign exchange transactions.

These ideas were tacitly founded on the existence of fixed exchange rates. Such a regime, provided by the Bretton Woods arrangements after the end of the Second World War, seemed so much a part of the planned common market, that nobody bothered to include it explicitly in the Treaty. The presumption of fixed exchange rates gave rise to some of the early inconsistencies in the overall conception of EEC stabilization policies.

1.2. Facts

To appreciate the force of conviction carried by arguments such as those of the Segré Report and to understand why those initial successes were blocked in the late 1960s and finally reversed in the course of the 1970s, one needs to trace the background. The first element relates to the broad historical perspective: the lessons of the Great Depression—when many countries attempted to maintain employment through competitive devaluations and by resorting to exchange and trade restrictions—were deeply engraved in the minds of post-war policy-makers. The Bretton Woods agreement, the United Nations Charter, and especially the Rome Treaty reflect a keen awareness of interdependence, a strong political will to promote integration and co-operation, and growing acceptance of the need for an agreed code of conduct in international trade and financial matters. Policy-makers were

---

[2] Commission of the European Communities 1966.

firmly convinced of the self-defeating nature of beggar-thy-neighbour policies and of their contribution to lower global employment and welfare.

Secondly, the interpenetration of financial markets and the openness of the industrial economies were much less pronounced than they are today, so that policy-makers were less fearful of uncontrollable exogenous developments impinging on their domestic autonomy. As regards the financial markets, for example, longer-run net private capital flows within the Community totalled less than \$1 billion in 1960, while 'classic' foreign bonds issued within the EEC amounted to only \$200 million in 1961.[3] The Euromarkets were, for their part, just beginning to see the light of day. On the 'real' side of the picture, the major European economies were much less open than they are today: measuring openness by the ratio of total exports to GDP, in 1960 it ranged from 12 per cent for Italy, 14 per cent for France, and 18 per cent for Germany (compared with respectively 25, 22, and 30 per cent today).[4]

Thirdly, the general economic climate of the late 1950s and early 1960s was also propitious to a process of relatively harmonious and shock-free integration. This was a period of steady, non-inflationary growth, of plentiful and mobile labour, of low and declining energy and raw-material costs, and of asynchronous cycles among the major industrial countries: factors that were all favourable to a generally convergent economic performance and a reduction of per capita income disparities among the original six members of the Community. In this environment, the dismantling of capital controls seemed to lie in the mainstream of developments and to be in the natural order of things.

1.3. Policy analysis

The macro-economics of open economies prevailing in the early 1960s focused on insular (i.e. basically independent) national economies and governments. Between any two countries, a real and a financial relationship was considered to hold in the case of fixed exchange rates. The 'real' relationship linked domestic poli-

---

[3] Commission of the European Communities 1966: statistical annex, tables 13 and 15.

[4] Commission of the European Communities 1981 and 1982*a*.

cies to the trade balance: if a national government conducted expansionary policies, the trade balance would worsen via increased domestic spending on imported goods. The 'financial' relationship meant that international capital flows reacted to interest rate differentials: a rise in nominal interest rates in a given country would increase capital inflows, thereby improving the capital account.

The analytical combination of these two relationships demonstrated how international flows of financial capital fitted into national stabilization policies. Take, for example, the case of a slow-down in economic activity. A policy of budgetary expansion would stimulate the economy, while restricting monetary policy would keep domestic interest rates high enough to attract capital inflows. Overall balance-of-payments equilibrium would be maintained, as the trade deficit would be financed by interest-sensitive capital inflows from abroad. The result is a policy mix in which monetary policy is not directed towards domestic goals, but becomes a tool for balance-of-payments financing, working via the interest sensitivity of international capital flows.

Thus, the economic wisdom of the early 1960s suggested that, in a fixed exchange rate regime without capital controls, there was in principle no room for an independent national policy mix. In particular, monetary policy was constrained to act as a tool for external stabilization. This consequence followed from the coexistence of free capital flows and fixed exchange rates. Both these conditions were built into the Treaty of Rome, however. Free capital flows were explicitly considered as an objective. Fixed exchange rates were an implicit pillar of the Treaty. It should follow that the use of monetary policy for domestic purposes is ruled out, that is, that national monetary policies are constrained by balance-of-payments considerations. We cannot aim simultaneously at (i) free trade, (ii) capital mobility, (iii) independent domestic monetary policies, and (iv) fixed exchange rates. The circle cannot be squared: one element has to be surrendered in order to avoid inconsistency. The incompatibility between fixed exchange rates, free capital movements, and independent national monetary policies has been referred to in economic literature as the 'inconsistent trinity'. I have turned this trio into the 'inconsistent quartet' by adding a fourth element, free trade, which is a pillar of the Treaty of Rome and an aspect

which cannot simply be taken for granted in our present economic environment. As Henry C. Wallich has observed, the
incompatibility of these elements is 'a fact well known to economists but never recognized in our institutional arrangements or
avowed principles of national policy'.[5]

Given the Treaty's explicit provision for the free flow of goods,
services, and capital, the choices were between giving up either
the autonomy of domestic monetary policies or the system of
fixed exchange rates. The latter option being hardly conceivable
at the time, the Community's founding fathers made a definite
choice in favour of the co-ordination of policies, overcoming the
incompatibility of the various objectives by indicating that in the
'inconsistent quartet' it is the autonomy of national policies that
would have to yield to the needs of co-ordination, to enable fixed
exchange rates, free capital flows, and free trade to coexist. There
are a number of articles in the Treaty bearing this out: Article
145, in particular, sets the task of ensuring the 'coordination of
the general economic policies of the Member States' alongside
'the power to take decisions', as one of the two fundamental
Council tools for the attainment of the Treaty's objectives. The
fact that, in a regime of fixed exchange rates and free capital
movements, economic policy is necessarily constrained by external considerations is recognized in Article 104: 'Each Member
State shall pursue the economic policy needed to ensure the equilibrium of its overall balance of payments and to maintain
confidence in its currency'.

The analytical foundations of the Treaty are therefore sound
and conceptually consistent: the subsequent inconsistency and
related difficulties have arisen because the principle of economic
policy co-ordination, enunciated in the Treaty, has remained no
more than a principle. Its practical implementation continues to
rest on loose and largely ineffective arrangements, so that co-
ordination remains without any bite, at times degenerating into a
mere exchange of information on policy actions decided unilater-

---

[5] Wallich 1972. A similar dilemma faced the Bretton Woods negotiators. They
solved it by agreeing that members of the IMF should be able to control capital
transfers (except for current transactions). Already in HM Treasury 1943, Keynes
had declared that no country could safely permit unwanted movements of fugitive
funds, for which reason it was 'widely held that control of capital movements,
both inward and outward, should be a permanent feature of the post-war system'.
See Gold 1977.

ally. That is the main shortcoming and the root of the problem: the Treaty set co-ordination as a condition and an objective, but failed to provide for implementing norms and concrete instruments to render it a reality.

2. THE EARLY 1980S

2.1. The legal framework

The two Council directives of 1960 and 1962 marked the last progress so far achieved towards the liberalization of capital movements. In fact, since then there has been a retreat. A third directive, aimed at a stepwise further liberalization, was submitted by the Commission in 1967, but had to be withdrawn after ten years of fruitless negotiations in the Council. A decision is still pending on a more recent proposal (1979) to broaden the scope of the first directive (inclusion of investment fund certificates). To be sure, there have been other directives with some, albeit indirect, bearing on this matter: the 1973 directive on financial institutions (freedom of establishment and freedom to provide services) and the 1977 directive relating to the taking up and pursuit of the business of credit institutions. There have also been directives on insurance, and two directives (in 1979 and 1980) on the admission of securities to official stock exchange listing and the particulars to be published for such admission.

In so far as capital market integration requires some harmonization of regulations and institutional structures, these measures are undoubtedly important. But as regards the main stage of the direct liberalization of capital movements, the account remains negative. The overall degree of liberalization is lower today than in the early 1960s, and differs widely from one Community country to another.

Two other points are worth making about the legal aspects of the liberalization of capital movements in the Community. First, liberalization of capital flows in the Community continues to depend, from a legal point of view, solely on directives issued on the basis of Article 69 of the Treaty. This is to say that even today, after a long transitional period, the general principle of free capital flows (Article 67) does not, by itself, constitute directly binding law. This point has been clarified recently, for the first time, by the European Court of Justice (*Casati* case, decision of 11 November 1981). Hence, the legal framework still makes it necessary to follow the long road of issuing directives, building European capital market integration step by step.

Secondly, there are very long internal decision lags within the Community itself. The time seems to be gone when it took the Council only a few months to approve a proposal put forward by the Commission, as was the case with the first two directives in 1960 and 1962. Today, we sometimes have to wait for years until a proposal by the Commission is approved by the Council, if it ever is (Table 2.1).

To the length of the decision-making process, it is also necessary to add the very long implementation delays and/or grace periods granted when proposals are finally approved. A good example is the time it took certain member states to apply the 1973 directive on the freedom of establishment and the freedom to provide services of financial institutions, risking the initiation of formal proceedings as a result.

2.2. Facts

To depict the background of the present situation, the financial, real, and policy phenomena of the early 1980s will be examined in turn. The detailed regulations that constrain many national capital markets in the EC contrast sharply with the growth of international financial markets that are global in scope and highly flexible since they are not subject to official regulation (Table 2.2). Against this background, the continued existence of nationally regulated capital markets in the Community appears somewhat anachronistic.

This contrast appears even sharper if one considers that the failure to build a European capital market was one of the reasons why Euromarkets came into existence. The absence of a liberalized and integrated official capital market *within* the Community constituted a vacuum which was filled by private activities, with the informal construction of a free and integrated capital market *outside* the Community. There is some analogy here with the way in which US multinationals have been able to

TABLE 2.1. *Internal lag of Community directives on capital markets and related issues*

Directive (subject)	Commission proposal	Council approval	Decision lag
First Council Directive implementing Art. 67 of the Treaty of Rome	1960	11 May 1960	2 months
Second Council Directive, completing and amending the First Directive	1962	18 Dec. 1962	7 months
Modified proposal for a Third Directive implementing Art. 67, submitted by the Commission pursuant to Art. 149(*a*)	1967	withdrawn in 1977	120 months
Directive on financial institutions	1965	28 June 1973	95 months
Council Directive 72/156/EEC on regulating international capital flows and neutralizing undesirable effects on domestic liquidity	1971	21 Mar. 1972	9 months
Council Directive 79/279/EEC co-ordinating conditions for admission of securities to official stock-exchange listing	1976	1979	38 months
Council Directive 80/390/EEC co-ordinating requirements for the drawing up, scrutiny, and distribution of listing particulars to be published for the admission of securities to official stock-exchange listing	1972	17 Mar. 1980	90 months
First Council Directive 77/780/EEC on co-ordination of laws, regulations, and administrative provisions relating to the taking up and pursuit of the business of credit institutions	1974	12 Dec. 1977	36 months

take fuller and better advantage of the opportunities offered by the common market than most European firms.

The golden period of steady, non-inflationary growth which accompanied the early steps on the road to liberalization has been followed by one of poor growth, price, and employment performance throughout the industrialized world (Table 2.3). More importantly, the structural disequilibria in the balance-of-payments situation of the major country groupings, and

TABLE 2.2. *Growth of international financial markets, 1970–1981* (US$ '000 millions)

	1970	1975	1981
Eurocurrency market estimated size			
gross	110	460	1,800[a]
net	65	250	905[a]
Eurocurrency bank credits, publicly announced in period	4.7	21.0	133.4
New international bond issues	4.6	19.9	53.0

[a] Provisional.

Source: Morgan Guaranty Trust, *World Financial Markets*, various issues.

TABLE 2.3. *The early 1960s versus the early 1980s: some indicators for the Community*

	1960–1965	1980–1982
GDP volume growth	5.3	0.8
Consumer prices	3.3	12.3
Unemployment rate	2.1	7.7
Net lending (+) or net borrowing (−) of general government (% of GDP)	in balance	−4.5
Real short-term interest rates	+0.4[a]	+2.1[a]
Share of exports in GDP (%)	18.5	29.5
Current account balance (% of GDP)	+0.3	−0.8
Cumulative change in ECU/USD rate	+1.3[b]	−28.0[b]

[a] Average 1961–5; and April 1980–1982.

[b] For 1960–5, change between the two yearly averages: for 1980–2, change between January 1980 and May 1982 (+ sign indicates ECU appreciation).

Sources: Commission of the European Communities, Directorate-General for Economic and Financial Affairs, *European Economy* and *European Economy: Supplement A, Recent Economic Trends*, various issues; and Commission staff internal calculations.

particularly the persistence of a large deficit for the non-oil developing countries, continue to imply a sustained need for financing, i.e. for compensating international capital flows, giving an essential role to international financing markets as recycling vehicles. In 1981 the OECD countries raised medium- and long-term loans on the Euromarkets amounting to some $100 billion; adding the $35 billion they raised through international bond issues, this gives a total of $135 billion, which surpasses by far the current account deficit of the OECD countries in the same year ($29 billion). In general terms, there is thus a saving–investment dissociation at the international level calling for a high degree of international capital mobility.

Finally, in a world of generally floating exchange rates, the currency area of the European Monetary System has existed since March 1979, with fixed (but adjustable) exchange rates. There is a clear contrast between the EMS, which provides unrestricted convertibility of European currencies within fixed exchange rate margins, and the continued existence of nationally regulated European capital markets. In other words, while at the short end of financial capital transactions money markets are tied together and integrated by means of the EMS, the longer term end of European capital markets, comprising long-term loans as well as the issue and circulation of securities, is still segmented.

2.3. *Economic analysis*

Theoretical developments as well as factual experience have modified the analysis of 'insular' economies outlined above for the early 1960s. It is now clear that full insulation from external influences is impossible in a world of capital mobility even with floating exchange rates.[6]

This conclusion is supported by the following line of reasoning. The basic determinants of exchange rates—relative cost and price developments and balance-of-payments positions—operate consistently only in the long run. In the short run, exchange rates may be pushed in either direction away from their fundamental equilibrium level by rapidly changing expectations influenced by a variety of factors. Recent analysis of exchange rate determination has explained the frequent overshooting of the equilibrium level (defined in terms of purchasing power parity or other determinants) by treating exchange rates as financial asset prices, i.e. prices which are determined in the short term by portfolio adjustments in asset markets and influenced by often unstable

---

[6] See Tobin and Braga de Macedo 1980.

expectations.[7] Short-run changes in exchange rates are thus brought about by massive flows of short-term financial capital, generated by and transmitted via efficient international financial markets.

The deviation of exchange rates from their 'normal' level, i.e. their over- or undershooting, has important real effects on domestic economic activity and industries exposed to international competition. It follows that national authorities of widely open economies cannot afford benign neglect of their exchange rate.

The policy reaction of national authorities varies according to their possibilities: returning to the inconsistent quartet, Community countries have dealt with the resulting policy dilemma by adopting different combinations and yielding on one or more of the various fronts. In very general terms the situation can be described as follows: the smaller open economies, such as the Benelux countries, have sacrificed the independence of their domestic monetary policy on the altar of exchange rate stability and free capital flows. On the other hand, France and Italy have broadly aimed at insulating their domestic monetary policy and at maintaining their currencies' exchange rate via the use of exchange controls (and other direct controls, such as credit ceilings). The United Kingdom has followed yet another course: it did not join the EMS because it felt that an exchange rate commitment was incompatible with the lifting of exchange controls and the pursuit of quantitative monetary targets, to which it gave priority.

One could object that Germany, at least, has in some way succeeded in squaring the circle. To the extent that this is true, it is clearly due to Germany's pivotal position in determining monetary conditions in the Community as a whole. But if the horizon is enlarged beyond the confines of the Community, it is sufficient to look at developments over the last decade (the 1970s) to realize the extent to which even Germany first had recourse to capital controls (special minimum reserve requirements, cash deposit requirements, and limitations on the sale of domestic fixed-interest securities to non-residents) in the early 1970s[8] and, more

---

[7] For various versions of the asset market approach to exchange rate determination, see Lindbeck 1976.

[8] Causing the German Export Council to remark that 'in restricting international capital movements, the Federal Republic has embarked on a path which will lead us away from a European monetary union'. Quoted in Walter 1976.

recently (1982), has had to design its monetary policy in the light of external considerations; in the words of its own monetary authorities: 'During the year under review (1981) the Bundesbank was unable to take as much account as in previous years of domestic economic problems (which it always kept very much in mind) in its policies, which had to be oriented more towards external requirements at times'.[9] In the present international monetary system, a truly independent monetary policy is feasible only in what could be termed the nth currency country, i.e. the USA.

3. LOOKING AHEAD: THREE POSSIBLE APPROACHES

The picture of the changed economic environment should now be completed with an attempt to look ahead, to define a new Community policy for European capital markets. Comparison of the early 1980s with the early 1960s reveals the persistence of the old problem in a new environment: we still have to reconcile the four elements of the inconsistent quartet. The problem, and the whole question of capital-market liberalization in the Community, has to be tackled on the basis of a Community-orientated organization of these four elements. We can think of trade, money, control, and policy as constituting the four rings of what must be an organized chain, and we can distil three policy approaches that could bring about full consistency between them. In what follows, they will be briefly described in their pure and conceptual form, i.e. for clarity of exposition the existence of political difficulties and the constraints of gradualism will be deliberately ignored.

3.1. Following consistent macro-policies

If the policy line followed by each member country were consistent with that of its partners and orientated towards commonly agreed objectives, no tensions would develop in the chain. Thus policy co-ordination looks like the road of wisdom and simplicity. So much so that, starting with the Treaty, a whole library of

[9] Deutsche Bundesbank 1982.

Community texts has laid down detailed procedures by which groups, committees, and councils of experts, officials, central bankers, and ministers, should reach *ex ante* consistency, as if *one* policy were followed in the whole of the area. In the Commission in Brussels every effort is made to maximize the effectiveness of co-ordination, but my experience there made me profoundly aware of the formidable limits of this exercise: what appears to be the road of wisdom and simplicity is, in many ways, the road of over-simplification and deception.

Complete and systematic harmony among the macro-policies pursued by a group of sovereign governments is, to say the least, extremely difficult to achieve, for a variety of reasons. Each government ultimately responds to its own electorate; there is little probability, and we constantly have evidence of this, of voters of different countries voting for the same policies at the same time. In addition, policy calendars do not coincide; even the definition of the fiscal year varies, budget proposals for a given year are presented at very different points of time in different countries. For monetary policy, the difficulties are just as great, since they concern not only the calendar but also the choice of targets and instruments and the structures of the banking industry and financial intermediaries in general. Finally, policy mixes are shaped in very different ways according not only to choice but also to the institutional relationships between national central banks and Treasuries. And more reasons could be given.

Complete and systematic consistency of policies achieved without any institutional infrastructure is a dream, a beautiful and dangerous one like the anarchist dream of universal altruism. On the other hand, the attempt to create an international infrastructure permitting the dream to be turned into reality would encounter enormous difficulties and resistance, much greater than those met by more limited institutional steps in the areas of capital-market or monetary integration.

To the extent that co-ordination does not work, or at best, in the words of J. J. Polak, is only 'a relatively weak form of international influence on national policies',[10] we have different distortions in the other rings of the chain. One is the development of controls, including capital-market controls, as we have already

---

[10] Polak 1981.

seen. Another, of course, is the widening of economic divergences that create tensions in the EMS and threaten trade and agricultural arrangements, thus endangering the very foundations of the Community. In other words, if the policy co-ordination ring in our chain of four elements does not hold, at least one of the other elements is bound to come under tension and perhaps break: trade, money, or controls. To prevent such negative consequences, ways have to be found to strengthen policy co-ordination, either indirectly, via capital-market integration, or directly, via the completion of monetary union.

3.2. Capital market integration

The idea of capital-market integration conforms closely to the fundamental principles of the Community and is based on the logic of strengthening policy co-ordination in an indirect way through the institutionalization, or organization, of a European capital market. Detailed proposals to enact further liberalization directives and to revitalize the legally established supervisory functions of the Commission and the Monetary Committee[11] are its basic practical ingredients. It might be objected, however, that the integration of *European* capital markets has become an obsolete or redundant goal: financial markets are already linked *world-wide* via the Euromarkets, which have repeatedly proved their worth as efficient vehicles for international capital mobility. It can be argued that there are market pressures towards conformity and co-ordination. As Lindbeck observed: 'The internationalization of credit markets and the integration of governments in those markets as regular lenders and borrowers, as well as the increased importance of market forces for exchange rate determination, mean that the coordination of government actions is increasingly brought about by the "invisible hand of markets", rather than by the more visible hand of government authorities'.[12]

This may be partially true, but it does not mean that the

---

[11] This advisory body was set up in 1958 pursuant to Article 105 of the Treaty of Rome. It is charged with monitoring the monetary and financial situation of each member state and of the Community as a whole, and with providing opinions on international monetary matters.

[12] Lindbeck 1977.

problem of government action in terms of management and surveillance can be avoided and reliance placed solely on market
forces. This is borne out by the tendency over the last decade for
all major countries to increase their authorities' regulatory and
supervisory powers, in many cases enacting far-reaching legislation for the first time since the 1930s (another crisis period), and
by the attempts to increase the transparency of the international
financial markets, which have tended to grow faster than the
authorities' ability to supervise them.

The fact is that money and financial markets do not manage
themselves. To the extent that there remains a need for control
and supervision, the question arises of the scope they should
have, and in this regard there is a solid case for their being carried out at the Community level. In this respect the EC can be
seen as constituting an optimum regulation area. This would certainly be preferable to a completely independent use of controls
by individual member countries, which may work at cross purposes and invite retaliation and competitive restrictive measures.
A rational use of controls based on Community co-operation and
consultation would alleviate such difficulties: its intention would
not be to extend the area of government regulation, but on the
contrary to forestall conditions leading to the widespread expansion of restrictions.

The Treaty in fact advocates a Community approach of this
type in Article 70, providing for 'the progressive co-ordination of
the exchange policies of Member States in respect of the movement of capital between those States and third countries. For this
purpose the Council shall issue directives, acting unanimously. It
shall endeavour to attain the highest possible degree of liberalization.' This article provided the basis for the 1972 directive on regulating international capital flows and neutralizing their
undesirable effects on domestic liquidity.[13]

This directive was approved in the wake of the unsettling
events following the demise of the Bretton Woods system (and to
respond particularly to the formidable short-term capital inflows

[13] The directive provided that member states 'adopt measures immediately in
order to have available, should occasion arise, the appropriate instruments for the
purpose of discouraging exceptionally large capital movements, in particular to
and from third countries', seen to cause 'serious disturbances in the monetary situation and in the economic trends in Member States', likely to 'hinder the establishment by stages of an economic and monetary union'.

recorded by Germany in 1971). The implementation of this strategy is none the less highly 'legislation intensive'. There are not only extremely long decision lags with the Community, as already mentioned, but more importantly the legislative process in the EC is paralysed, as national governments are increasingly absorbed in resolving domestic problems. Regarding the building of the necessary institutional arrangements to conduct systematic Community-wide policies in monetary and financial matters, national governments are passive and immobile. Nevertheless, since this paralysis can be overcome if the political will is there, this road is to be tried seriously. Its implementation would be a major step towards exploiting the above-mentioned potential of the EC as an optimum regulation area.

3.3. Complete monetary union

The third approach, monetary union, is well-known and was attempted after the collapse of the Bretton Woods system had deprived the common market of the vital monetary organization required for its proper functioning. It is therefore not necessary to expound on it further here. Suffice it to say that intellectual support for European monetary union stems from acknowledgement that the twin goals of freedom of capital movements and fixed exchange rates (explicit or implicit in the Treaty) imply a single currency area and a single monetary authority. Within a single country—where there are of course unrestricted capital flows and a single exchange rate—it is clear that 'the various branches of the central bank cannot pursue independent monetary policies. The Federal Reserve, whose 12 regional banks were established on the contrary assumption, learned this early in its career, and most other central banks never tried.'[14]

Fully fledged European monetary union is thus the high road to policy co-ordination and economic convergence, implementing these directly by replacing a number of monetary authorities with a single, central authority. Its realization should in practice be easier than the capital-market-liberalization approach; it would not be necessary to overcome a multitude of intricate, difficult obstacles and regulations. It would be sufficient to realize one

[14] Wallich 1972.

major achievement: monetary union. Here too, implementation would conform to an optimum concept: that of the Community as an optimum currency area.

4. CONCLUSIONS

Where do we stand today in the Community as regards these three approaches of: (i) following consistent and co-ordinated policies; or arriving at such policies through either (ii) capital market integration or (iii) monetary union? It would seem that on all three fronts we are, to a greater or lesser extent, at a sort of half-way house between purely national policy formulation and policy-making that is entirely lodged at the Community level. It is a situation in which the Community is still contending with the problem posed by the inconsistent quartet. Until a coherent, Community-orientated organization of all these four elements is found, the temptation is to yield a little on each, including even the principle of free trade, thus calling into question the very foundations of the Community. There is no point in assuming an attitude of moral or legalistic condemnation in the face of such developments and risks: the problem needs to be tackled, and in this regard there would seem to be two broad possibilities.

The first, and certainly preferable solution, would be the complete implementation of one of the three alternatives examined above: complete co-ordination of policies, full capital-market integration, or monetary union would square the circle. There is no need to illustrate the considerable difficulties that will have to be overcome before arriving at the final destination along any one of these three roads: the experience of the Community to date is unfortunately eloquent and sufficient testimony in this regard. But if the will to take the important qualitative leap which is involved were to materialize, it would seem that the way of monetary union is likely to offer the least 'mechanical' resistance and the greatest chance of success.

The second, less satisfactory but in practice more probable, alternative is that of gradualism. Here the transition from purely national approaches to a Community-orientated organization is seen as a progressive shift in a spectrum, as a gradual but nevertheless ongoing process. The EMS, for example, by focusing attention on convergence, can be seen as a crucial catalyst in this process of integration, enhancing the legitimacy of each participant's concern for the others' policies, and inducing member states to discuss fundamental issues sooner, in greater depth, and in terms of more concrete policy options than in the past.

Barring a great leap forward to full Community co-ordination, a fully integrated European capital market, or monetary union, we therefore appear to have no choice but to persevere on all three fronts, taking a series of steps, lengthening our stride where possible, and gaining momentum until the leap—which will then perhaps not have to be so 'great'—to effective integration provides the natural and logical culmination of our efforts since the early 1960s.

3

Lessons from the European Monetary System

1. INTRODUCTION

Fifteen years ago policy-makers believed in, and operated under, a fixed rate regime, while most academic economists were advocating a system of floating rates and were pointing to the fundamental weaknesses and drawbacks of the Bretton Woods arrangements. These arrangements subsequently broke down and the search for national independence in macro-economic policies came to be conducted in the context of floating rates. Since the collapse of the Bretton Woods system academic research has taken several directions. One strand that developed while attempts were still being made to reconstruct the system sought to reconcile a regime of fixed exchange rates with the advantages of easy adjustments to changes in economic conditions: crawling pegs and the like. Subsequent contributions came from the study of the causes and possible costs of excessive variability in exchange rates, of overshootings. Recently, the study of the relationships between sovereign countries in the area of monetary policy, and more generally of macro-economic policies, has developed with increasing use of game theory, which, at least for policy-makers, probably makes more sense than much of the preceding literature, although it does not always bring very concrete results.

Few proposals have been made for reforming what used to be called the international monetary system. This subject seems to be out of fashion among both practitioners and academic economists. The latter have so far tended to ignore the experience of the EMS in their research. To analyse the EMS and understand the essence of its six years of life, economists would have to work

December 1985, Badia Fiesolana (Florence). Lecture given at the European University Institute. The EMS had successfully performed its disciplinary function. The negotiations on the Single European Act were near to conclusion.

with experts on legal matters and economic institutions. The EMS experience has certainly not yet been fully incorporated into the academic research of economists. The following, subjective and non-technical, account of this experience is divided into four parts. It starts by examining the functioning of the EMS and then looks at the lessons that can be learnt. Next it considers possible and, in my view, desirable developments in the System. Finally, it examines the difficulties such developments are likely to encounter.

2. THE FUNCTIONING OF THE EMS

A detailed account of how the EMS has functioned in its early years will not be given. Elsewhere,[1] I have analysed the performance of the System in terms of exchange rate variability, interest rates, links with the dollar, and macro-economic convergence in the member countries, by comparing the performance of the EMS countries in the years before and after the System was established, as well as the performance of the EMS and leading non-EMS countries. Both these comparisons show that the System has been fairly successful in achieving its immediate objectives, namely to have more stable real and nominal exchange rates[2] and a certain degree of convergence in intermediate monetary objectives such as interest rates and the growth of monetary aggregates. There is also evidence, though weaker, that the final objectives—inflation rates in particular—have moved substantially closer.[3]

Turning from these quantitative results to more general considerations, the achievements of the EMS in these six years can be summarized in three points. First, the EMS has saved free trade inside the Community in a period in which it was threatened by

---

[1] Padoa-Schioppa 1985*a*.

[2] The figures given for the periods before and after the inception of the EMS point to a particularly significant reduction in variability, measured as the standard deviation of the monthly % changes in the effective exchange rates of the leading EMS currencies: from 1.4 to 0.9% for the DM, from 2 to 0.7% for the lira, and from 1.4 to 1% for the French franc.

[3] The correlation between the domestic rate of inflation and that of Germany increased from 0.35 to 0.85 for France, from 0.15 to 0.65 for Italy, and from 0.34 to 0.61 for the UK.

numerous factors: the tensions following the second oil shock, the very large inflation differentials, and the highly divergent economic policies—one could almost say ideologies—to be found in the period. To take an example of the last aspect, the roles assigned to macro-economic policy by the newly elected government in France in 1981 and its counterparts in the United Kingdom and more recently Germany were poles apart. In these conditions, the strains were very serious. The EMS can justifiably be said to have preserved the trade links inside the Community: this is its first and most important achievement.

Secondly, the EMS has significantly promoted macro-economic adjustment in member countries. Even though it has often been insufficient, the EMS has been a force pushing very strongly for such adjustment in France, Italy, Belgium, and Denmark; indeed, in all the countries with serious macro-economic imbalances. This was true not only for countries with high inflation. For instance, Belgium did not have an inflation problem, its major problems were unemployment and external disequilibrium. This was probably because, being a small and very open economy, Belgium could not take the inflationary route followed by Italy and France and had to pay for its lack of adjustment more in terms of unemployment, external disequilibrium, and external debt. In all these countries, the EMS has been the catalyst of a change in policy, a catalyst that some have seen as tardy and insufficient, but which is still an important one when the situation today is compared with that in 1979.

Thirdly, the EMS has helped to shield the Community from the crisis of the dollar. The last few years' movements in the US currency would have had a much greater impact on the cohesion of the European economies if the EMS had not existed.

I am naturally well aware that no proof is provided here of these three points. It cannot, of course, be said that these goals would not have been achieved at all without the EMS, or that they have been fully achieved, or that actual achievements have been entirely due to the EMS. What I claim is that in all three respects the EMS has exerted a decisive influence.

3. THE LESSONS

3.1. In the economic field

What lessons can be drawn from the EMS experience? The focus is on those of interest to economists, but other lessons are highly significant for the life and development of the European Community at large. From an economic point of view, there are three main lessons. First, the EMS has shown that there is a way out of the dilemma often presented to policy-makers: whether to move back to some sort of Bretton Woods system of exchange rate relationships, which is inevitably too rigid and probably not feasible today, or to live in a world of totally unregulated exchange rate relationships, with all the problems, dangers, and difficulties that were a feature of the 1970s.

When the EMS was set up, it was presented (and probably also conceived by its creators) as a kind of local Bretton Woods, with official rates that member countries were committed to defending, plus the possibility of modifying them. This conception gave rise to not entirely unjustified scepticism about the viability of the System, since the prevailing idea was that the Bretton Woods system had broken down for good reasons that were still valid when the EMS was invented. The EMS has developed, however, rather differently from the Bretton Woods model and cannot be seen, after five or six years of life, as a repetition, not even a successful one, of the Bretton Woods scheme.

Several elements have emerged as essential components of the System that were either not included in the written provisions or, if they were written, were not originally considered essential. The first, and the most important, is that realignments have become a truly collective decision. The setting of new central rates in the EMS is a Community decision, in the same way as the decisions on agricultural prices. This procedure was not built in from the start, but developed gradually.

The first realignment took place in September 1979, less than six months after the System had started. I remember vividly that the Secretary of State of the German Ministry of Finance—it was Mr Lahnstein at the time—came to the realignment session with a list of what the new parities were to be, saying: 'We have thought about the situation and have come to the conclusion that the following parity changes have to be made.' The session was rather difficult. It succeeded in setting new parities, which were in the direction indicated by that list, but not identical. It was clear to all that the next realignment would have to be made differently. At the first meeting of the Monetary Committee after the realignment, Mr Lahnstein himself expressed the view that the Commission should propose the new parity grid on the next occasion. In a sense, this episode can be seen as the switch from the 1972 agreement on exchange rates (the so-called Snake) to the EMS. In the Snake there were only small countries and minor currencies grouped around Germany and the Deutschmark. Proceeding in the way tried in the first EMS realignment was probably feasible and desirable in the Snake, but it was not possible in the full Community context of the EMS.

The second realignment was totally unilateral. At a European Council meeting in Dublin a member of the Danish delegation came to me—I was then a Director-General in the Commission and a member of the Monetary Committee—and announced: 'We have decided today in Copenhagen to change the parity; please tell the other members of the Community; we are devaluing by 5 per cent.' The Community institutions swallowed the decision, but at the next Monetary Committee, speaking on behalf of the Commission, I clearly stated, and the Committee agreed, that it was totally unacceptable to arrive at a realignment in that way ever again.

The third realignment, however, was still of a unilateral nature. It was made by Italy, over the telephone, in April 1981. The Italian authorities asked to devalue by 6 per cent, and this was probably reasonable because Italian inflation was running at almost 20 per cent. The competitive advantage that Italy had acquired by allowing the lira to depreciate before the start of the System had been consumed and a parity change was necessary. But there was renewed agreement that this procedure could not be accepted again in the future. The Italian authorities informed the chairman of the Monetary Committee late on Saturday night; there was literally no time to call a meeting since the Italian coalition government itself had reached agreement only shortly before and to pack two big negotiations—one national within a government coalition, and the other at the Community level between ten partners—into a weekend is almost impossible.

Thus, what can be called the hegemonic method was abandoned after the first realignment and the unilateral method typical of Bretton Woods after the third. Since then, all the realignments have been made properly, in the sense that on each occasion there was a meeting at the Community level, with the realignment being decided only after all the member countries had had an opportunity to propose a change in parities alternative to that asked for by the applicant country.

Another factor that makes the EMS very different from Bretton Woods, is that realignments have generally been accompanied by a change in the domestic policies of the applicant countries. In other words, realignments have been part of comprehensive policy packages designed to bring about adjustment. This means that changes in exchange rates have not simply been a way to ratify differences in inflation rates, but have been actively used as a necessary element of a change in policy designed to bring national economies closer into line with that of the Community.

In conclusion, the first lesson is that there is indeed a possibility, at least for a group of countries like the Community countries, to organize their monetary relationships in a way that is neither an impossible repetition of the old Bretton Woods system nor the kind of monetary anarchy that was seen in the 1970s and still rules at the world level. The second lesson, and it is perhaps an even more surprising one, is about 'parallel currencies'.[4] I am referring to the success of the ECU.

I will not describe the facts, which have been widely published in the press, concerning the unforeseen growth of the ECU in private markets. What is important is that they show that there is considerable potential for an international currency used by private agents, and that the development of this potential only requires a very small legal, and one could say 'official', platform. In reality, the only difference, as regards the ECU, between the situation before and after EMS started in 1979 is the name; the European Unit of Account had its name changed to ECU,

---

[4] The meaning of this term has gradually changed during the debate on European monetary unification. In this chapter the concept of a 'parallel currency' is comparable to that of the 'common currency' referred to in Chapter 8, where it means a currency existing alongside the others and possessing an autonomous monetary creation capacity.

everything else remained the same. Of course, the EMS was also created, but the Exchange Rate Mechanism, which is its centre-piece, does not affect the private ECU directly.

The development of the ECU in the last few years suggests that the markets have recognized its potential as the future currency of the Community. It also shows that, unlike the Special Drawing Right, the ECU is more than a simple basket currency, because it comprises currencies bound by mutual commitments that the currencies composing the SDR do not have. Moreover, the 'intangible' element of political commitment which is behind the EMS—intangible because it is not operational in relation to private markets—is very powerful indeed in showing private agents that if they want to develop a basket currency for their operations, they would do better to choose a standardized, easily negotiable basket, with some official endorsement, rather than creating their own on each occasion, with the aim of optimizing its composition.

In one way this is surprising, but in another it is not, because in the international financial sphere there have been other important developments that are almost entirely the fruit of private initiative. The Euromarkets are one, and they have filled a gap left by the official authorities, which were slow in meeting the needs of economic and financial integration; private agents simply stepped in and filled the gap. More fundamentally, it is worth noting that in most countries central banks came after, and not before, money. In the case of the ECU, there is still no central bank, but we seem to be getting the currency.

This is a second very important lesson. When people first spoke about it more than ten years ago, a parallel currency was simply an idea. I myself did not know what attitude to take towards it, but in practice we have seen that it is a possibility, and problems may even arise from the ECU being too successful. The third lesson of the EMS concerns regional systems. In the organization of international monetary relationships it is both possible and necessary to have a level between the national and the world levels.

It is worth asking what would happen if some of the leading European countries agreed to enter into new arrangements linking their currencies to the dollar or the yen. Without an intermediate step consisting of some kind of arrangement at the regional

Community level, such as the EMS, there would probably be a very serious threat to intra-Community relationships, because the other countries would hardly accept the constraints imposed by a system in which they did not participate. Besides, orderly and balanced intra-Community relationships are essential to the well-being not only of the Community countries but also of the world economy. It is hard to imagine that the European currencies could participate directly in a more co-ordinated system of world monetary management, or readily accept explicit leadership by one of their number.

Moreover, in the absence of an international monetary system, the EMS at least provides order in a region as important as Europe. Other regional examples can, of course, be given. The IMF now has almost 150 member countries and most of their currencies participate in some kind of local arrangement, so that the problem of ordering monetary relationships really involves three areas, three key currencies: the US dollar, the Japanese yen, and a European currency, which is something between the ECU and the Deutschmark. I regard this third lesson as very important for the question of how the world economy can and must be organized.

3.2. For the development of the Community

If we move from the economic standpoint to the broader one of the general development of the Community, the list of lessons to be drawn from the EMS experience becomes even longer. It has frequently been claimed that the only important success achieved by the Community in the last few years has been the EMS. This in my view is an exaggeration. There have been other important developments, notably the enhanced role of the European Parliament following the direct election of its members: universal suffrage is such a fundamental aspect of political life that it can alter the course of the Community on its own. Even so, the EMS is undoubtedly a most important innovation in the life of the Community and worth examining in its general features, independently of the fact that its object is money rather than some other matter.

In the first place, the EMS was conceived and created outside the normal Community procedures. This may not be a praiseworthy feature, but it is a reality. The original proposal was made by President Roy Jenkins in a speech that took his colleagues in the Commission almost by surprise. The speech would perhaps not have been made if there had been more prior consultation within the Commission. Subsequently, the bones of the System were negotiated and prepared by a small group of representatives of some, not even all, of the Community countries, completely outside the normal channels and in spite of the lack of enthusiasm of technicians and several central banks. Again, it is not implausible to imagine that without these exceptional procedures such a major step would not have been possible.

A second lesson is the usefulness of variable geometry in the Community. Again, we may not like it, but the EMS is nevertheless the first important case in which the decision was taken to move ahead without the full participation of all the members of the Community. The future will tell whether the EMS can become the system of the whole Community.

A third element is that the EMS owes much of its success to the fact that it has mobilized private agents to a much greater extent than many other Community initiatives. In a sense those who have worked most effectively for the EMS are the banks, firms, and others who have developed the ECU in the markets, simply by exploiting the initial push given by the creation of the System.

A fourth and essential element is that the operational constraints of the EMS make the threat of disaster so strong that it is virtually impossible to postpone decisions. In normal times intervention becomes obligatory when currencies reach their bilateral fluctuation margins. The rule is very simple, leaving no room for interpretation; everybody knows exactly what has to be done. When the realignment procedure is invoked, the System switches to a very different mode of operation based on a crisis procedure in which the rule is replaced by discretion, and technicians by ministers. The operational constraint is the fact that the markets open on Monday morning, that you cannot stop the clock, that decisions cannot be put off. This concentrates the mind and forces the parties to reach agreement in a way that is very difficult to achieve in other Community negotiations.

A fifth interesting element is that the EMS constitutes a 'parallel' system. It does not replace national legislations or existing realities, but creates a Community level, a Community dimension—in particular the ECU—without replacing national currencies. It thus shows that in some areas Community legislation can deal with the same object as national legislation, and in a way compete with it, offering a Community level to those who want and need to move at that level.[5]

4. THE POSSIBLE DEVELOPMENTS

This section considers the future of the System: not the ultimate goal of creating a monetary union, with a single currency and a single central bank for the whole Community, but the possible and desirable developments that could occur before that goal is reached. The first aspect is the growth in the private use of the ECU. It can be both a widening and a deepening.

In the financial sphere the ECU can easily be used to denominate monetary assets, in addition to long- and medium-term financial assets, for which this role is already firmly established. Some first steps have been taken: credit cards, traveller's cheques, instruments that can be used to make payments. Another field where widening is possible is the non-financial area, the area of trade, where the ECU could be used to denominate non-financial contracts. A number of ideas and proposals have been put forward. One promising area is East–West trade, another is trade in primary commodities. There is, of course, a big difference between simply using the ECU to pay for certain commodities and using it to price them. The big change would take place the day a commodity was priced in ECUs, making the price of that commodity to Community buyers independent of the dollar exchange rate. The movements of the dollar have been a strong incentive to advance in this direction, and further progress is possible.

The deepening of the ECU can be conceived as the gradual disappearance of the ECU's basket nature. While the ECU was originally defined as the sum of given amounts of the various Community currencies, there are no technical impediments why it should not become a currency in its own right, owing nothing to

[5] This possibility is important in the subsequent development of the concept of subsidiarity.

the fact that it was originally conceived as a basket. Indeed, no official commitment of any kind stems from the fact that the ECU is a basket; the private market functions without agents being bound by the basket definition, and both the interest rate and the exchange rate of the ECU could at some point become independent of the basket. As a matter of fact, the former is already independent: the interest rate of an ECU-denominated bond is not the weighted average of the interest rates of the component currencies. The same could conceivably happen for the ECU's exchange rate. Here is a possible development that would take the ECU very far along the road to being a fully fledged currency.

A second development—which is very important in itself and which would be even more important if the first actually took place—is the need to devise controls over the ECU. Those hoping for the development of a European currency may perhaps have been happy at first that there were almost no controls on the ECU and that it could take advantage of this situation. However, looking ahead, it is necessary that the same steps should be taken for the ECU as have historically been taken for all currencies: namely to develop a system of controls whereby responsibility for the stability, good quality, and legal status of this particular currency are entrusted to a legally constituted institution.

This point would require a lengthy explanation that goes beyond the scope of this essay, but in my view it would not be particularly difficult to establish such controls. All, or almost all, the technical means necessary are already there, though this claim may seem surprising. A private market for the ECU already exists; we should soon have—and this would be a decisive advance—an organized clearing system for the ECU attached to the Bank for International Settlements in Basle. If this happens, the private circuit of the ECU will be complete and have a link with the BIS, the home of the official ECU and the regular meeting-place of the governors of the Community central banks. The ECU clearing would thus be linked to an institution that is fully capable of acting as a bank. Nor is there any operational obstacle preventing the critical contact between the official and the private ECUs. And this contact, namely the exchange of private ECUs against official ECUs, is the essence of monetary control. So, if central bankers one Sunday in Basle decided to allow their agent, the Bank for International Settlements, to swap private ECUs against official ECUs, we would have, qualitatively, the whole system in place. Thus, in this essential operational sense, control is possible. Of course, it is still embryonic; yet, though they are small, all the organs exist in the System—it is complete.

A legal framework is also needed. German monetary policy, which has been the most successful in the post-war period, owes much to monetary legislation, as well as to monetary operations. The forbidding by law of indexation clauses in contracts denominated in Deutschmarks is a most important requirement for a sound monetary constitution. Legislation of this kind is still lacking for the ECU. When the Commission made such a proposal, surprisingly enough it was the German authorities who objected. The legislative capacity is in place: the Community's legal institutions are fully empowered to legislate on the ECU. Some steps will have to be taken in this domain, since the legal aspect of controls is very important.

The third area of future developments, after the private ECU and monetary controls, is the shift from monetary to financial integration. It is surprising that integration is proceeding faster where it is more difficult to achieve, that is, at the monetary end of the financial system, which is the most volatile and potentially the most destabilizing, while there is so little integration at the financial end which has a stabilizing role. This is even more surprising when we consider that the Treaty of Rome hardly touches on monetary integration, whereas much is said about financial integration.

Financial integration is desirable from the point of view of the efficient allocation of resources, but the European financial industry (banking, insurance, stock markets, and capital movements) is almost as segmented now as it was ten years ago. The development of the EMS, however, necessarily entails progress towards financial integration in two areas: mobility of capital and the integration, or harmonization, of financial structures, legislations, and institutions. With regard to capital mobility some countries, particularly France and Italy, are out of line, but the EMS is a continuing source of pressure on laggard countries to remove existing obstacles. As regards the integration of financial structures and legislation, it is rather difficult to classify countries according to their readiness to remove existing barriers and restrictions. For instance, the strongest opposition to further integration of the insurance industry comes from Germany.

5. THE DIFFICULTIES

Finally, it is worth looking at the difficulties to be encountered ahead: some of these are 'false' difficulties, that is, they are more apparent than real. Sterling is one. It is said that the EMS cannot progress without the participation of sterling. I do not share this view: sterling's joining is desirable, but it is not true that the EMS cannot advance without it. Progress has been made and more is possible. But such progress must not discriminate in any way against the members of the Community who do not participate in the EMS. This is an important legal problem for the experts to research. My own, non-expert view is that while the so-called *acquis* of the Community must be preserved for all members, it would not be harmful for the Community, nor illegal, for some countries to integrate more than others. If a group of countries decided on closer co-operation, without discriminating against other member countries, this would not be incompatible with the spirit of the Community. Nor should there be impediments to those countries making full use of Community procedures and the Community system, including its ultimate safeguard—the Court of Justice. The EMS has shown that this is possible. When a realignment is made, the British are present; they participate in the debate, albeit not as full members. There do not appear to be any technical or legal impediments to further progress along this road.

A second false difficulty is the dollar. People say that the success of the EMS is attributable to the strong dollar and that with a weak dollar the System will be hard put to survive. But the EMS was originally created in 1978 to face the problems posed by a weak dollar. The strength of the dollar in recent years has accustomed us to thinking that the strong dollar has underpinned the System, and in many ways it has. It is, of course, true that the problems created by a weak dollar are not the same as those created by a strong dollar, and it would be very unwise and dangerous for the EMS to face a weak dollar with the same policies as it has faced the strong dollar. However, it is totally wrong to think that the EMS cannot cope with a sliding dollar.

Let me outline three real and important difficulties. One can be called 'breakdown before progress': the System could break down before the kind of developments I have described take place. There is little need to expand on this. The System is fragile; it has been surprisingly successful and resilient if we bear in mind its intrinsic fragility—a member country could decide to opt out at any point, leading to a sudden collapse. At realignment meetings agreement is often reached between 11 p.m. and midnight, but one day it might not be reached, and 24 hours later the System could cease to exist. These are very real dangers. Alternatively, after a perfectly democratic debate and vote, a country might decide that it simply did not want to stay in the System, that it wanted autonomy of action. France came close to this during the run-up to the March 1983 realignment. Fortunately, the breakdown did not occur; but the danger is always there.

The second difficulty will take longer to explain. It is what I call the inconsistent quartet. In a system of sovereign countries it is logically impossible to have free trade, free capital movements, fixed exchange rates, and full autonomy of national macroeconomic policies at the same time. This is not because countries act in bad faith or disregard the Treaty, but rather that it is impossible for all of them to reconcile the four elements of the quartet. Of course one country—Germany—may be strong enough to accept the three external constraints and still pursue its preferred policies. Its economic size and strength mean it can remain relatively unaffected by the policies of other countries while exerting an influence on theirs. In the present situation in Europe, the small countries (Belgium, Luxemburg, the Netherlands, and Denmark, and Austria as well) have accepted the monetary sovereignty of the Bundesbank, while two large countries—France and Italy, which make the difference between the EMS and the Snake—have accepted an exchange rate constraint, but for the time being have made little progress towards full capital mobility. For these two countries this can be regarded as better than the opposite choice (understandably made by the United Kingdom, which has liberalized capital movements but not entered the EMS) because exchange rates are, generally speaking, more important than capital movements in terms of both allocative efficiency and safeguarding free trade in the Community. But these countries could well change their position, or—as France did in 1981–2—claim more autonomy in macro-economic policies, even to the point of breaking the exchange rate constraint. The fact is that the problem is not one of good intentions but of economic consistency. Real progress towards freedom of capital movements can only come from member countries accepting a further erosion of their macro-economic sovereignty.

The third difficulty can be baptized with the somewhat provocative name of German reluctance. Owing to its economic strength, political importance, and remarkable record of monetary stability, the Federal Republic's stand *vis-à-vis* European monetary integration is of crucial importance.

The difficulty is not basically a legal one. It is not, as some seem to think, the special legal and institutional independence of the Deutsche Bundesbank that prevents the European political institutions from proceeding towards closer monetary integration. No serious scholar of constitutional or Community law, in Germany or elsewhere, would claim that a decision furthering monetary unification adopted by the Council of the Communities under article 235 would not be legally binding on the Bundesbank. And in the unlikely event of the debate among scholars ending in a legal contest as a result of the Bundesbank failing to comply with such a Council decision, Germany would be taken to Court—presumably the European Court of Justice in Luxemburg. Now, it is very hard to imagine this body denying the power of the Community to take decisions, even far-reaching decisions in the monetary field; and the principle of the superiority of Community over national legislation is undisputed. The legal argument is thus not a difficulty in itself, but it reveals a serious political and institutional problem.

Nor does the present stance of the German monetary authorities *vis-à-vis* the private ECU constitute a serious difficulty, that is their reluctance to grant the ECU currency status because of an article of the German *Währungsgesetz* forbidding the use of indexation clauses in connection with Deutschmark-denominated monetary obligations. This certainly does not enhance the ECU's image. However, even though this somewhat paradoxical interpretation of the law appears open to question, we must not forget that it still leaves German citizens freer to hold ECU-denominated assets than citizens of countries such as Italy and France, where the ECU has the status of a foreign currency but exchange controls severely restrict residents' foreign currency operations. The attitude of the German authorities *vis-à-vis* the ECU, after all, creates more problems for German banks (which are partly prevented from doing profitable business and partly led to do it through their subsidiaries in Luxemburg) than it causes to the ECU, which in any case could not easily compete with the Deutschmark.

Where then is the problem? Let me try to spell it out in my own way, from the standpoint of a sympathetic observer of Germany. First of all one has to stress the remarkable success of Germany and the Bundesbank in maintaining monetary stability over almost forty years, even in periods in which most of the surrounding world was plagued by severe inflation. Such an outstanding performance can only command the greatest respect and admiration, particularly from a central banker operating in a country which is still striving to recover from ten years of double-digit inflation. It is only natural that the institution deserving most of the credit for this performance should be extremely cautious in considering the possibility of becoming mixed up with less virtuous partners.

Monetary success has constituted a political and historical success for post-war Germany. Since the end of the Bretton Woods system and the decoupling from the dollar, achievement of full international autonomy in the monetary field has had a significance beyond the monetary sphere. Penetrating observers have drawn a parallel between the French stance in problems of Western defence and the German posture in monetary matters. In both cases there is deep attachment to the strategies and institutions which made certain accomplishments possible.

Finally, there is the concern about preserving the independence of the central bank. This independence has two dimensions: a national one, relating to independence from international (or supranational) constraints, and an institutional one, relating to independence from the government. In matters concerning the EC these two dimensions are often confused, especially when the central bank enjoys a high degree of autonomy. This is epito-mized by the fact that the decision-making institution at the European level is the Council of Ministers. The Council is a leg-islative body in the European framework, but central banks see it as the offshoot of the executive branches from which they claim independence in the national context. Consequently, Council decisions may be resented as being imposed by the executive on the central banks. Thus, these two institutional dialectics may cumulatively strengthen the reluctance and hesitation of a central bank to accept institutional changes.

These motives help us to understand German reluctance, but not necessarily to share it; the long-term interests of Germany do not appear to be best served by such reluctance. I will not develop this claim in full, but just state my deeply rooted convic-tion that, in an ever smaller and more economically integrated world, it will become increasingly difficult, and in the end impos-sible, to save both domestic independence (*vis-à-vis* other deci-sion-making bodies) and national independence (*vis-à-vis* foreign partners). A policy of every man for himself is a dangerous dream, particularly when the country has the size, geographical position, and history of Germany. It is none the less hardly sur-prising that the temptation to take refuge in this dream is strongest in the areas of success, such as monetary policy for Germany, rather than in those of weakness.

The scope for building a monetary authority at the European level, endowed with the same safeguards of strength and indepen-dence as the Bundesbank enjoys today in Germany, is much greater in the present state of incompleteness of the European construction than it might be at some later time when the politi-cal and institutional process of unifying Europe will have gone further. Today, a European monetary authority could only be created as part of a federal political system, that is, one based on a plurality of mutually independent powers, because a centralized European constitution does not exist and is not on the cards. Thus, it is not unrealistic to think that the best way to save the special institutional position of the central bank is to place it safely at the Community level, where the hold of the executive and budgetary authorities is weak.

If this analysis is correct, then to urge further progress towards the monetary unification of our continent is not going against the fundamental interest of the Community's strongest monetary institution, although from time to time it may entail friendly debate. Treating the difficulty facing the Germans with the understanding and respect it deserves means action to promote further monetary integration will have to ensure that the legal, technical, and institutional safeguards of independence at the Community level are at least equal to those that underlay the remarkable monetary performance of the Bundesbank. It is also important to give sufficient substance to the proposals for a further strengthening of monetary integration so that its political value and links with the fundamental interests and orientations of Germany are more perceptible.

6. CONCLUSIONS

Basically, the three difficulties I have described are manifestations of one and the same problem, that of sovereignty and institutions. The general conclusion is, therefore, that the essential problems of the EMS, the obstacles to the System's full success, to its possible and desirable progress, are not technical or even economic in their essence. They are basically institutional problems and involve finding a way of shifting sovereignty that is at the same time feasible, successful, and acceptable. The role of the economist and the expert is to look for the *technical* solutions by means of which to overcome this fundamental institutional and political problem. But if it is not clearly recognized that these technical issues are just secondary aspects of a basically political problem, the essential point will be missed.

4

The ECU's Coming of Age

1. INTRODUCTION

While world monetary relationships are still wandering in a
non-system some fifteen years after the collapse of the Bretton
Woods arrangements and the SDR is at best living a wretched
life twenty years after it was invented, at the European level two
remarkable monetary processes have developed in parallel since
1979: the rise of the EMS and the growth of the ECU. The former has promoted orderly intra-European trade relationships and
greatly enhanced macro-economic co-ordination and stability.
The latter has resulted in many of the essential elements of a
common European currency being put into place. The EMS is
the work of the authorities. The ECU is essentially a market phenomenon. The close link between the two is clearly recognized:
on the one hand, the establishment of a common currency is the
natural completion of a process of monetary union of which the
EMS is the first step; on the other, the ECU owes much of its
success to the expectation that this process will run its full
course.

This article is about the main 'qualitative' aspects of the
ECU's past, present, and future development: the formal establishment of the clearing system, the *de facto* overcoming of the
basket phase, a reassessment of the lender-of-last-resort problem,
and the need for a link between the private and official ECUs.
The customary nature of the process whereby a monetary system
takes form has been long recognized. In the words written by
Karl Menger in 1892:[1]

Money has not been generated by law. In its origin it is a social, and not
a state-institution. Sanction by the authority of the state is a notion
alien to it. On the other hand, however, by state recognition and state

July 1987, Rome. Paper. The debate on the possible role of the ECU in both
policy and markets was lively before the idea of EMU was launched.

[1] Menger 1892.

regulation, this social institution of money has been perfected and adjusted to the manifold and varying needs of an evolving commerce, just as customary rights have been perfected and adjusted by statute law.

2. THE ECU CLEARING SYSTEM

In the early years of the EMS the nature of the ECU was closely associated with that of the basket of component currencies. Typically, the banks involved in ECU transactions (deposits and loans) had to create matching assets or liabilities by bundling national currencies. The need to economize on the transaction costs incurred in this bundling and unbundling gave rise to a bilateral clearing system, similar to that operating for other Eurocurrencies. Under this system, called MESA (Mutual ECU Settlement Agreement), ECU banking transactions were cleared by a group of five banks linked together through bilateral arrangements. The excess of claims or liabilities denominated in ECUs none the less still gave rise to costly bundling or unbundling of the component currencies.

In February 1982, prompted by Robert Triffin and Paul Caron, I convened the banks that were then active in the ECU market and invited them to set up a study group for the creation of a multilateral clearing system.[2] As to the location of the system, after envisaging the creation of an *ad hoc* institution, it was finally decided to ask the Bank of International Settlements to act as the clearing house. The system was set up in February 1986 and became fully operational at the beginning of 1987. It is based on a few banks holding ECU accounts for other member banks and clearing their net positions through the BIS. The clearing banks hold deposits with the latter in the component currencies as backing for their ECU transactions. These deposits ensure that the system is equipped to cope with temporary imbalances.

The results of the clearing system's few months of activity have been encouraging. The number of transactions has steadily increased from a daily average of 1,950 in January to about 2,500 in May, which is more than twice the daily figure recorded

---

[2] At the time the author was serving in the European Commission in Brussels.

in 1986 with the MESA system. In May 1987 the daily turnover amounted to about 10 billion ECUs, against less than 3 billion in 1986. No serious problems have so far emerged in the technical functioning of the system, which is due to be rapidly enlarged to include other clearing banks, in particular from EC countries that are not yet represented.[3]

The functioning of the multilateral clearing system has improved the marketability of ECU-denominated assets and avoided the need for individual commercial banks to create or destroy ECUs in the event of imbalance in their net uncovered asset positions. The size and depth of the ECU interbank market have increased accordingly. In 1986 the ECU ranked fifth among the major denomination currencies for Eurobond issues and banking intermediation. Market participants apparently expect this role to increase further in coming years.

3. FROM A BASKET TO A CURRENCY

In parallel with these developments, the basket characteristic of the ECU was itself questioned in the early 1980s. There were talks and proposals to free the ECU from its original definition in terms of member currencies and to move to what was then called an 'abstract' ECU or an 'ECU-grid': an ECU defined exclusively in terms of its exchange rate *vis-à-vis* other currencies or its position in a parity grid. Such a transformation was considered a further step towards the establishment of the ECU as a currency in its own right. It was thought that this development would require a change in Community legislation, that it should not be pushed through prematurely before the ECU was well established in the market, and, finally, that it should be accompanied by the creation of an institution responsible for the ECU, much as central banks are responsible for our national currencies.

Reflecting on the possible developments of the ECU, in 1983 I argued that the transformation of the basket into a currency was a matter of *habit*, not of *decree*. The argument ran as follows:

---

[3] This aspect was particularly emphasized by the Committee of Governors of the EEC Central Banks when it examined the conditions of the agreement between the BIS and the EBA setting up the ECU clearing system.

Let us investigate the logical and practical process by which the ECU could become a 'true' money. In doing so, let us not face the question whether this process is likely or desirable. We might then consider three different stages. The first stage is 'definition'. The ECU does not exist in any form or for any function. Only its definition exists. 'Someone' declares that the ECU is worth DM 0.828, plus Fl. 0.286, etc. Such a declaration has no practical market effect. We have had this stage already. The 'someone' was the EC Council in its decision of 18 December 1978.

The second stage is 'free-floating'. On the basis of the declared definition, some operators begin to bundle ECUs and to deal in them. This adds a new line and a new column to the exchange rate matrix. If exchange arbitrage produces consistent values, the figures in the ECU line and column will probably, at least initially, be a mere reflection of the movement of the other currencies. The ECU will be influenced, but will exert no influence of its own. Behind the other lines and columns of the matrix, there lie whole systems of production, trade, income, and prices expressed in those currencies; and behind them, states, armies, and central banks. In contrast, the ECU is backed by little more than the EC agricultural prices denominated in ECUs, but in fact administered in national currencies and controlled by a 'green rate' system. Neither an army nor a central bank, merely an EC Council decision and the idea, once expressed even by De Gaulle, that 'cette Europe, un jour il faudra bien la faire'. However, the fact that exchange rate impulses run only one way, from national currencies to the ECU, is not a logical necessity, it is only a practical probability. Rather than the consequence of the will of legislators and official authorities, it is only the result of behavioural choices made by operators. Indeed, nothing prevents a businessman from quoting the price of a newspaper or a service or a bond in ECUs and then actually dealing in them in an another currency.

If ECU trading were to outstrip trading in other currencies, it could well happen that the ECU would become something different from a mere sum of other currencies: it would become a currency on its own, with an identified supply and demand. It is even conceivable that impulses in the exchange rates would also flow from the ECU rather than only towards it. Obviously arbitrage would continue to make sure that currency rates in the matrix were consistent, but there is nothing that forces the ECU market rate to be always identical to the one declared. In a sense, the definition of the ECU as a basket would become a relic of the past in the same way as the gold definition of paper currencies. The ECU would be a free-floating currency. This would bring us to the height of the second stage. In a different scenario,

Hayek has explored this process in his essay on *The Denationalisation of Money*.[4]

The third stage is 'governed exchange'. 'Somebody' buys or sells ECUs in order to regulate the price. To do so efficiently, he has to be able to create ECUs or, if he wants to buy them, to offer something attractive in return, such as another currency, financial assets or gold. If his objective is not profit but stabilization or, more generally, to offer the public a high quality monetary standard, he will in fact be acting like a 'government'.

The process described here is only partly a chronological sequence. Each of the three stages may exist in part, or coexist with parts of the other two. Today we find elements of the first stage together with seeds of the second and third. Some of these seeds have grown and multiplied at impressive speed. There is no certitude that we will ever see the complete picture. But no reason to assert that we never shall.[5]

I would still subscribe the above argument, though I would add one proviso: the need for fuller consideration of the fact that ECU-denominated contracts generally include clauses enabling debtors to fulfil their obligations by bundling ECUs at the 'basket' exchange rate. Such clauses are actually a customary and not an institutional feature of the ECU system. As such they do not invalidate the argument that nothing institutional or logical ties the market value of the ECU to the basket value ('calculated' as the weighted average of the rates of the component currencies). Furthermore, these clauses in ECU contracts are a powerful stabilizer of the value of the ECU, a force that greatly reduces the practical possibility of divergence between the market and the calculated exchange rates of the ECU.

This leads me to stress, even more than in the text above, that the dividing line between a basket and a currency is pricing. Indeed, the fundamental economic forces underlying the determination of an independent exchange rate will only come into play when a significant range of goods and services is originally priced in ECUs. In this way the ECU will gradually cease to be a basket of currencies to become a basket of goods and services. This process, it should be repeated, involves a change in habits, not in legislation.

In advance of these fundamental changes, the growth of the ECU market and the creation of the clearing system has gener-

[4] Hayek 1976.   [5] *ECU Newsletter* 1983.

ated a tendency for prices and rates of return to be determined more by the prevailing supply and demand conditions for ECU-denominated instruments and less by the mere computation of the average price of the component currencies. It is therefore worth assessing the accuracy of my earlier considerations, in particular with respect to what I then called the 'free-floating' stage of the ECU's development.

4. THE RATE OF RETURN ON THE ECU

A comparison between the market and calculated rates of return of ECU-denominated assets is of course possible only for those assets that exist with similar characteristics for each of the component currencies. Table 4.1 shows that such equivalent instruments exist, if at all, only for the major component currencies. Certain instruments, such as commercial paper and zero-coupon bonds, exist in ECU denomination but are not yet available even in some of the major EMS currencies. Obviously, in all these cases it can be said that the ECU rate is determined autonomously. The market for these instruments has developed rapidly in the last few years, giving the ECU a prominent role in the process of financial innovation.

Figure 4.1 shows substantial differences between the market and calculated rates of return for Eurodeposits of various maturities, for which there is a complete mapping. Several factors contribute to these differences. The transaction costs incurred in the arbitrage between the ECU market and those of the other Eurocurrencies may vary, especially in relation to expectations of parity changes. On the eve of a realignment the bid and asked prices tend to diverge, both in the foreign exchange market and in the Eurodeposit market, thereby rendering arbitrage operations more costly. This helps to explain the large spread observed before the March 1983 realignment.

Revision of the weights of the component currencies also modifies the pattern of the ECU rate of return. In the early months of 1984 the expectation of an increase in the weights of the currencies that had previously depreciated and whose nominal rate of interest was higher tended to raise the market rate of interest of the ECU, thereby increasing the spread *vis-à-vis* the calculated

TABLE 4.1. *Euromarket availability in component currencies of certain ECU-denominated financial instruments*

ECU financial instruments	DM	£	F.Fr.	Lira	H.Fl	B.Fr.	Lux.Fr.	D.Krone	Irish.P.	Gr.Dr.
EURODEPOSITS										
O/N, S/N, 1W, 1, 2, 3, 6, 12 months	yes	yes	yes	yes	yes	yes	yes	yes	yes	yes
FACILITIES										
Commercial paper	no	yes	dom.	dom.	dom.	no	no	no	no	no
Certificates of deposit	yes	yes	yes	yes	yes	yes	yes	yes	no	no
Note issuance facilities	no	no	no	no	no	no	no	yes	no	no
Multiple options facilities	yes	yes	yes	yes	yes	yes	yes	yes	no	no
Medium-term notes	no	yes	no	no	no	no	no	no	no	no
BOND ISSUES										
Fixed rate	yes	yes	yes	yes	yes	yes	yes	yes	no	no
Variable rate	yes	yes	yes	yes	yes	yes	yes	yes	no	no
Zero coupon	yes	yes	no	no	no	no	no	yes	no	no
Equity warrant	yes	yes	yes	no	yes	no	no	no	no	no
Convertible	yes	yes	yes	dom.	yes	no	no	no	no	no
BANK LOANS										
Revolving standby credits	yes	yes	yes	yes	yes	yes	yes	yes	no	no
Term loans	yes	yes	yes	yes	yes	yes	yes	yes	no	no
FUTURES AND OPTIONS	yes	yes	yes	opt.	yes	opt.	no	yes	opt.	no

dom. = available through domestic market facilities
opt. = options only

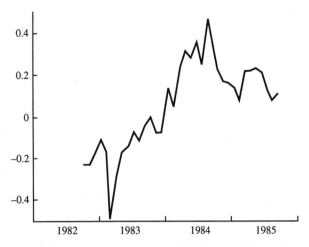

FIGURE 4.1. Differences between quoted ECU 3-month deposit rate and calculated Eurocurrency 3-month interest rate (%)

Source: Tullio and Contesso 1986.

rate. Indeed, Figure 4.1 shows that the positive spread increased until September of 1984, when the revision actually took place, and subsequently narrowed.

Another factor is the risk diversification property of the ECU. In equilibrium, the market return is likely to be lower than the calculated one if the interest rates of the component currencies are negatively correlated, either because of imperfectly correlated movements in individual rates or because of changes in exchange rates among member currencies. Conversely, a positive correlation between the component rates would cause the market rate of the ECU to be higher than the calculated rate. Figure 4.1 provides some evidence in this respect, since it shows that the market interest rate of the ECU was lower than the calculated rate before the realignment of March 1983, as well as in the following months, when foreign exchange expectations were not entirely stabilized. After 1984 increased economic convergence and the closer relationship between movements of member countries' interest rates reduced the risk diversification characteristic of the ECU and gave rise to a positive spread.[6]

[6] Similar evidence can be found in Levich 1987 and Lézardière 1987.

Recent research on the determination of the ECU interest rate[7] also shows that, whereas the relative influence of the rates of interest of the component currencies on that of the ECU coincided with the theoretical weights implicit in its definition in 1982-3, more recently (1984-5), short-term ECU interest rates have tended to follow the rates of the Deutschmark and the guilder, while for longer maturities they have been influenced mostly by those of the French franc and the lira. This differentiated pattern seems to imply that ECU-denominated assets diversify foreign exchange risk, especially for short maturities, in so far as the timing and size of realignments have not usually been perfectly anticipated. For longer maturities there seems to be less scope for diversifying foreign exchange risk.

5. THE ECU EXCHANGE RATE

The relationship between the market and calculated exchange rates of the ECU can be analysed in a similar way. With a growing number of transactions denominated in ECUs, it has become one of the many currencies quoted in the foreign exchange markets where it has the status of a foreign currency. As the size of the ECU market increases, the factors underlying its price tend to reflect not only those of the component currencies but also the conditions regarding its overall supply and demand, while the exchange rate of the component currencies is influenced by the factors affecting the exchange rate of the ECU. The direction of causality is hard to deduce from the data, however, since arbitrage will maintain the exchange rate of the ECU in line with that of the weighted average of the component currencies. The two alternative hypotheses are in a way observationally equivalent.

Figure 4.2 shows significant differences between the market and calculated rates of the ECU. However, since the data refer to the exchange rates fixed sequentially in the Italian foreign exchange market, with the ECU fixed after the component currencies,[8] the market conditions underlying the exchange rates of

---

[7] See Tullio and Contesso 1986.

[8] Between the fixing of the DM and that of the ECU there is a lag of about 40 minutes. Figure 4.2 starts in October 1984 to avoid problems with the measure-

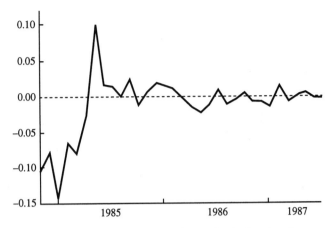

FIGURE 4.2. Differences between market and calculated exchange rates of the ECU (%)
Source: Banca d'Italia.

the latter may have changed by the time the ECU comes to be fixed. Regression analysis actually indicates that there is a positive correlation between the rate of change of the exchange rate of the Deutschmark and the measured spread between the market and calculated rates of the ECU.

The institutional setting and functioning of the foreign exchange markets can be of help in evaluating the degree to which private agents consider the ECU as an autonomous currency and the extent to which there is a specific ECU pricing mechanism. In the first place, contracts denominated in ECUs explicitly accept the official EC Commission definition ruling at any given time.[9] This so-called 'open basket' characteristic means that the ECU is considered not so much as an indexing scheme but as a currency that serves as a unit of account and has

ment of the calculated exchange rate of the ECU at the time of the change in the weights of the component currencies in September 1984. The ECU was first quoted in the Italian foreign exchange market on 14 September 1981. Evidence of the recognition of the ECU's status as an independent currency is to be found in the fact that since 27 November 1989 it has been fixed immediately after the dollar and before the component currencies. There is an interval of several minutes between the fixing of the ECU and that of the DM.

[9] See Allen 1986.

institutional backing, an important feature for market participants.[10] Another important institutional feature is the position of the ECU among the currencies quoted in the foreign exchange market. In Paris and Brussels, for instance, the ECU is the second currency to be fixed, immediately after the US dollar, which implies that its official quotation is determined before that of its components.

The volume of ECU transactions has become quite large: in Paris, for instance, the ECU is the third currency in terms of turnover, after the US dollar and the Deutschmark.[11] The relatively large size of the ECU market strongly suggests that transactions there have some influence on the exchange rates of the components. This does not mean that the quotation of the ECU is determined independently of the latter, but at least it is fixed concurrently. Finally, the ECU is quoted in some markets, such as futures markets, where the component currencies are not listed. The average daily volume of ECU trading on the Chicago Mercantile Exchange is around 3 billion.[12] The ECU is the sixth-ranking currency, while the only component currencies to be quoted are the Deutschmark, and marginally the French franc. Futures contracts in ECUs are therefore priced quite independently of the quotations of the component currencies and the related arbitrage, even though the value of the ECU is clearly affected by the exchange rate expectations regarding the latter.

6. THE POLICY INSTRUMENTS

In this chapter, it was first argued that the obstacles to the evolution of the ECU from a basket to a currency were not of a logical or institutional nature, but rather customary. Then, turning to the observation of market behaviour, it was shown that (modest) progress had been made from the first to the second stage of a logically possible evolution from a basket to a currency, in so far as there are grounds for believing that the market ECU interest and exchange rates show signs of independence of the calculated rates. Although my belief that the mutation from a basket

---

[10] See Levich 1987. Continuing to treat the ECU as a basket currency, as does Allen 1988, is therefore rather restrictive.

[11] Committee of Governors 1985.

[12] *ECU Newsletter* 1987.

to a currency can come about simply through a change in habits is not widely shared, the growth of the ECU market and the possibility of its expanding further have raised the problem of providing the ECU with the policy instruments typical of a currency system.

Influenced by the technical apparatus normally found in a full monetary system, the debate on the initiatives in the official sphere that could bring the ECU closer to a true currency tends to focus on the instruments that are allegedly missing in the present ECU system. Recently the debate has flourished around two issues: the lender of last resort and the creation of a link between official and private ECUs. These two issues will be briefly discussed below.

7. THE LENDER OF LAST RESORT IN ECUS

It is often stated that the lack of a lender of last resort is a major weakness of the present ECU system and an impediment to a deepening of the ECU market. Private operators, it is claimed, would only be justified in having complete confidence in the ECU by the existence of an institution providing such backing for ECU transactions, which would also have to supervise the clearing process and ensure orderly and fair market practices, thus improving the physiology of the market. Without denying the advantage of having a lender of last resort in ECUs, I would argue that this problem has been overstated.

First, economic history shows that currencies can live and develop without a central bank necessarily acting as lender of last resort. The Federal Reserve System, for instance, was created in this century, by which time dollars had already been in circulation for more than one hundred years, and permitted the extraordinary development of the American economy.

Secondly, liquidity problems arising because of the low quality of the assets held by commercial banks must be distinguished from those due to the difficulty of obtaining ECUs at a certain moment in time from an otherwise liquid counterpart.[13] In the first case, the ECU market is no different from any other

---

[13] See Allen 1986 and Goodhart 1986.

Eurocurrency market, for which no lender of last resort exists to support the solvency of private agents. In the second, which involves short-term liquidity problems, the need for a lender of last resort tends to be limited by the existence of a developed and efficient money market. In reality, the ECU interbank market is continuously growing and the present multilateral clearing system seems to provide a safety net for this type of short-term liquidity problem.[14] As the bundling of ECUs becomes less costly, it will be possible to overcome any residual difficulty that may arise in the ECU interbank market through the Euromarkets of the component currencies.

Finally, more attention should be paid to the fact that some lender-of-last-resort functions already exist for ECUs. The central banks of EMS member countries provide this service in their domestic markets and could be resorted to in the event of liquidity problems in view of the close interaction between national and Eurocurrency markets. Furthermore, the Exchange Rate Mechanism of the EMS incorporates intervention rules that envisage the supply of liquidity in the event of exchange rate tensions.

The above considerations suggest that the existence of a lender of last resort for the ECU does not represent a necessary condition for the working of the private ECU market. This is not to say that such a function would not greatly enhance the role of the ECU; nor does it mean that lending of last resort would be impossible within the institutional setting that already exists to regulate the activities of the European Monetary Co-operation Fund (EMCF). As shown in the next section, the 'Agent' of the EMCF (the BIS) could conceivably play this role, following guidelines set by the central banks of member countries.

If a qualitative innovation is to be introduced, I believe it should concern the setting of interest rates. The 'official' interest rate of the ECU today is a weighted average of the official rates of the component currencies. As such it is not a policy variable in the way official rates are for national currencies. Decoupling

---

[14] Between January 1989 and December 1991 daily clearing turnover increased from 18 to 44 billion ECUs. Following the review undertaken by the central banks of the Group of Ten countries of the functioning of international clearing schemes, the Committee of Governors of the EEC Central Banks identified a number of measures aimed at ensuring that the security of the system is adequate and promoting the distribution of liquidity among the participants.

the official ECU rate and making it a rate that EMCF central banks could set at their discretion would provide both the EMS and the ECU market with a policy instrument that is at present lacking. The missing element to permit more direct involvement by the central banks is 'only' political consensus and not technical feasibility, nor the necessary legal basis.

8. LINKING THE PRIVATE AND OFFICIAL ECUS

Two types of ECU exist today. 'Official' ECUs, a liability of the EMCF, are created by member central banks contributing gold and dollars to the Fund. 'Private' ECUs, an 'inside' instrument, are created by private agents bundling component currencies in the market. Official ECUs are used as a means of settlement between central banks; private ones as a convenient denomination for a wide range of financial contracts, including monetary instruments. The lack of a point of contact between the two ECU circuits is often cited as one of the major shortcomings of the present situation. Helmut Schmidt in 1984, and others before and after, have insisted that the establishment of a link between the two ECUs would remove a serious impediment to the development of a more complete European Monetary System. At the technical level, various ways have been suggested to create such a link by transforming official ECUs into private ECUs.[15]

A fully fledged monetary system of the kind we know today is, of course, one in which inside and outside money coexist and interact in the special relationship of complementarity-substitutability that vests commercial banks with the main role of money creation and a central bank with the policy function of determining the quantity and the price of money. The evolution of the ECU system towards this model is accordingly seen as requiring the establishment of a link between the two ECU circuits. Without denying the validity of this view, I would none the less argue that this problem is often badly presented.

The link that really matters is not so much between ECUs of different origin as between economic agents with different objectives and motivations. The line that separates inside from outside

[15] See Masera 1986 and Allen 1988.

money lies at the border between the profit motives of commercial banks and the policy motives of central banks. The instruments that are used are important only in as much as they condition the pursuit of the objective.

Thus, a central bank that intervenes in the ECU market does link the two circuits, whether the ECUs used are of private or official origin. In this sense the link between the two circuits is already in place, since interventions in private ECUs are currently being undertaken by the central banks of EMS countries, although in very limited amounts, as can be seen from Table 4.2. The limiting factors are technical, such as the regulatory restrictions that existed until recently in certain foreign exchange markets with respect to the ECU. But the main reason why a policy function has not yet developed is that the market does not really need it. And this is so because the market is small and is still primarily stabilized by the mechanism of the basket.

The scope for interventions in ECUs may increase in the future as the use of the ECU widens and the need for a stabilization policy emerges. In the working of the EMS, as the group of stable currencies grows larger and pressures tend to concentrate on individual currencies in connection with external shocks or particular national policy developments, the ECU may increasingly become the most efficient instrument for interventions.

From a practical point of view the possibility of intervening in the ECU market is limited by central banks not holding large amounts of 'usable' ECUs as reserve assets. To borrow them from the market would weaken the effectiveness of their interventions. The need to improve the use of the ECU for intervention purposes may be better satisfied by increasing the liquidity of the official ECU, which at present is basically only used as an accounting device for transactions between EMS central banks and the EMCF. In this 'quantitative' sense a closer link between the official ECU and the private ECU is important. Even within the present institutional setting, there appear to be no major technical or legal difficulties in linking the two circuits so as to increase the ammunition available to the policy authorities for stabilization purposes.

Improving the use that can be made of the official ECU depends primarily on its wider acceptance as a reserve asset among the central banks external to the area. From a technical

TABLE 4.2. *Gross interventions (billions of dollars)*

	EMS countries				Italy			
	All currencies		Private ECUs		All currencies		Private ECUs	
	Purchases	Sales	Purchases	Sales	Purchases	Sales	Purchases	Sales
1983	25,236	33,655	39	0	9,553	5,429	39	0
1984	16,960	21,356	46	0	5,760	4,238	46	0
1985	19,231	30,123	1,213	611	4,107	12,890	190	518
1986	38,121	47,974	55	137	14,656	10,265	55	137
1987	59,006	47,935	766	87	18,244	17,295	210	13
1988	26,342	30,539	670	166	10,349	9,777	199	128
1989	28,588	36,191	2,436	2,706	12,195	7,765	1,347	1,766
1990	40,804	33,071	4,767	7,419	10,868	12,126	2,719	5,996
1991	13,943	35,735	1,462	6,245	3,850	9,968	1,462	4,516
1992	76,947	189,394	222	15,666	3,335	39,189	222	8,665

Source: BIS.

and legal point of view, since the status of 'third holder' has been officially envisaged for a potentially large number of institutions, it would be sufficient to convert official ECUs into private ECUs through the balance sheet of one that was willing to consider acquiring official ECUs in its process of reserve diversification, given the attractiveness of the latter as an investment asset. This could be done by any of the EMS central banks with any institution that has been granted third holder status or collectively by EMS central banks with the 'Agent' of the EMCF. Both solutions would improve the liquidity of the official ECU without affecting its overall quantity and hence without impinging on the ability of monetary authorities to control domestic aggregates.

9. CONCLUSIONS

The emergence and development of the ECU is a most interesting case to study because it amounts to an experiment in the creation of a new monetary system. The official origin of the ECU is undeniable: the creation of a unit of account, the change in its name in 1978, the official definition of the basket, and the establishment of the European Monetary System. The mark of official decisions is so strong that many observers of the ECU tend to underestimate the importance of the customary element in its recent development and in its future prospects. The institutional dimension of the ECU is overstated both in interpreting the past and in designing the future. This chapter suggests that many of the elements of a complete ECU monetary system are either already in place or can be developed with little or no changes in legislation. Most of the basic components are there, but they are difficult to detect with the naked eye, as in the early stages of an embryo's life. Some of these elements will develop naturally in the growth process.

Should one conclude that nothing needs to be done on the official side in order to move closer to a complete ECU system? This is not my view. The strong connection between the market and the official side has been, and remains, the key aspect of European monetary developments. Without the EMS, the ECU would not have taken off, although the basic provisions of the EMS say almost nothing about the ECU. Without further development of the EMS, sooner or later the ECU will wither. The ECU draws part of its strength from the expectation that European monetary integration will progress, and it is on the basis of this expectation that it helps to meet the strongly felt need for a common European currency. What the official side has to do, however, is not so much to devise technical mechanisms for the functioning of the ECU market as to provide the fundamental public good that the Community needs in the monetary area: the stability of exchange rates in a system of capital mobility, better monetary relationships *vis-à-vis* the rest of the world, macro-economic convergence, etc. If this is done, and no legal impediments are put in the way of the ECU's development, the system is likely to grow by itself. And the means to control such a system are mostly in place or can be created without too much difficulty.

II

THE SINGLE EUROPEAN
ACT AND ITS LIMITS

5

After the Single European Act: Efficiency, Stability, and Equity

1. THE FACTS

The problems the Community is facing today stem from two decisions taken in 1985: the decision to enlarge the EC by accepting the applications of Spain and Portugal and the decision to create a single market without internal frontiers by 1992. These are extremely important decisions, of a kind that the Community has not often taken in its history. Since its creation, the Community has, of course, taken other decisions that have reshaped its structures and future. In general, such decisions have always required a combination of favourable circumstances: a sense of urgency with respect to the aim of giving renewed impetus to the Community machine; a propitious economic and political climate in most of the member states; and experienced political leadership possessing both courage and vision. Such a combination recurred in 1984 and the two decisions taken in 1985 were the tangible result.

The following summarizes the contents of the report on *Efficiency, Stability and Equity* prepared at the request of the EC Commission by a group of experts chaired by the author of this book. The group was asked to examine the problems posed by the Single European Act and to propose guidelines for action.

The decision to accept the applications of Spain and Portugal to join the Community might appear relatively simple. After all, it was not the first time the Community had been enlarged. However, compared with the adhesion of Greece, this enlargement had much more far-reaching implications, owing to the

September 1987, Paris. Opening address to the annual meeting of the Association Française de Science Économique. A summary of the report on *Efficiency, Stability and Equity* (April 1987), prepared at the request of the EC Commission following the approval of the Single European Act and the adhesion of Spain and Portugal.

large gap between average economic conditions in the Community and those in Spain and Portugal, coupled with Spain's size. The 1985 decision is thus comparable only with the admission of the United Kingdom, Denmark, and Ireland in 1973.

The approval of the Single European Act was even more important. At first sight it appears to do no more than give renewed impetus to the pursuit of a goal already set out in the Treaty of Rome. In practice, however, its effects will profoundly change the very nature of the EC economy. The objective is to dismantle non-tariff barriers, eliminate internal frontiers, and extend the single market to include sectors, such as services, finance, and public procurement, that have so far remained closed to competition. The fixing of a time limit for the creation of the single market (1992) is another key factor; this date will serve as a landmark not only for the action to be taken but also—and this is of cardinal importance—for economic agents' expectations. Indeed, it is already possible to discern a tendency to conform with the orientation of the new rules, even before the relevant directives have been formally adopted by the Community. The method envisaged for the implementation of the single market contains two highly significant innovations: mutual recognition and much more systematic recourse to majority voting.

The principle of mutual recognition involves each country granting access to its markets to goods and services that comply with the provisions in force in another member state. In other words, each Community country undertakes to recognize the standards and regulations of all the other member states. Applying this principle enormously simplifies the process of legislating for the single market. The approach previously pursued by the Community envisaged a complete redrafting of economic legislation at the Community level with the aim of creating the completely uniform legislative and regulatory framework considered essential for an integrated market. The adoption of mutual recognition signifies the abandonment of the 'monolithic' approach to the creation of the single market, implies acceptance of a plurality of laws, permits experimentation with different standards and regulations, and means that harmonization can be limited to a small set of key aspects that need to be safeguarded throughout the Community.

Identifying these aspects is one of the most difficult tasks to be tackled in the new situation, but the two methodological principles introduced in 1985 with the adoption of the Single European Act (mutual recognition and majority voting) will greatly simplify, and accelerate, the steps required to create a market without internal frontiers.

2. THE ANALYSIS OF THE PROBLEMS

The Single European Act and the enlargement of the Community have determined the broad lines of the EC's development in the coming years. They can be seen as stemming from concerns and objectives relating to the allocation of resources; since the obstacles to a more efficient allocative process are to be removed, economic growth and welfare are bound to benefit. These innovations none the less involve problems and create new difficulties. The Report seeks to identify and analyse them so as to indicate guidelines for the action to be taken. In the first place there are problems linked to the actual implementation of the programme; some are of a conceptual nature, others are practical.

The most complicated of the conceptual problems concerns the demarcation of the fields in which to apply the two methods that the Single European Act envisages for achieving market integration: the harmonization of key provisions by way of directives and, where harmonization is judged to be unnecessary, the application of mutual recognition. Economic theory suggests that legislative harmonization is desirable when there is a public good to be safeguarded at the Community level, a good that would not be guaranteed if competition between national rules were allowed free play. The definition of such public goods implicitly adopted by the Community before the approval of the Single European Act was extremely broad. It is sufficient to look at the matters on which the Community legislated to realize that EC law was often concerned with details and hardly at all with truly public goods. The institutional model underlying this approach was undoubtedly taken over from the experience accumulated by most of the Community countries during their economic and legislative unification. For instance, in nineteenth-century Germany the setting up of the *Zollverein*, a major factor in the unification process,[1] was followed by the formulation of a single commercial code for all the German states. The approach of the Commission and the Community in the early years bears the imprint of Hallstein, who had a legal background and was probably influenced by the history of his own country.

When the principle of all-embracing legislation is abandoned in favour of a plurality of laws and regulations, as is the case with the Single European Act, it becomes necessary to tackle the intellectually and technically difficult problem of determining the matters that really need to be dealt with in minimal Community legislation. In the financial field, for instance, it is necessary to establish the minimal Community rules that will be required to prevent competition between national regulatory systems reducing investor protection below the level needed to ensure the stability of financial markets. Similar problems arise in other parts of the single market programme.

The practical problems are of two kinds: the exceptional legislative burden that will weigh on the Community in the coming years and the need to complement legislation with effective measures by the executive and the judiciary to enforce Community law and repress violations.

Turning now to the second set of problems, which concern the logical consistency of the single market programme, it can be seen that the most important can be formulated in the following way: complete mobility of capital, which is one of the key features of the programme, implies the creation of a monetary union or at least of a system ensuring very close co-ordination of national macro-economic and monetary policies, but neither monetary union nor such co-ordination is provided for in the programme. As it stands, the programme will therefore create a situation in which the EMS, a system of nearly fixed exchange rates, is accompanied by complete freedom of capital movements, without any effective Community constraint on the economic and monetary policy autonomy of the member states. Such an arrangement is inconsistent and has never worked in the past. One reason why the Bretton Woods system was able to function

[1] The events that led from the customs union of 1834 to the monetary union that was completed with the creation of the Reichsbank in 1876 have recently been re-examined by Holtfrerich 1989, with the aim of drawing lessons for the monetary unification of Europe.

is that capital mobility was restricted; its collapse can be seen as the transition from a fixed exchange rate regime with limited freedom of capital movements to a floating rate regime with capital mobility, both of which were consistent with a high degree of monetary policy autonomy.

The difficulties inherent in this lack of logical consistency have already emerged on two occasions: at the beginning of 1987, when central rates were realigned within the EMS even though the economic fundamentals did not really justify such a step, and more recently when the lira came under heavy and prolonged speculative attacks, leading to the reintroduction of restrictions on corporate foreign currency transactions.

A third set of problems concerns the cohesion of the Community and the distribution of income. Here, I shall do no more than mention these issues. The Community is a very heterogeneous entity, with large differences in per capita income and pronounced disparities between the richest regions and the poorest. Strains are bound to develop when competition is extended to sectors that had previously been protected. A Community in which the benefits of an improved allocation of resources are not distributed uniformly is unlikely to be seen as 'fair' and will be accused of disregarding the bond of solidarity, which is one of its deep motives.

Finally there are problems concerning growth. They have a special importance because faster growth is likely to ease the other problems and vice versa. In the 1960s, when the first steps towards market integration were taken, the rate of growth was close to 5 per cent. A growth rate of this order of magnitude in the coming years would enormously simplify the solution of the foregoing problems, particularly as regards the distribution of income. Slow growth, by contrast, would inevitably make the problems much more difficult to overcome. Of course, growth is likely to be stimulated by the process of market integration itself, but even the most optimistic estimates of the economic impetus deriving from the opening of markets point to growth rates far below those of the 1950s and 1960s.

3. GUIDELINES AND RECOMMENDATIONS

What guidelines does the Report propose? Its policy analysis is based on an approach that has become standard since it was first formulated by Musgrave in his work on public finances. Three functions for economic policy are distinguished: an allocative function, a stabilization function, and a distributive function.[2] Musgrave uses his model with reference to budgetary policy, but it can be applied to economic policy as a whole and thus to monetary policy and regulation as well. It should be noted that these three economic policy functions are to be found not only in national economies, which we know best, but also in the organization of the international economy. The allocative function, for example, has traditionally been entrusted to the treaties that govern world trade (the GATT and even more the arrangements defined in the Havana Charter).[3] The stabilization function has been assigned to a monetary order (the Bretton Woods system in the post-war period). While the World Bank and other organizations providing assistance to developing countries have been engaged in the redistribution function.

There is probably an underlying need for these three functions to be performed at every level of the organization of economic activity, whether regional, national, or international. They are to be found in the European Community right from the start. The provisions of the Treaty of Rome are primarily concerned with the allocation of resources. A part deals with the problems of stabilization, where reference is made to a system of fixed exchange rates and to a strengthening of Bretton Woods through specific procedures for the co-ordination of economic policies. Lastly, there are the various Community institutions and instruments involved in the distributive function—such as the European Investment Bank, the Social Fund, and the Regional Fund.

[2] Musgrave 1958.

[3] The Havana Charter was intended to establish the principles that would foster a recovery of world trade after the Second World War by avoiding protectionism and bilateral agreements. The General Agreement on Tariffs and Trade was reached as an interim measure, but in fact the Charter never took effect and the International Trade Organization, which was to have supervised international trade with the aim of ensuring its stability, was never set up.

I have often wondered whether, in making provision for these three functions, the authors of the Treaty were consciously applying the Musgravian model, or simply responded to the perception of a political necessity. In the light of this analysis of the three functions of economic policy, it can be seen that the programme established in 1985 for the enlargement of the Community and the creation of a single market is concerned almost exclusively with the allocation of resources and that its implementation is likely to run into serious difficulties owing to the problems it will engender in the other two areas of economic policy.

The basic recommendation of the Report can be summarized as follows: it is highly desirable that the single market should be implemented, but if the programme is to achieve its objectives, it will have to be supplemented by action in the two areas of economic policy—redistribution and stabilization—that the decisions adopted in 1985 do not consider. The Commission's 1985 White Paper describing the steps to be taken in constructing the internal market contains many indications that its authors were aware of these problems. But this recognition is not translated into action in the fields of stabilization and distribution. By contrast, the document sets out in detail some original, and probably effective, solutions in the field of resource allocation.

The Community already provides scope for action in all three areas of economic policy. Simplifying somewhat, it can be said that the policy instrument for implementing the resource allocation function is the law, together with a mechanism for controlling and safeguarding competition entrusted to the Community's executive and judicial authorities, i.e. the Commission and the Court of Justice. The stabilization function is basically confined to the area of exchange rate relationships and is performed by the EMS, which has replaced the Bretton Woods system within the Community. As to the distributive function, this is largely performed by way of activities impinging on the Community budget. It cannot, of course, be claimed that the Community budget is exclusively an instrument of redistribution; indeed, most of it is related to the common agricultural policy, the logic of which, at least originally, was rooted in resource allocation. However, it remains true that most of the measures concerning the redistribution of income are of a budgetary nature.

The Report recognizes the importance of the stabilization and distributive functions already performed by the Community. It claims, however, that more is needed to strike a balance that is political as well as economic and also to ensure that the single market programme continues to be supported by the member states. It therefore recommends both that the stabilization function should be enhanced by strengthening the EMS and that the distributive function should be made more effective by reorganizing and increasing the action carried out via the Community budget.

There are two problems as regards stabilization. The first is whether the aim of restoring consistency between capital mobility and monetary policy autonomy requires the Community to switch from the present system of quasi-fixed exchange rates to a floating rate system. The conclusion of the Report—arrived at after some tribulation, since several members of the group were only convinced of its validity as the work proceeded—is that, at a time of very high unemployment and a consequently strong temptation to engage in economic protectionism, breaking up the European Monetary System and renouncing exchange rate fixity would probably destroy much of what has been achieved so far in the integration of the European market. The Report therefore comes down squarely in favour of strengthening the EMS and economic policy co-ordination.

The second problem is whether it is sufficient to co-ordinate the member states' monetary policies or whether mandatory co-ordination of their fiscal policies is also necessary. For the Community as a whole, fiscal policy is enacted through the budgets of the member states and that of the Community. The latter is none the less too small to produce a macro-economic impact, so that the budgetary function is performed primarily at the national level.

There are grounds for claiming that monetary policy co-ordination is not sufficient and that fiscal policy co-ordination is also necessary. The conclusion of the Report is, however, very cautious in this respect, for both practical and theoretical reasons. On practical grounds the Report notes that such co-ordination would involve very serious difficulties because budgetary powers are intimately related to sovereignty, national parliaments, and the problem of suffrage. At all events, it would be much harder to constrain national budgets by means of an institutionalized mechanism than to co-ordinate and limit member states' autonomous powers in the monetary field. In theoretical terms, moreover, fiscal co-ordination is probably not even necessary. In a system leaving no scope for countries to 'monetize' their public debt, and in which national budgets would be subject to the judgement of an integrated capital market, national budgetary policies would be under a common discipline notwithstanding their formal autonomy. In most federal systems the members of the union—for example, the German *Länder* and the individual states in the United States of America—are not subject to budget rules imposed from above but simply lack the power to print money and have to comply with the discipline of an integrated capital market.

4. TWO QUESTIONS FOR ECONOMISTS

The authors of the Report have used rather than produced economic theory. It is of some interest to note that basic propositions of economic doctrine, propositions which are stated in textbooks rather than being at the centre of advanced economic analysis, have proved extremely useful in understanding new problems, such as those posed by recent Community developments. But there are also problems whose solution would undoubtedly benefit from new research. It is worth mentioning just two of them by way of conclusion.

The first concerns the assignment of the various policy functions to the different levels of government—local, regional, national, and Community. The key feature of the 1985 decisions is that they deliberately opt for a pluralistic organization of economic management and abandon the idea of adopting an economic constitution for the Community as centralized and monolithic as those of most of the member states. The choice of this diversified approach means that the level of government to which policy functions and powers are to be assigned has to be decided case by case, according to the nature of the problem. In constitutional theory the principle that guided the work of the group is known as 'subsidiarity'. It requires functions to be attributed to a higher level of government only when they cannot be performed satisfactorily at a lower level. It is the principle upon which federal systems are based and derives from the classical concept of minimum government.

Economics also offers some useful indications in this field, such as the theory of 'optimal monetary areas' and the theory of fiscal federalism, but there does not exist a 'general' theory of the assignment of the functions of economic management to the different levels of government. The approach to follow in the search for such a theory should start from the definition of a public good and the identification of the geographical, economic, and institutional context in which a good can be said to be 'public' and in which it should therefore be produced. The organization of economic policy at different levels of government is an issue to which theory still provides only very incomplete answers.

The other problem is to identify second-best solutions to situations characterized by capital mobility, fixed or at least stable exchange rates, and monetary policy autonomy. There is general agreement among economists that the real solution to the problem is to suppress independent monetary competences and establish a monetary union. It is easy to arrive at this theoretical conclusion, but in practice it is not possible to ignore the question of intermediate arrangements, or the path to be followed to arrive at the union. It is therefore necessary to establish rules, and institutions, permitting a second-best solution to be adopted before the optimal solution is arrived at. In practice, the search for this solution is subject to constraints that are more political than economic, in view of the difficulty of reconciling different positions through negotiations. Economists could none the less make a contribution to this reconciliation by focusing attention on the need for logical consistency. Only in this way will it be possible to devise solutions that are both conceptually sound and institutionally feasible.

6

The EMS is not Enough:
The Need for Monetary Union

1. INTRODUCTION

This essay examines the long-term prospects of the European
Monetary System from a non-technical standpoint, considering
the System as a variable rather than as a given. The reasons for
this approach are that the EMS is now sufficiently well established to justify expectations of its having a long life, while the
tests it has still to pass may be so demanding as to change its
shape. In what follows three concepts will be central to my argument: 'long term', and the 'performance' and 'evolution' of the
System.

What do we mean by long term? Rinaldo Ossola used to say
that the time horizon of a central banker is about three months.
Between this extreme and Keynes's definition of less than a life-
time, a period of several years can be taken as a fair compromise. However, a definition based exclusively on the time
dimension is too restrictive. It is more helpful to base it on the
well-known distinction that the German language makes between
Prozesspolitik and *Ordnungspolitik*: the former operates within
existing institutions, instruments, and markets; the latter acts on
the existing framework. In the light of this distinction, the long
term can be related to *Ordnungspolitik* and is the time that
elapses before a change in the existing order becomes necessary
and is enacted. I shall argue that the problem of the long-term
evolution of the EMS may well require our attention earlier than
is generally believed.

The performance expected from the monetary organization of

October 1987, Perugia. Address delivered to the conference on 'The European
Monetary System'. The Basle–Nyborg agreements had just been signed. The sin-
gle-market legislation was being prepared and the liberalization of capital movements speeded up.

a group of economically interdependent and institutionally linked countries, such as the member states of the Community, is to foster trade integration and promote domestic price stability. An arrangement that is optimal for one purpose may not be the best for the other. For example, a fixed exchange rate regime could be optimal for the promotion of macro-economic discipline, but it might distort price competitiveness, leading to commercial imbalances and perhaps even disrupting trade. On the other hand, a crawling-peg system would ensure the stability of real exchange rates, thereby preserving the relative competitiveness of member countries, but might undermine macro-economic discipline by fully accommodating inflation differentials.

A monetary system must be based on a satisfactory balance between these two objectives. In this chapter, the desired performance of the EMS for today and tomorrow is taken to be satisfactory trade and macro-economic discipline.[1] This implies that exchange rates are managed so as to avoid overaccommodation of price differentials or unwarranted changes in real exchange rates. Since 1979 the System has been quite successful in promoting such a balance, compared with what has occurred outside the area.

Finally, the evolution of the EMS concerns the ability of the System to maintain or improve its performance as circumstances change. Adaptation of the System should build on what has already been achieved, without giving ground on the price stability front or any other. The programme set for the development of the Community in the areas of trade, financial services, and capital mobility will require the EMS to evolve to a *de jure* or *de facto* monetary union. I am not advocating the creation of a monetary union as an end in itself, as a means of strengthening European integration or of fulfilling a political commitment that dates back to 1969. Rather, my arguments are based on the less ambitious aim of maintaining a System that will be able to provide the performance defined above and support the programme of completing the single market.

The long-term evolution of the EMS can be seen as comprising three periods: the first, of consolidation, can be considered concluded; we are now living through the second, in which the 'inconsistent quartet' emerges; and we start to foresee the third,

[1] For a broader definition of the concept of performance, see Padoa-Schioppa 1987.

that of monetary union. In examining the main features of these three periods, I shall pay only limited attention to external factors and relations with the rest of the world. In part this is for the sake of simplicity, but it owes more to my conviction that the determinants of the development or failure of the EMS lie within the System itself and in the Community, not outside.

2. THE FIRST PERIOD: CONSOLIDATION

The first period in the life of the EMS was one of consolidation, aimed primarily at protecting the acquired degree of Community trade integration from disruptive fluctuations in real exchange rates and promoting convergence on a low rate of inflation in member countries. The performance of the System was quite satisfactory, notwithstanding the second oil shock—an event that would have perhaps discouraged the entire enterprise if it had occurred on the eve instead of the morrow of the Jenkins–Giscard–Schmidt initiative. Average inflation in the EMS countries fell from 11 per cent in 1980 to 2 per cent in 1986; the difference between the highest and the lowest inflation rates narrowed from 16 to 6 percentage points. Despite high and rising unemployment (from 6 per cent in 1980 to 10.5 per cent in 1986), trade relationships within the Community were not strained or infected by the protectionist pressures that emerged world-wide.

The period of consolidation was also fruitful in establishing important practices and interpretations, thereby fleshing out the System's written constitution. Three such features, which we now consider an integral part of the EMS, were not taken for granted from the start and should be mentioned. The first is the successful blend of rules and discretion by means of which the System functions. The rules apply to the management of exchange rates, which have to be maintained within compulsory margins between realignments. They enhance co-operation in intervention, market confidence, and the credibility of the System itself. Discretion governs the timing and the magnitude of realignments. It is necessary both because the events that lead to a realignment are themselves difficult to forecast and because predictable parity changes would generate such strong speculative pressures that the System would break down.

The second feature is that central rates are the result of a collective decision. In this respect, the management of exchange rates has been effectively taken away from national hands and is conducted at the Community level. This is a crucial advance, and one the Bretton Woods system failed to make, since changes in parities were normally decided unilaterally by the country concerned and simply communicated to the IMF to obtain a sort of multilateral blessing.

A third important feature is the positive interaction the System has fostered in the last nine years between exchange rate policy and other policies (both monetary and real). In a way, this has put an end to the debate that flourished between 'economists' and 'monetarists' at the time of the Werner plan.

Acceptance of the principles and objectives of the System has reinforced policy co-operation both *between* member countries and *within* countries, between such policy-making bodies as central banks, fiscal authorities, trade unions, and employers' organizations. Italy (July–September 1980), Belgium (February 1982), and France (March 1983) are the most significant examples of the behaviour of one or more macro-economic agents having conformed to the stability-orientated choice embodied in participation in the System.

Undeniably, the System's successful performance in the period of consolidation owed something to the help of special factors and circumstances. First, the strong dollar attenuated intra-EMS pressures by diverting financial flows away from Deutschmark-denominated assets. Further, the gain in competitiveness of European producers *vis-à-vis* important non-EMS competitors partly offset the contractionary effects of disinflationary policies in EMS countries. Overall, the external environment was propitious in the consolidation period, notwithstanding the inflationary effects of the rising dollar and their different impact on member countries' economies.

Second, capital controls reduced the exchange-rate pressures associated with the higher inflation rates of France and Italy, whose participation in the System is the main difference between the Snake and the EMS. Finally, recognition of the need to give priority to the reduction of inflation also resulted in relatively easy acceptance of the policy leadership of the Federal Republic of Germany, the member country that is both economically strongest and most committed.to monetary stability. The sensitive issues of co-ordination, leadership, and symmetry were thus not a major problem for several years.

3. THE SECOND PERIOD: THE INCONSISTENT QUARTET

The end of the first period coincided with the disappearance of the favourable factors mentioned above. The reversal in the trend of the dollar was largely exogenous to the EMS and the Community. Improved inflation convergence and the relaxation of exchange controls were made possible, on the other hand, by the very success of the System, although they are now posing new problems for its existence. Consolidation led to lower inflation, and hence has made consensus on monetary objectives more difficult to achieve, since national priorities may shift in favour of growth in some countries and away from it in others. The success of the stabilization policy has also meant that the complete liberalization of capital movements, provided for in Articles 67–73 of the Treaty of Rome, is once again a credible item of the Community agenda.

The second period of the EMS is marked by the emergence of a fundamental challenge to the System: the removal, following the implementation of the programme set by the Single European Act, of exchange controls and all the remaining non-tariff barriers in the trade of goods and services. Unless new items are added to the agenda, the Community will be seeking to achieve the impossible task of reconciling (i) free trade, (ii) full capital mobility, (iii) fixed (or at any rate managed) exchange rates, and (iv) national autonomy in the conduct of monetary policy. These four elements form an inconsistent quartet: economic theory and historical experience have repeatedly shown that they cannot coexist, and that at least one has to give way.[2]

The full effects of the inconsistency have not yet been felt in the second period, which can be seen as having started in 1986, because capital mobility is still incomplete. Short-term capital is not yet wholly transferable and the national markets for financial services are not open. However, the main allocative decisions of

---

[2] See Padoa-Schioppa 1985*b*.

businesses and households regarding production, consumption, and investment can already range freely across frontiers and no serious obstacles hinder the execution of payments. The difference between the second and third periods is the extent to which this inconsistency manifests itself.

The question is whether the EMS mechanisms are adequate to allow the System to survive and to perform, as defined above, as effectively as it did in the first period. Perhaps the challenge in this new phase arises less from the objective of maintaining price stability (since inflation has been substantially lowered), than from the active dismantling of barriers to the exchange of goods and services and the liberalization of previously heavily protected sectors. The importance of making the EMS mechanisms adequate has been highlighted by the recent Basle–Nyborg agreements, which modify and improve certain aspects of the System, making it less likely that there will be another round of revision during the present period. The EMS will therefore have to rely solely on what is already available.

The existing arrangements and mechanisms of the EMS appear sufficient to preserve its performance, provided a significant change takes place in the way the System is managed, and provided participants are constantly aware of the dangers of the System's fragility. Of course, there will continue to be instances in which pressures on exchange rates are wholly justified by cost and price divergences. As in the past, a realignment accompanied by other policy measures will be the appropriate response. In contrast with the first period, however, there will be many other instances in which tensions will be fuelled by capital mobility, with minor 'real' divergences being nothing more than a pretext. The required change in attitude consists in *not* considering pressures in the exchange markets as a sufficient condition for a realignment. The only effective way to counter financial disturbances is by defending the exchange rate through enhanced co-operation among monetary authorities and being willing to subordinate domestic goals to exchange rate stability when circumstances require.

Interventions will be the first line of defence, and they may have to be on an unprecedented scale. Co-ordinated movements in interest rates, as agreed in Nyborg, would provide the second line of defence. The problem is that these two instruments may be insufficient, even if used jointly and aggressively. First, the financial assets that economic agents can ask their central bank to convert into foreign currencies are a large multiple of official reserves, and secondly, the size of the interest rate changes needed to offset the expected return from a realignment may far exceed the central bank's room for manœuvre.

In these circumstances, the two lines of defence mentioned above would need to be supplemented by a third. This would consist in a recycling mechanism that would permit the System to counter destabilizing capital movements by providing temporary accommodation of the demand for currency diversification, for the time and in the amount necessary to change market expectations. If a large number of economic agents in the area want to convert financial assets (not necessarily *monetary* assets) from currency A to currency B, the System should accommodate the change in preferences by withdrawing assets denominated in As and issuing assets denominated in Bs. If central banks are successful, this operation will end with a profit for the authorities and a loss for private agents, because assets denominated in As are likely to carry a higher nominal yield than assets denominated in Bs.[3]

There is an analogy here with the textbook case of how a central bank responds to a run on banks: the demand to convert deposits into banknotes should be fully accommodated, without worrying about the monetary statistics, in order to restore full confidence in the 'parity' between banknotes and deposits. The EMS case differs in that runs and the lender-of-last-resort function are transnational and 'intercurrency'.

The technicalities of such a mechanism are not too hard to work out in detail. The difficulties are of another kind, and there are several. First, it may be difficult both to decide what is causing the market pressures and to agree that their nature makes defence of the existing parities appropriate. Some lack of convergence in price and cost developments will always exist and make

---

[3] Attempts to defend the parity with funds raised in the market would not reduce the excess supply of the currency under attack in the Community market as a whole. To offset the pressure of market participants, monetary authorities must take an equal and opposite exchange rate position. With unchanged parities, this would not inflate the aggregate money supply of the EMS, nor stimulate demand in the country whose currency is most in demand. The overshooting of the monetary targets set for that country is offset by a fall in velocity.

the 'easier' option of a realignment appear more attractive, with the full burden of adjustment being put on the exchange rate. In such circumstances a realignment would not serve the interests of the Community as a whole, nor serve those of individual countries. It could severely damage the export industry of the appreciating country and the pursuit of price stability of the depreciating one.

Secondly, the need for decisions and action to be taken jointly is much greater than it was between realignments during the earlier period of the System. While joint discretionary action in the first period was basically confined to realignments, it will now be needed during the week and not only at weekends. This will require intense consultation and co-operation among central banks, almost to the point of their acting as the departments of a single monetary authority.

My conclusion with regard to the second period is that its objective is the survival of the System, and it is my hope that it will not last too long.

4. THE THIRD PERIOD: MONETARY UNION

The third period will be characterized by the full implementation within the Community of the first two elements of the inconsistent quartet—free trade and capital mobility—to the point of eliminating all distinctions based on nationality between economic agents, services, and products. Note that 'trade' is to be taken as comprising services, and 'capital' as including financial assets of all possible maturities, including cash. The time horizon for reaching this stage and completing the internal market is 1992, the date set by the Single European Act, which has been approved and ratified by member states as an amendment to the Treaty of Rome.

In the monetary and financial area, the implementation of the programme implies the elimination of all the remaining restrictions on the full mobility of capital and the complete freedom for households, firms, and financial intermediaries to engage in transactions throughout the Community as in a single market. The monetary and credit instruments available to economic agents in the Community will correspond to the money and credit supply of the area as a whole and be limited only by their ability to gather information and cover transaction costs.

If nothing is done about the last two elements of the inconsistent quartet, however, the inconsistency will emerge in full and the process of restoring consistency could develop in an uncontrolled and destructive way. It could take several alternative routes, possibly leading to the breakdown of the common market as a result of failure to complete the internal market by 1992, the reintroduction of capital and exchange controls or the return to floating exchange rates. This would be only the first step towards a 'remise en question' of the whole 'acquis communautaire'. Sooner or later, the existing degree of trade integration and the painful problem of unemployment in most European countries would inevitably cause today's Community arrangements to unravel. Breaches of Community law, failures to adopt the national legislation necessary to implement Community directives, congestion in the presentation and examination of cases before the Court of Justice, a weakening of the policing action of the Commission for infringements of the law, and growing recourse to safeguard clauses and retaliatory measures against foreign producers would all be part of this unravelling scenario. The process would not necessarily be dramatic; it could advance in a creeping way and take the form of a historical decline.

In the long term, the only solution to the inconsistency is to complement the internal market with a monetary union. It would be unrealistic to hope the Community could square a circle that has never been squared—that is, to let national monetary policies follow their own course and yet expect macro-economic and trade discipline to survive for the area as a whole. Monetary unification has an institutional and a functional aspect. The former concerns the legal provisions and procedures of approval, etc.; the latter, the definition of the monetary regime. The debate on this subject, particularly in official circles, gives the impression that the functional aspects are sufficiently well identified—as regards both the definition and the solution of the problems— while the institutional aspects are the difficult ones. Since in most countries central banks occupy a rather delicate and special position, it is understandable that they should be particularly sensitive to the institutional problem. Moreover, it is in the institutional and legal field that the crucial questions of sovereignty and responsibility emerge in full. It is possible, however, that the alleged difficulties of the legal and institutional aspects of the problem actually conceal problems of political will or a natural reluctance to consider fundamental changes in the seemingly solid ground on which the existing institutions rest. If a satisfactory solution were found to the functional aspects of the problem, it should not be too difficult to settle the institutional issues.

It is obviously not possible to undertake a comprehensive analysis of the problems of creating a monetary union here, nor even to identify all the aspects that would have to be considered. I will confine myself to some considerations concerning the functional and institutional aspects.

5. FUNCTIONAL ASPECTS OF A MONETARY UNION

If the monetary union were set up, with one currency being declared the currency of the area and one central bank being created to issue and control it, the solution of the functional problems would be straightforward and the process would repeat the historical experience of many nation states. The difficulty in a top-down approach of this kind would be mainly political, the replacement of national currencies and central banks would be such a momentous move that most of the parties involved would be unwilling to consider it, except as part of a plan for full political union.

It is questionable, however, whether this move is really necessary. My own opinion is that less is required to produce the substance of a monetary union than is usually thought. In reality, it could be built on the foundations that already exist with little need for change in what is presently visible to economic agents. It is worth briefly listing some of the things that appear to be dispensable.

It would not be necessary for the existing visible symbols of national monetary systems to disappear: currency denominations, banknotes and central banks could well continue to exist in a monetary union. This would not require much more 'tolerance' than was required in allowing Banco di Napoli and Banco di Sicilia to issue banknotes for more than sixty years after the unification of Italy, or the Bank of Scotland to issue pounds sterling today.

Fiscal policy does not have to be formally unified either. In every political system the budgetary function is shared by central and local governments; this is also true for the Community. However, the allocative considerations that guide the attribution of different tax and expenditure functions to different levels of government do not necessarily coincide with those underlying the choice of an optimal currency area. Indeed, full coincidence of the geographical jurisdiction of the bulk of budgetary and monetary powers offers an opportunity, but also entails a danger. The opportunity is to conduct fiscal and monetary policy in a coordinated way. The danger is to use the printing-press to finance the deficit. In a political union, the budget would almost by definition reach a size that would involve its having a macroeconomic impact, since essential public goods such as defence, internal security, and justice would be provided at the level of the union. A political union thus offers the opportunity of combining monetary and fiscal policy, but it also brings the danger of their mutual contamination.

The crucial question about fiscal policy, however, is whether the monetary union runs a serious risk of being undermined by independent and possibly unco-ordinated budgetary policies conducted by member countries. In other words: should the fourth element of the inconsistent quartet include monetary policy only, or should it include fiscal policy as well?

In a monetary union with a fully integrated internal market but decentralized fiscal authorities, national governments would be subject to two disciplinary factors that are now lacking in the Community. The first would be provided by their having to fund their requirements in a large (and for them uncontrollable) capital market encompassing the whole area. Member states would be assessed according to the logic of the market, simply as borrowers endowed with legislative powers and no longer as the source of regulation and control. They would be treated according to their creditworthiness, although the debt problem experienced in recent years shows how difficult the assessment is for sovereign borrowers. The other new disciplinary factor would be the impossibility of monetizing the debt, since the printing press would be at the level of the union.

Historically, the combination of these two factors has been considered, and proved, to be sufficient to promote fiscal discipline and co-ordination. With the exception of Australia, there is no constitutional system—not even in countries with a high degree of decentralization and federalism—in which local government budgets are subject to the authority and control of the union.

In Europe, the size of member states relative to the size of the union—both in general economic terms and in terms of their respective budgets—makes it questionable whether a more binding process of fiscal policy co-ordination would be necessary to make the monetary union work. Of course, national fiscal policies will have to be consistent with participation in the union. They will have to react to real shocks that cause exchange rates to diverge from their equilibrium levels and avoid determining such divergences. The disciplinary forces described above should generally put sufficient pressure on member countries to bring about such consistency, although their existence does not rule out fiscal irresponsibility on the part of one member country with regard to the burden of taxation and the use of fiscal deficits for stabilization purposes. Nor should it be forgotten how technically and politically difficult it would be to limit fiscal sovereignty for the purpose of stabilization, since budgetary power is tied to the exercise of an allocative function and firmly placed in the hands of elected national parliaments. Formal co-ordination would certainly be desirable, but I do not think it has to be regarded as a *sine qua non* for establishing the union.

Finally, turning to exchange rates, it is at least questionable whether definitive and irrevocable fixity needs to be a feature of the monetary union from the start. I would suggest that it does not, although I am aware that this runs counter to well-established convictions. Provided they remained under the firm control of the federal monetary authority and were decided only in special circumstances, parity changes could be the best policy instrument for coping with unusual developments in one country (exceptional developments in the labour market or in the social field come naturally to mind).

The notion of a 'currency area' is economic, not geographical. The same territory may (and usually does) belong to more than one monetary area, corresponding to the markets in which goods are traded. A vast area such as the Community might well include sub-markets where local currencies could continue to be efficiently used. If monetary union is compatible with a plurality of currencies, decentralized fiscal policies, and even with movements in exchange rates, what exactly is required to make such a union possible? The simple answer is: that there be just *one* monetary policy and hence a single monetary authority, entrusted with the necessary decision-making powers and operational instruments. This means that the supply of money for the whole Community—the supply that will be available to every single economic agent in each country when capital markets are fully integrated—should be based upon the same monetary base: that is, one base money aggregate should be the ultimate source of total money and credit in the whole Community.

This may not require the replacement of the national high-powered monies in the two layers of the system of money creation that exist in our countries, as described in textbooks. It may require the addition of a third layer, a Community monetary base that, *vis-à-vis* national base monies, would play the role that the latter play *vis-à-vis* bank deposits. This role is made up of customary and regulatory elements, such as the legal-tender and lender-of-last-resort functions, wide acceptance of such money as a means of settlement, and the requirement that reserves proportional to the outstanding national base money be held in that instrument. The creation of such a third layer would not be a novelty. Indeed, it used to be occupied by gold; after which it was occupied by the dollar until the 'Triffin dilemma' came into full effect;[4] contrary to the hopes of its promoters, the SDR has failed to occupy it.

It is natural to envisage the ECU as the base money of the Community. Each central bank would be allowed to expand its monetary base according to the high-powered ECUs in its balance sheet, in much the same way as commercial banks can expand deposits only up to a maximum multiple of their holdings of high-powered money. ECU deposits with the European central

---

[4] Triffin was the first to point out the potential long-term instability of the Bretton Woods mechanism for the creation and control of liquidity. This 'systemic' weakness stemmed from the fact that the only way the USA could provide the international money markets with sufficient liquidity was via a balance-of-payments deficit, but the consequent drain on the country's gold reserves was bound to end up by undermining the dollar as a reserve currency (Triffin 1960).

bank would be the instrument for final payments between central banks, and perhaps between commercial banks as well. In the meantime, the ECU we know, the so-called 'private ECU', would continue to function as a parallel currency,[5] with all economic agents in the Community free to use it as they liked. Only a small share of the Community payment system would be occupied by the official ECU, but that share would be a sufficient lever to organize a monetary union.

Of course, the main problem in this respect is that of defining the rule and the techniques by means of which to govern the creation of high-powered ECUs. These should be created through the purchase of assets by the European central bank. As for the rule, it should not be purely mechanical, but allow the European central bank discretion in fulfilling its statutory mandate of promoting exchange rate and price stability in the Community.

6. INSTITUTIONAL ASPECTS OF A MONETARY UNION

If the foregoing functional problems could be dealt with in a satisfactory way, what are now regarded as the most difficult aspects—namely the institutional ones—would probably prove less intractable than they seem today. The following discussion focuses on the relationships between political and monetary union and the legal basis of the monetary union.

It is often claimed that without political union there cannot be monetary union. While it would be paradoxical to think of a political union without a monetary union, economic analysis and historical experience show that the converse is possible. Neither the gold standard nor the Bretton Woods system, which to some extent performed as a monetary union for several decades, were based on a political union. From an economic point of view, the relevant meaning of the term 'political union' is (i) that the 'rule of law' should apply to the whole area and (ii) that certain public goods should be provided at the highest level of government. As to the first proposition, the Treaty of Rome and the body of Community legislation that already exists, or will exist by 1992, provides a unified rule of law for the whole Community in the

---

[5] The change that has occurred in the meaning of this term is discussed in Chapter 3 note 4.

field of economic activity. As to the second, it has been shown above that a wider budgetary policy for the union is desirable but not actually indispensable, and also that it involves some danger for the independence of the monetary authority at the Community level.

This does not mean, of course, that the creation of a monetary union is simply a technical decision. It is a political decision of the greatest importance, since it touches fundamental questions of sovereignty and modifies the economic constitution of member countries. This is why technical institutions and authorities, such as central banks, have neither the right to impose it nor the right to impede it. The contribution they can (and should) be asked to make to the sound development of the monetary order of the Community is to explain and clarify what can (and cannot) be achieved with a given type of technical authority, help design an appropriate new regime when the decision to implement one has been taken, and operate the regime in force at any time as effectively as possible. However, recognizing these links between the technical and political spheres of a monetary union does not mean that the latter is impossible without political union. It means that the new order needs to be created by an act of political will and provide for an appropriate relationship between the technical and political levels of responsibility. This would be very difficult to achieve by a loose group of countries without institutional links. It is possible for a structured constitutional system such as the Community.

The second aspect is the legal basis of monetary union. Without a new treaty, it is said, there can be no monetary union. This proposition is widely accepted and was at the origin of the insertion in the Single European Act of Article 102A, the second paragraph of which states that 'if the further development in the field of economic and monetary policy requires institutional modifications, the dispositions included in Article 236 of the Treaty apply'. None the less, neither historians nor economists would necessarily agree. Historians would once again recall that the gold standard was never formally legislated, and could go back to the old eighteenth-century debate about the advantages and disadvantages of having a written constitution. Economists cannot ignore the very strong customary element embedded in every monetary system. Money was not invented by legislators, nor was it the consequence of creating a central bank. It was created by the needs of commerce and only subsequently was it regulated by law and managed by central banks.

Theoretically, it is possible to envisage an entirely customary or an entirely formal route to monetary union. The customary route would pass through growing *de facto* acceptance of the ECU as a convenient instrument gradually performing all the functions of money. In this process the ECU would develop an 'independent' exchange and interest rate, as it came to be used to price a growing range of goods and services. There is room for ECU pricing both in the wholesale area of large contracts for primary goods and commodities and in the retail area for goods and consumers spread throughout the Community. As the need arose, the central banks of the member states would perform important stabilization functions, either individually or collectively. A suitable structure is already in place at the EMCF and the BIS, where central-bank governors meet at the same interval as the meetings of the Federal Open Market Committee at the Fed. The BIS is the institution that hosts the ECU clearing system and acts, with full operational capacity, as agent for central banks. The monetary base function is now performed for the ECU system by member currencies and member central banks, but it could be carried out collectively and based on the ECU if open-market operations in ECUs were developed further and the use of official ECUs for such operations permitted. An operational connection between the ECU clearing and the official ECU would be the natural way to promote such a development.

I have argued elsewhere[6] that if the wind of habit blew with sufficient strength, developments along the customary route could go very far indeed without meeting insurmountable legal or logical obstacles, perhaps to the point of eventually imposing the formalization of a monetary union. The system would be one of monetary federalism, the ECU would be a widely and increasingly accepted parallel common currency in the Community markets. Consistency with the other currencies and monetary policies would be imposed jointly by the complete and irreversible mobility of capital and growing co-operation among central banks. A similar (though not identical) customary route seems to be envis-

[6] See Chapter 4.

aged by the Bundesbank when it outlines a situation in which many Community currencies would, after achieving the same degree of stability and 'openness', be fully interchangeable and provide equally attractive alternatives to the dollar.

The formal route, in turn, would involve a new treaty creating a European monetary authority and defining its status and functions, with a procedure similar to that establishing the Federal Reserve System and the International Monetary Fund. The new institution would replace or federate the existing central banks, and a common currency would replace or parallel the existing currencies. Decentralized solutions of monetary federalism, such as those outlined above, could be adopted as an alternative to the more traditional centralized ones, the functional and the institutional choices being largely independent.

The two routes correspond to two extremes, both of which are possible, though unlikely. I regard it to be not only more realistic but also more desirable to envisage a sequence of events in which the customary and the legal elements are dynamically intertwined. Of the two components of any modern monetary system, one—the currency—will be pushed primarily by the customary factor, while the second—the central bank—will require more legal and institutional initiatives to provide the necessary independence and operational capacity. Market forces and the political will would thus interact, with each contributing in its own field. Monetary authorities would remain as a technical entity placed in between, operating in markets for policy purposes.

7. CONCLUSIONS

The European Monetary System that we have known since 1979 is based on two obligations subscribed to by each participant: to maintain the market exchange rate within given margins around central rates, and to change the latter only in accord with the other participants. For nine years the two obligations have been fulfilled and the System has made a substantial contribution to lowering the average inflation rate in the Community and narrowing the earlier large inflation differentials, as well as helping to preserve open trade in a period of rapidly rising unemployment in Europe and growing protectionism in the world at large.

Partly as a result of this success, the Community has set itself new and ambitious objectives to be achieved by the year 1992. These include the complete dismantling of all physical and regulatory barriers to the free circulation of goods and services, and the complete liberalization of capital movements, including short-term capital and monetary instruments. In implementing this programme, the problem will emerge of the contradiction between fully integrated trade, complete mobility of capital, fixity of exchange rates, and as yet unchallenged national autonomy in the conduct of monetary policy. This contradiction is demonstrated by economic analysis and confirmed by historical experience.

I have argued that the only solution to this contradiction that does not entail the undoing of the common market is to move towards a monetary union. Basically, this means adding a third obligation: to link the process of money and credit expansion in each country to that of a single monetary base for the whole Community. A monetary union requires a single policy, but not necessarily a single currency and even less a unique name. In turn, the unitary nature of policy requires operational instruments and regulatory powers to be entrusted to an institution with full authority and operational independence.

The historical and political importance of creating a monetary union in Europe can hardly be underestimated. It would be a decisive step towards full political union, as the creation of a defence Community in the early 1950s would have been. As such, it will have to reckon with traditions and attitudes that are deeply rooted in the customs, ideas, and sometimes prejudices of economic agents, institutions, analysts, and politicians. That such difficulties and obstacles can be surmounted is far from obvious, and perhaps is not even likely. The considerations developed here are thus by no means meant to minimize the difficulty of moving to a monetary union; they are reflections developed on economic and technical grounds, not the programme of a politician. At this technical and economic level, it can be argued that a monetary union is a necessary complement of a fully integrated market, that there are no insurmountable technical difficulties to setting it up in a way that builds on existing realities and that an institutionalized budgetary union is not a prerequisite. This in no way lessens the political difficulty, but it may promote recognition of its true nature.

III

FROM THE DELORS COMMITTEE TO THE MAASTRICHT TREATY

7

The Delors Report: From Intentions to Action

1. INTRODUCTION

One can hardly discuss European affairs at this time without being very strongly affected by the onrush of events around us. It would perhaps be going too far to say that our feelings are exactly the same, but in every European country people are being powerfully moved by the images transmitted from Berlin and Germany and are conscious of the importance of the hour.

2. MONETARY UNION IN THE DELORS REPORT

What are the prospects for European monetary union six months after the presentation of the Delors Report? To answer this question, I shall examine three points: the definition of monetary union, the link between economic union and monetary union, and the question of gradualism. Then I shall give you my views on what should be done *now*. Though it may seem strange, neither in its Report nor in its preliminary work did the Delors Committee explicitly examine what should be understood by monetary union; rather, it simply took over the Werner definition. Yet I think the Delors Report results in a fundamental clarification.

The Werner Report defines a monetary union as a regime that satisfies three conditions: fully convertible currencies, complete freedom of capital movements, and irrevocably fixed exchange

November 1989, Kronberg (Frankfurt). Address to the European League for Economic Cooperation. The Berlin Wall had just fallen, marking the start of German reunification. Following the publication of the Delors Report in the spring, the European Council held in Madrid in June had accepted the principle of an intergovernmental conference but had not fixed a date. The timetable of the conference was established in December at Strasbourg.

rates. These three elements are to be found in the Delors Report, though convertibility is no longer a real issue in our countries. Capital mobility has been agreed on and there does not appear to be any doubt that the last directive will be implemented, though this may be clearer now than it was when the Delors Committee was working. The key factor is thus the irrevocable locking of parities. However, even though the Delors Report takes over the traditional definition, it qualifies the concept of monetary union in two important ways. First, it indicates that in addition to full mobility of capital it is necessary to have complete liberalization in the field of financial services. In a way this is rather obvious. Since such liberalization involves services, it is usually classified as economic rather than monetary. Yet the link with monetary matters is very close in the field of financial services, and for banking services in particular, so that it is right to include the liberalization of all financial and banking services in the definition of monetary union.

The second qualification is much more important: the Delors Report clearly indicates that the crux of the matter is that there has to be a single monetary policy. The best way to understand this is to make it very clear that what will still be lacking from monetary union once the 1992 programme has been fully implemented, with the complete liberalization of capital movements and of banking and financial services, will be the shift from twelve formally independent monetary policies to one single monetary policy. A monetary union is *neither* an exchange rate regime *nor* a tightening of the rules of the EMS; it is an institutional change in the way monetary policy is formulated and organized.

In its present form, the EMS is based fundamentally on two rules: that of keeping the exchange rates within the margins and making interventions or adopting other economic policy measures when these are reached, and that of changing central rates only by collective agreement and not unilaterally. The key point is that a monetary union is not a reformulation of these two rules, for instance by stating that the margins will shrink to zero and that there will be no more realignments. The distinguishing feature of monetary union is the addition of a third basic condition: the unification of the procedures of monetary policy decision-making. Naturally, the exchange rate system will also change and there will be irrevocably locked parities, to use the language of the Delors and Werner Reports, but this is not the crucial factor. In the EMS, of course, the crucial factor was, and is, an exchange rate rule that is supposed to retroact on monetary policy decisions and hopefully also on economic policy decisions; the focal point is the commitment concerning exchange rates. A monetary union includes the irrevocable fixity of exchange rates, but the focal point is the way monetary policy is conducted. This is a most important distinction and it is not always fully appreciated, even by experts.

3. HOW MUCH ECONOMIC UNION DOES A MONETARY UNION REQUIRE?

Of all the themes examined in the Delors Committee and its Report perhaps the most critical is the question of how much and what kind of economic union is necessary for a monetary union to be viable. The answer of the Delors Report can be summarized in the following way. An economic union has three components: (i) the single market; (ii) regional and structural policies; and (iii) budgetary and fiscal macro-economic policies. The programmes already in place or being prepared are broadly sufficient in the first two fields. As far as the single market is concerned, it is, of course, important to make sure that the programme is implemented, but the objectives have already been set and the instruments identified; moreover, the necessary lawmaking capacity exists, so no institutional changes are called for. In a sense, the same can be said of regional and structural policies because the fundamental channels of these policies—which are budgetary, but not only budgetary—are also in place. The question of how effective they are is debatable, as is the question of whether the resources allocated are sufficient, but there is no need to construct any entirely new parts in the Community system. By contrast, the Delors Report advocates a fundamental change in the third component, with the introduction of so-called 'binding rules' for national budgetary policies.

4. HOW CAN GRADUALISM BE ACHIEVED?

The difficulty in answering the question of how to be gradualist is due to there being both technical and political reasons for being non-gradualist, together with equally strong technical and political reasons for being gradualist, so that some sort of balance has to be struck. The Delors Committee agreed that monetary policy was not divisible and that responsibility for its conduct should be clearly assigned to a single body, either at the national level or at the Community level. Indeed, it would be dangerous to stay for long in an intermediate situation in which it were not clear in whose hands responsibility for monetary policy had been placed or, worse, in a situation in which too many hands shared this responsibility. At one stage of the Committee's proceedings proposals were put forward for the partial transfer of operational competences, especially as regards exchange market intervention, but the strong opposition of some members prevented their adoption.

The solution proposed by the Committee is based on a different distinction, between what I would call the container and the contents of monetary union. As a first step, the structure is created (with a treaty and institutions, etc.) and subsequently the competences are transferred. The three stages proposed in the Delors Report reflect this approach. In stage one there is no new treaty, but the existing procedures are strengthened; in stage two a new treaty is adopted and the legal framework (the container) is put in place; and in stage three, in which parities are irrevocably locked, responsibility for monetary policy is actually transferred. This is an original solution to the problem, but it is also a traditional one because it mirrors the approach followed with the Treaty of Rome, which also involved the creation of a new institutional structure within which a certain process was supposed to occur. Thirty years later the process is still under way, but the institutions are still those put in place at the very beginning, when they had a very narrow range of competences.

5. THE DEBATE THAT FOLLOWED THE DELORS REPORT

Since the Delors Report was published the debate has proceeded at the level of both governments and observers. Broadly speaking, there has been a sort of division of labour, with observers focusing on the content and governments on the calendar. Many of the arguments used in connection with the latter have been couched in terms of content, but the fundamental issue for governments has been, and still is, the timetable for monetary union.

A special tribute needs to be paid at this point to the quality of the discussion that took place, at the 'observer' level, in the United Kingdom and the British press. It has been by far the most penetrating and objective debate on these issues and deserves an anthology of some of the articles. The discussion among observers has focused mainly, though not exclusively, on the issue of budgetary discipline. This requires more thorough treatment than is possible here, but it is worth noting that the debate has rightly drawn attention to the questionable nature of the position adopted in the Delors Report: the proposition that binding rules have to be imposed on national budgetary policies can, of course, be defended with very strong arguments, but there are also valid counter-arguments. The question of the real meaning of monetary union has received less attention. I may be mistaken, but it would appear that the importance of this point—that a monetary union is not the application of an exchange rate mechanism but the substitution of several decision-making authorities with a single one—has not yet been fully grasped.

The discussion about the calendar was at the centre of the Madrid European Council meeting in June 1989, where a sort of compromise solution was found. Many people believed that the choice to be made by politicians after the Delors Report was between no more than two options: either to adopt the Report *in toto* or to shelve it and make it material for doctoral theses. A decision to move ahead would have meant, and this was clear to everybody, starting work on a new treaty and setting up an intergovernmental conference as the instrument for negotiating and producing it. Accordingly, the Madrid summit was expected either to take a decision on this business and fix a calendar or simply to pay tribute to the quality of the Report and postpone its implementation to a later, unspecified date. What happened in Madrid was that it was found possible to divide the first decision into three separate agreements on the holding of a conference, the fixing of the date, and the actual start of the conference. Only the first of these three matters was decided in Madrid.

One should certainly not underestimate the importance of the principle of the conference having been accepted; it implies acceptance of the need for a treaty and therefore agreement to take economic and monetary union seriously, since everybody concurs that the existing treaties are not a sufficient basis for such a union. However, the calendar was left open in Madrid and in many respects this is creating uncertainty.

6. WHAT MUST BE DONE AFTER MADRID

It is absolutely vital now to 'close' the calendar, namely to give certainty to the dates, not for the full implementation of economic and monetary union, but for the conference and the drafting of the treaty. It is also vital that the calendar should be short rather than long. At issue is the economic and technical dilemma the Community will inevitably face, once the Single European Act and the single market have been completely implemented, if monetary union has not been set in motion. I shall not dwell on the importance of completing the single market in all its parts, but this should not be taken as indicating lack of attention to this fundamental need. The single market will be marked by a contradiction that has no precedent. Broadly speaking, there will be the now generally recognized inconsistency between complete freedom of capital movements, unrestricted trade in goods and services, exchange rate discipline, if not fixity, and national autonomy in the conduct of monetary policy.

Even in a narrower sense, the traditional components of our monetary and financial systems will be transformed by the complete mobility of capital, including monetary items. With complete freedom to provide banking services throughout the EC, banks will be able to operate in every Community country in a regime of full capital mobility under the control of the supervisors of their home country, but they will be faced with twelve independent monetary policies. Bankers must surely be losing sleep when they think about this situation, in which each bank will depend on its home country for supervision and on its host countries for monetary policy, two aspects of banking that are inextricably intertwined. Such a situation can hardly last for long and this is the technical reason why people who have no direct interest in the political dimension of European integration, such as observers and economists in countries outside Europe, affirm that there is no alternative to a monetary union.

7. EXPECTATIONS, INTENTIONS, ACTION

To ensure the proper functioning of markets and advance safely towards the 1992 objective, it needs to be made very clear to all economic agents that the contradiction will be overcome by moving forwards and not by trying to go back to protected and segmented markets. At present, the contradiction is concealed, in a sense suspended, because of the very strong expectation that monetary union will indeed come. Let me clarify this point.

Since the Single European Act was adopted, steps have been taken year by year to build up and justify the expectation that the single market objective was being seriously pursued. In 1988 there was the decision of the Hanover European Council—greatly helped and encouraged by the earlier work of the Giscard–Schmidt Committee.[1] The Report of the Delors Committee followed. It is the report of a committee of which the twelve governors of the EC central banks were members; they all signed it. More recently, there has been the decision of the Madrid European Council. Brick by brick, all these developments have built up a very strong expectation, which, in a sense, can be seen as performing the stabilizing role of tomorrow's monetary union.

[1] The Committee for the Monetary Union of Europe, founded by Valéry Giscard d'Estaing and Helmut Schmidt, met for the first time in Brussels in December 1986 and aimed to give new impetus to the process of monetary unification. The Committee drew up a series of proposals, published in April as 'A Programme for Action'. The programme included: the setting up of a European central bank, the unification of the public and private ECU circuits, the development of private-sector transactions in ECUs, the liberalization of capital movements, and the overall convergence of economic policies.

We must be aware that it would be a big mistake to interpret the fact that we are currently living in a relatively quiet and peaceful monetary environment as proof that we can do without monetary union. First of all, some of the main elements of the 1992 programme are not yet in place: in particular, full mobility of capital and the integration of banking services. Secondly, today's strong expectation, like all expectations, will last for some time, but not for ever unless it is supported by facts. It is important to appreciate that processes, such as the creation of a monetary union, have their own dynamics. There is a chain of events, a continuity of movement, that has to be maintained if the process is to be effective and credible.

The fundamental distinction here is between action and intentions. Economic and monetary union has been a stated intention and the object of a political commitment since 1971, and I am sure it will remain a firm political commitment. But this is not the problem. What is important is to see whether the chain of events going back to 1986 that I have just described will continue or be interrupted. What would happen if there were an interruption? In all probability, every two or three meetings of the European Council the final communiqué would restate, in appropriate language, the commitment to economic and monetary union, just as for years and years there were similar reaffirmations of the need to complete the single market, without anything actually happening. One possibility is thus to return monetary union to the sphere of intentions.

If we move from the sphere of intentions to the sphere of action, and this is what has been done in the last few years, things are completely different and the time-scale is much shorter. It is worth recalling that the Bretton Woods Conference lasted for about three weeks, that the American Constitutional Convention lasted for about eight weeks, and that the Treaty of Rome took only a few months to write. There are no technical or other reasons for it to take more than a few weeks or months to draw up a treaty on economic and monetary union. Of course, there are some very difficult political and institutional questions to negotiate, but none of these issues will be resolved until a conference is called, because there will be no concentration of minds unless the parties reach the point of sitting round a table to conclude a treaty.

If the momentum gained in 1986 and 1989 is lost, we will fall back into the sphere of intentions and a new painstaking build-up of action will be needed in the future. Before this occurs, the political situation will have changed, the political leaders will have been replaced in most countries, and we will have to start again, as we did with the Single European Act. This does not add very much to the Treaty of Rome, but it was necessary to start all over again, to restate the objectives of the Treaty, simply because things had stood still for too long.

8. THE 'SOVEREIGNTY' COUNTER-ARGUMENT

The arguments used by those who do not share the view that it is important to close the calendar and make the time-scale short can be divided into three strands. The first is the radical sovereignty counter-argument associated with the United Kingdom: we do not want monetary union because we do not want to cede our sovereignty. The development of the Community has made it increasingly clear, however, that sovereignty is not something indivisible: there has already been a loss of sovereignty in many areas.

The Community's banking law (the Second Co-ordination Directive), for example, has been adopted to all intents and purposes without the favourable vote of the German delegation. This is highly significant because it shows that, even in such a fundamental field as banking law, new legislation can be 'imposed' on no less a country than Germany. Hence, it is not a question of metaphysics and philosophy, the sovereignty issue is extremely serious, but it cannot be claimed that no sovereignty has been transferred to date and that the process would only begin with the creation of an economic and monetary union. It should also be noted that proposing a counterplan for achieving economic and monetary union, as the British Government did a few weeks ago,[2] puts the supporters of this argument in a very weak position, especially because the counterplan does not stand up to close scrutiny. Saying 'We accept that this is the way to do

---

[2] See Chapter 8 note 7.

it, but we just do not want to do it' would be much more effective and understandable.

9. SOME SMALL COUNTER-ARGUMENTS

There are also several small counter-arguments that deserve to be briefly mentioned. The first is that we are not ready for the conference. It may be hard to judge whether or not we are ready politically, but technically we are ready, there is a clear plan. This does not mean, of course, that all the problems have been solved; there are important issues still to be settled, but they will not be settled simply by further analysis conducted outside the framework of a conference called specifically to find solutions. It is worth noting, moreover, that decisions on difficult issues do not necessarily take a long time to reach; difficult decisions are one thing, slow decisions another.

The second is that some countries are not ready: Italy has a huge budget deficit, inflation in other countries is too high. There is, indeed, some truth in this argument, but I think it is now universally recognized that the EMS experience shows causation to act in both directions; while countries' economic performances must be at a certain level in order to permit changes to be made in institutional arrangements, the latter also interact very powerfully with policy processes within countries. Such positive interactions have to be set in motion and exploited.

The third small counter-argument, if readers will forgive me for calling it small, is that the UK would not sign the treaty. I do not consider this to be a decisive issue because I have the following scenario in mind. If there is a clear will to move ahead and the only major country with fundamental objections is the UK, it will have three options. The first would be to accept to participate fully with the other countries. I regard this as very unlikely if the move comes in the next eighteen months. Secondly, to cause a fundamental crisis in the Community by using its power of veto over the adoption of a new treaty. Thirdly, to disagree, but in a friendly way: in other words, to sign the treaty but after obtaining conditions, not just for one country but for several, whereby the pace of the advance would not have to be the same for all countries. I regard this to be by far the most likely outcome, a choice consistent with the great British tradition of political pragmatism. It saves all the benefits of participating in the Community as it is today. Accordingly, there does not appear to be any reason—even in the mind of the most rigid, and in a way ideological, political leader in the UK—to follow the second course of action leading to complete crisis in the Community. Hence my belief that this is a small counter-argument.

10. THE 'DEUTSCHMARK ANCHOR' COUNTER-ARGUMENT

The third strand can be called the big Bundesbank, or German, counter-argument. Briefly, it is that the degree of monetary union the Community needs, for all the reasons given earlier, can be assured by the EMS with German leadership or with the Deutschmark 'anchor'. It is claimed that there is no need to go beyond this because it satisfies all the needs, including the guarantee that the fundamental aim of monetary policy, which is to preserve price stability, will be pursued by a credible institution which has an excellent track record and which, it should not be forgotten, led the disinflation process in most European countries in the first half of the 1980s.

This is a very serious argument, clearly the most serious. It is not always formulated as explicitly as this and often those whose opposition is basically rooted in this big counter-argument refrain from using it explicitly and use instead what I have called the small counter-arguments to resist a sufficiently rapid move to a new treaty. Though serious, this argument is probably fallacious, both technically and politically. Technically, it is clear that a national currency cannot perform the role of international currency for long without being caught in a dilemma that will undermine one or perhaps both of its roles. In my view the German currency and the monetary policy of the Bundesbank are approaching this situation and the period in which the Deutschmark was most successful in this context is probably drawing to an end or may even have ended already.

Secondly, Germany is not America. The importance of Germany in the world economy or, for that matter, even in the Community economy is not comparable to that of the USA in the world economy at the end of the 1950s and in the 1960s. Moreover, the EMS is not the Bretton Woods system. The latter had rules and support mechanisms, such as limits on capital mobility and limited financial integration: factors that will be completely lacking in the post-1992 EMS. Thirdly, the Deutschmark is not the dollar and probably neither Germany nor the other member countries would be willing to see it play the role the US currency played under the Bretton Woods system. It should not be forgotten, just to give an example, that there are currently severe restrictions on the international use of the Deutschmark such as were never imposed on users of the dollar.

Politically, a system that would go a long way towards formalizing the Deutschmark's anchor role would not be readily acceptable, and this appears to be generally recognized. In short, the example of Bretton Woods cannot be followed. Under this system one currency was formally the leading currency and yet it collapsed because of the contradiction between the national and international roles of the dollar. Such a leading role in our system is unlikely ever to be accepted to the same degree as in the Bretton Woods system; and if it were, the system would probably collapse for the same reasons.

11. CONCLUSIONS

We have no choice but to close the calendar and move ahead with a short time-scale. Underlying the whole of this discussion is the crucial problem of credibility. This applies to all the participants. Countries such as Italy are frequently reminded that their economies are not convergent or sufficiently stable, that they are probably not ready for an economic and monetary union based on a new treaty. However, there is also a problem of credibility for the countries that claim to be committed to economic and monetary union but which reject the idea of moving relatively fast to a new treaty. When this 'yes but slowly' slogan is decoded, it means that economic and monetary union is accepted at the level of intentions—an objective to be periodically restated—but not in terms of action. The only way to resolve this twofold credibility problem is to maintain the recent momentum by proceeding to a new treaty embodying all the necessary guarantees of gradualism and economic soundness. In other words, if we want to be slow, let us be slow *after* concluding a treaty but not *before*.

8

Monetary Union and Competition

1. INTRODUCTION

The debate triggered by the publication of the Delors Report has revived the classic confrontation between the 'institutional' and 'market' components of monetary systems. Institutions and the market are the warp and woof of monetary theory and policy; together they form the connective tissue of every monetary system. In the institutional component public action is fundamental and there is an element of monopoly; legislation, rules, and public bodies play the decisive role. In the market component, private action is fundamental and individual decisions and competition are at work; the customs and habits of individuals are the key factors.

The preparatory work for the intergovernmental conference that will draft the EMU Treaty is complete as the summer of 1990 draws to a close. It is a moment both of clarity, because the problems have been thoroughly analysed, and of uncertainty, since the debate within and among the member countries is still open and perhaps has still to confront the most delicate issues. It may yet engender developments and ideas that could require further study. These notes on monetary competition have as their leitmotiv the discrete and complementary roles of public and private action, institutions and the market, and central banks and currencies in the process leading to European monetary union.

2. PUBLIC ACTION

That the creation of money is and must be a prerogative of the prince is almost universally accepted. The principle of extensive intervention by the public authorities in vital aspects of the mon-

August 1990, Rome. Paper. The UK had just put forward its alternative plan for EMU, based on competition between currencies.

etary system, such as banking, the organization of markets, the payment system, and international monetary relations, is also universally accepted, even if variously applied. Neither the international economy nor groups of sovereign countries have a recognized 'prince' with powers similar to those of the public authorities in a nation-state. When commercial and financial relations create interdependence requiring at least a minimum of international monetary government, a remedy for the absence of a prince is sought, generally in the form of an exchange rate rule chosen from among the many possibilities, ranging from pure floating to completely fixed rates. The exchange rate rule is the means by which countries agree how each currency is to be priced against the others.

But if the essence of monetary policy is to decide *how much* money to create, clearly no exchange rate rule on its own answers the question of who should be the prince, since no such rule specifies who should decide the amount of money to be created in the entire area. Further, if interdependence means that economic and monetary conditions in one country influence the others, it is plain that no exchange rate rule can guarantee the local prince full power. In short, an exchange rate rule is not enough to fill the governmental vacuum: the conundrum known as the 'nth country problem'. Various solutions are possible: hegemony, when one country's prince acts as the prince for the others; anarchy, when each prince follows his own course and disregards the behaviour of the others; co-ordination, when there is an effective mechanism for collective decision-making, in other words a collective prince.

In the monetary field, public action can be based on the observance of a rule or the exercise of discretionary power. The distinction is valid and revealing in both the national and the international spheres. If it were possible to frame an unambiguous rule guaranteeing optimal economic results in every circumstance, there would be no need for a monetary institution; a supervisory body ensuring compliance with the rule would suffice. Institutions are essential for the exercise of discretionary power. Serious arguments have been advanced to show that national economic policy has too much discretionary power today, in fiscal matters no less than in the monetary field, and that this power should be restricted by statutory or constitutional law. Internationally, however, an even stronger case can be made for concluding that economic policy possesses too little discretionary power. International economic policy is usually entrusted to a rule rather than discretionary power being assigned to a supranational institution, because the limitation of sovereignty is felt less strongly. However, if the national level of government is the only one equipped to conduct discretionary economic policy, whenever discretionary action is called for in the international economy, the response will necessarily be inadequate.

The foregoing considerations show how far an exchange rate rule on its own is from providing a solution to the problem of the monetary government of a highly integrated economy made up of sovereign countries. The Werner Plan proposed a monetary union based on fixed rates and aimed in practice at implementing the co-ordination formula. The European Monetary System, an adjustable peg arrangement and thus something different from a monetary union, has operated in accordance with the formula of hegemony, the monetary policy of the EMS area having been that of the country with the strongest currency. The Delors Committee adopted a definition of monetary union couched in terms of fixed rates but interpreted this as a form of single currency, with union actually based on the transfer to a Community institution of the monetary policy powers that are currently exercised by the national central banks.

3. PRIVATE ACTION

Public action is so important that it risks obscuring the no less fundamental role of private action. The use of a numeraire and a means of payment had become widespread long before sovereigns began putting their effigy on coins, and the practices and customs of private economic operators are no less important today in making the monetary system work and determining its structure. Indeed, there is evidence suggesting that the influence of private action has been growing in recent years. In today's advanced economies, by far the largest part of the total stock of money is created by the 'private' action of commercial banks. Even clearing, one of the most delicate and crucial functions of the monetary system, is again tending to be organized on a private basis, in much the same way as it was before the rise of modern central banks.

In countries where foreign exchange and capital movements are unrestricted, the prerogative of the prince faces no formal challenge, but it is none the less limited in practice by the freedom of individuals to choose the currency in which they do business. Yet this very freedom has revealed how ingrained are monetary habits. The use of a national currency as numeraire is embedded in a mass of mental habits, accounting practices, commercial customs, and computer applications: a vast heritage based on the national unit of account that is modifiable only in the long run and at a high cost. The greater stability of another currency is an incentive for operators to alter their monetary habits, but it is a weak one and does not affect the dominant position of the currency they have always used.[1] Significant currency substitution is to be found only in countries with hyperinflation, where the local currency is abandoned for that of another country—notably the dollar.[2] When the inflation differential is small and largely compensated for by the interest rate differential, the advantage operators gain by choosing a more stable currency is more than offset by the cost of having to rebase their operations.[3] Moreover, by definition, the currency to be used in transactions cannot be chosen unilaterally; as long as some operators are forced to use a given currency for some operations, such as tax payments, currency substitution is hindered.[4]

Private action on its own cannot reach the point of creating a new and efficient system. Hayek proposed a monetary system institutionally founded on competition.[5] This formula envisages competition beyond that now found in the international field between different currencies. According to Hayek, the state should be ordered in such a way that the exercise of the prince's prerogative would be replaced by a system of private currencies competing for the public's favour (each with its own denomination and performing the functions of numeraire, means of payment, and store of value). Convincing criticisms have been made of this proposal. Monetary pluralism may be an efficient solution

---

[1] See Padoa-Schioppa and Papadia 1984.

[2] See, among others, Brillembourg and Schadler 1979, and Ortiz and Solis 1982.

[3] See Gros 1988.   [4] See Laidler 1978.   [5] Hayek 1976.

for the means-of-payment and store-of-value functions, but it is highly inefficient as regards the unit-of-account function, since it requires every operator, on both the demand side and the supply side, to consider not one but many price vectors. The benefits of a system that privileges monetary stability on the side of the issuer are achieved at a prohibitive cost for the users of the currency.

4. THE DYNAMICS OF MONETARY SYSTEMS

Both public and private action are essential to the working of a monetary system. Each has a specific task and is ill-suited to perform others. Left to itself, the market is unlikely to succeed in defining generally accepted standards—the numeraire in the case of money. On the other hand, public action and institutions cannot, simply by issuing decrees, change customs, which are notoriously slow to evolve. In France it is still common to count in old francs and in Italy the pre-unification names of money still survive in local dialects. Vice versa, custom or mere economic advantage are not enough to create or transform institutional arrangements. However inefficient existing arrangements may be, in a modern democratic society they can be changed only when a current of public opinion develops, followed by political and legislative initiatives.

If a change in the monetary system is to be as complete and effective as possible, public and private action must each play its part: public action is required to modify legislation, institutions, and the currency unit; private action to modify customs and accounting practices, as well as the stock of information necessary for economic comparisons and the calculation of economic advantage. Above all, expectations have to be adjusted, or the drawbacks of the pre-reform system will almost inevitably be carried over to the new one. And while it is normally the behaviour and needs of private operators that—at the political even more than at the economic level—trigger a movement for monetary reform and set its course, it is the architects of institutions who have to create the new framework within which a viable relationship with the private sector can be established.

Monetary reform does not always involve total and instant

change of the kind that has occurred in Germany and other nations in the wake of traumatic monetary or political upheavals. A 'monetary constitution' or system is made up of a number of components, some of which can be changed independently of the others. In some EC countries, for example, joining the European Monetary System was tantamount to a monetary reform. Any radical change in indexing mechanisms, or in the procedures for negotiating wages or determining interest rates is important for the monetary system. The same is true of shifts in relations between central banks and budgetary authorities. Even a new course of monetary policy, pursued to the point where it brings about a lasting transformation of market behaviour and expectations, is comparable to a monetary reform. In other words, it is not always easy to distinguish between monetary reform and a mere change of course by the monetary authorities.

One brief comment on the subject of timing. By definition, any institutional or legislative change materializes at a particular instant in time, albeit after a lengthy incubation. By contrast, customs, habits, and the organization of economic activity evolve slowly. Their intrinsic inertia is both a strength and a potential weakness. Monetary reform involves both aspects, and must therefore reconcile instantaneous change with gradual transformation.

5. THE DELORS REPORT EIGHTEEN MONTHS ON

Although its starting point is the Werner Plan, the Delors Report can rightly claim to be the first official blueprint for solving the question of European monetary union in terms of monetary reform and the creation of a monetary system similar in every way to those obtaining in single states. Based on the regulation of exchange rates, the Werner Plan left the nth country problem unsolved, it did not provide a clear solution to the problem posed by a multiplicity of monetary policy decision-making centres, and was even more vague on the institutional aspects of union.

The plan of the Delors Committee is based on the creation of a new institution, which would assume the monetary policy responsibilities now performed separately by each central bank within its national territory. The plan envisages a single currency, since once monetary policy decisions are made and implemented by a single entity existing as an institution rather than *de facto*, a fixed exchange rate arrangement ceases to be a vehicle for monetary co-ordination and the different currencies amount, in practice, to a non-decimal fractional currency: the rate of exchange is no longer a market-defined price but only the expression of that fractionalization; changing Deutschmarks into French francs or Italian lire ceases to be a transaction for the exchange dealer and becomes a job for the cashier.

While this reading is the only one that is consistent with the basic tenets of the Delors Report, it is precisely the latter's treatment of the currency to be adopted by the union that is its weak point. True, the Report asserts that the transition to a single currency is 'a natural and desirable further development of the process of monetary union', allowing the benefits to be reaped in full, but it says little else on this subject. It is as vague with regard to the single currency as it is explicit and detailed about the single monetary institution.

There are several reasons for this imbalance: the technical difficulty of planning the gradual transition towards a single currency; a certain reluctance to propose the suppression of the symbols of national monetary sovereignty; the hostility shown by some members of the Committee and by some countries to the development of the ECU.[6] The result is a half-hearted statement that the ECU could become the single currency of the union, a statement that is not followed by any elaboration of the proposal or by an examination of the technical problems involved in the actual transition. For a plan that is founded on the definition of a final stage and which describes the means and conditions for attaining it, this is a serious omission.

The two documents put forward by the United Kingdom following the publication of the Delors Report contain proposals regarding private action and the currency of the union.[7] While the Delors Report is largely concerned with the creation of a

[6] The preparatory documents published with the Delors Report show that there were positions more favourable to the ECU within the Committee. See Ciampi 1989, Larosière 1989, Thygesen 1989*a*.

[7] In a speech by the Chancellor of the Exchequer, John Major, on 20 June 1990 and in a subsequent paper by the Bank of England, a proposal was put forward to establish a European Monetary Fund (EMF), which would issue 'hard ECUs' and offer them to operators in exchange for national currencies; this

monetary institution endowed with the prince's prerogative, or monopoly, referred to earlier, and leaves private action to one side, the British proposal puts the latter at the centre of the stage and makes monetary competition the driving force of the union.

Without going into the technical details of the British proposal, it is essential to clarify that it can be seen from two standpoints.[8] On the one hand, it can be approached as a straight alternative to the solution advocated by the Delors Committee: spontaneous demand for ECUs would itself become the motor of monetary union, in accordance with 'Hayek-type' competition, and the institution (Currency Board, European Monetary Fund, or whatever) would be purely passive, with no monetary policy role of its own, nor any commitment to, or clear definition of, the monetary or institutional developments that might be expected to follow the stage of monetary competition. On the other hand, the proposal can be seen as a contribution of ideas for the transition stage within the framework of the overall strategy outlined in the Delors Report. Whereas the first approach appears difficult to reconcile with the positions of the other EC countries, the second seems far removed from that officially announced by the British Government. In the first case, monetary union would be entirely, and unrealistically, entrusted to private action; in the second it would be, as indeed it needs to be, the result of a combination of public and private action, a valuable supplement to the Delors Report.

6. THE CURRENCY OF THE UNION: DEFINITIONS

Like every other monetary system, the European Monetary Union will be built on two pillars: a central bank and a currency.

would avoid any additional creation of money (the hard ECU would thus not be a parallel currency). The promoters of this proposal expect that the relative stability of the hard ECU would make it attractive to operators and also have a disciplinary effect on national monetary policies, thus contributing to greater monetary stability in the Community. See HM Treasury 1989 and 1990.

[8] As of August 1990 the analysis of the British proposals cannot be said to be complete. They have not even been set out systematically in a single document, but are to be found in a series of speeches and papers that are not always wholly in agreement; it is also uncertain how far the British Government is committed to the proposals, which raise a number of technical issues that will need to be cleared up before the feasibility of the plans can be assessed.

The Delors Committee and subsequent studies have given careful thought to the problems connected with the first pillar: even where agreement on the solutions to be adopted has not been reached, the terms of the problem are clear. The debate surrounding the second pillar is less advanced, however; a number of studies have been carried out, but they have not been collated, nor have they been sufficiently assimilated in Community fora to provide the basis for decisions.

The first pillar of monetary union, the central bank, is concerned primarily with institutional aspects, public action, economic policy, and macro-economic issues; the second, the currency, with market-related aspects, private action, the interests of individual operators, and micro-economic issues. The transition from twelve central banks to one means changing from twelve monetary policies to one, and preparing the ground for macro-economic stabilization to be accomplished rationally and uniformly throughout the Community. The transition from twelve currencies to one means changing from twelve price systems to one and from twelve payment systems to one; it means extending the micro-economic processes of optimizing investment, production, and consumption to the whole Community economy, with information and transaction costs no higher than those now borne in each country: only in this way can monetary union become a reality for consumers and firms.

Expressions such as single currency, common currency, parallel currency, parity currency, and basket currency are often attributed different meanings by the participants in the same debate. An appendix to this chapter provides a glossary of the meanings that appear most suitable. Two comments will suffice here. First, the currency of the union can be (i) 'single', if it has definitively replaced all other currencies, (ii) 'parallel', if it is added to other currencies with its own capacity to create extra money, or (iii) 'common', if it circulates alongside other currencies through a process of substitution, but without any mechanism to create extra money.

Finally, the currency of the union will be a 'basket' currency if its official value is defined as the sum of predetermined quantities of the various Community currencies or a 'parity' currency if, like these, it is defined as an official rate of exchange against each of the other currencies. Both 'official' and 'value' are terms that require clarification, however. The 'value' of a currency can be defined as its capacity to purchase other currencies today, itself tomorrow, or a basket of goods and services: a rate of exchange, a rate of interest, and an index of prices are the corresponding expressions of these different meanings of value. The word 'official' means that the value or rate of exchange in question is an announced value, which may not necessarily be the same as that prevailing in the market.

The distinction between basket and parity currencies applies to the first of the three meanings of the value of money: for the third meaning, a value can be defined only where enough goods and services are priced in that currency for an index to be compiled. Clearly, in the final stage of union, with irrevocably locked exchange rates, the two definitions are equivalent. It is in the transition stage that the distinction between basket currency and parity currency becomes important. And it is in this context that the strategy for developing the common currency should be seen.

7. THE ECU SYSTEM: REALITY AND POTENTIAL

The reality before our eyes is not always easily related to this terminological framework, since the institutional and market components intertwine and change, each in response to its own internal forces. Let us take a look at its application to the ECU system. The ECU today is commonly held to be a basket currency whose functions as a common currency are limited to the financial markets; it is also generally believed that without some new institutional arrangement, without some public action as defined earlier, the ECU cannot break out of these narrow confines and come closer to being a truly common currency, on the way to the single currency: the lack of a lender of last resort, the separation between the official and private circuits, and the ECU's definition as a basket currency are all seen as impeding its development and as impediments that only public action can remove.

The ECU system is actually much closer to being a complete monetary system than is generally acknowledged and could, if its potential were given full scope, cover much of the road to single currency status. This thesis, which I have developed at length elsewhere,[9] can be summarized as follows. Under present conditions, there is nothing to prevent the ECU from being widely used for the three monetary functions of numeraire, means of payment, and store of value. Were this to happen, the ECU's value—in each of the meanings of 'value' referred to above—could increasingly be determined in the market independently of its official definition as a basket of currencies, which has the limited and operationally unmeaningful role of a parity that is *announced but not defended in the market* by any official commitment or authority. The clearing system set up at the Bank for International Settlements in 1986 has given the ECU a more advanced international payment system than any other currency. On paper, the fact that central banks hold private ECUs and the prospect of their operating via the clearing system, are in themselves sufficient to allow 'public' intervention in the ECU market, should this be decided.

The ECU is a currency whose market rate floats around the official basket rate. Its limited development is not the result of any specific institutional impediments, but of two other factors: the very high cost of promoting its use up to a 'critical mass', beyond which the advantages of a common currency would start to emerge, and the lack of that official and institutional backing without which economic agents are not aware of the existence of a monetary system in its own right.

8. PREPARATION OF THE SINGLE CURRENCY

Does it follow from these considerations that public action has done all it should and that private action alone can now carry the monetary union to completion by pursuing its own motives of profit and efficiency and using increased volume to develop mechanisms that already exist, albeit in embryo form? Or that public action can concentrate on the creation of a central bank while totally ignoring that other pillar of monetary union, the currency? I do not believe these are the right conclusions to draw. Whether or not the ECU's potential is realized depends primarily on private action, but public action is also necessary on

---

[9] See Chapter 4.

both the currency and the central bank fronts. The ECU needs to be managed, rather than promoted, by the central bank side of the system: public action must provide private action with the certainty of a point of arrival.

If it is true (i) that the completion of European monetary union calls for a single central bank and a single currency, (ii) that the transition to a single currency and the substitution of national currencies will not be simultaneous with the transfer of power over monetary policy to a single monetary institution, and (iii) that the adoption of a single currency is in any case not a short-term operation, since it involves the transformation of habits, accounting procedures, and organizational structures based on earlier systems, then the future single currency must somehow be managed and regulated *before* it takes over—if the process of unification is to be orderly, efficient, and as economical as possible. And until the single currency has completely replaced national currencies, the conduct of a single monetary policy with irrevocably fixed exchange rates will also raise problems requiring use of the future single currency by the European monetary institution in the discharge of its business.

The background against which to consider the various ideas and proposals that have been put forward on the subject of the ECU and monetary union includes: the preparations for a single currency, the transition to the final stage of monetary union, and the proper division of labour between public and private action.

Without distorting the Delors Report's approach to the implementation of monetary union, the gap with regard to the currency of the union can be filled by drawing on some of the proposals that have been formulated in recent years.[10] In the first place, the markets must be certain that monetary union will indeed be accomplished and that its ultimate stage will involve a single currency: this certainty will have to be provided by a treaty that is approved, ratified, and implemented. The markets must be given ample advance notice of which currency will be adopted as the single currency. A credible, official undertaking that this will be the ECU and that there will be no discontinuity between its value today and the value it will have on the day it becomes the single currency will give the markets a strong incentive to bear

[10] See Ernst & Young 1990, Association for the Monetary Union of Europe 1988 and 1990, and Ciampi 1989.

the initially high costs involved in adopting the ECU for monetary functions.

The use of the future single currency prior to its establishment as such must not complicate or even disturb the pursuit of a monetary policy aimed at price stability. This rules out any idea of a parallel currency as defined earlier. If the future single currency is to compete with, and gradually replace, existing national currencies, its value must be given maximum stability in terms of its present and future purchasing power, so that it can increasingly contribute to the Community's monetary system. So long as the ECU remains a basket currency, its market value will remain tied to the value of its component currencies. Thus the ECU's stability will have to be promoted through monetary policies directed at maintaining stability in all the member states and the participation of all their currencies in the Exchange Rate Mechanism. Alternatively, the ECU could be detached from the basket of currencies and based on fixed bilateral parities tied to the System's most stable currencies, as outlined in the British proposal to establish a hard ECU. In either case a monetary policy that, prior to the transition to a single currency, was closely co-ordinated in stage two, and then single in stage three, would benefit from wider use of the future single currency, which might even be a necessary condition for the working and regulation of a Community payment system,[11] policies *vis-à-vis* third currencies,[12] and the co-ordination of monetary policies.[13]

These options correspond to a series of measures and actions that are an integral part of the process of monetary union and which avoid the snags that have rightly been detected in other proposals for the ECU's development. A major feature is the proper interaction between public and private action.

9. CONCLUSIONS

European monetary union is a monetary reform with unprecedented features: it affects several countries rather than just one; it is being implemented while political union is still incomplete; the aim of advancing step by step is one of its key features; and the

---

[11] See Association for the Monetary Union of Europe 1990.
[12] See Larosière 1989.   [13] See Ciampi 1989 and Thygesen 1989a.

very sovereign authorities co-operating in its formulation will tomorrow be subordinate to it. Technically and politically it is a highly complex 'experiment'; at the theoretical level it sheds new light on the nature of monetary systems and helps us to understand them better.

The debate as to 'how' and 'when' monetary union is to be accomplished has revealed a diversity of interests, of political and constitutional concepts, and even of doubts as to 'whether' the union should be accomplished at all. At the same time, it has also revealed the complexity of the problems and the difficulty of finding technically satisfactory solutions; thus the positions that confront each other are often more compatible and complementary than even the participants immediately realize. It is not uncommon during a process of institutional change for a new order to emerge, born of the need for compromise between opposing interests and wills, and subsequently to reveal a consistency, durability, and ability to function beyond the expectations of either analysts or the protagonists themselves.

A monetary system can function efficiently only when the different elements—private and public action, competition and monopoly, institutions and the market, the central bank and the currency—contribute to promote the appropriate interaction and each one performs its tasks to the full. The jigsaw puzzle that must be pieced together to produce European monetary union is not yet complete: until it is, some of the pieces still waiting to be inserted may seem incompatible with others, unplaceable, or to belong to a different puzzle altogether. Often this is not the case and the considerations of the preceding pages strengthen my conviction that no piece should be discarded until the overall design is complete.

Glossary

Common currency: a currency used by Community operators that is different from member states' or third countries' currencies. It does not involve the creation of extra money, but the substitution of member states' currencies. It does not require, but neither does it exclude, the creation of a monetary authority to manage the substitution.

Parallel currency: a currency created independently of, and in addition to, national currencies; it circulates in parallel with national currencies and competes with them; it is created, managed, and administered by its own monetary authority.

Single currency: a common currency that has completely replaced national currencies and is the only currency officially in circulation in the Community; it is managed by a single monetary authority.

Parity currency: a currency whose value is based on an official exchange rate with each of the other currencies.

Basket currency: a currency whose value is based on fixed quantities of national currencies or goods. The ECU is currently composed of quantities of the twelve Community currencies that are fixed but adjustable every five years.

9

Fiscal Compatibility and Monetary Constitution

1. INTRODUCTION

This chapter deals with the issue of how much fiscal discipline and co-ordination are needed among member countries' budgets to ensure the viability of a monetary union. This is one of the key open issues on the European agenda at both the political level and the technical level. The *Report on European Economic and Monetary Union* (Delors Report) stresses the importance of fiscal co-ordination. It states that, although this objective should be achieved as much as possible through voluntary co-operation, there is a need for 'binding rules' and for the transfer of some decision-making power from member states to the Community to avoid unsustainable differences in public-sector borrowing requirements (paragraph 19).

This position has been strongly endorsed by several countries since the publication of the Delors Report. On the other hand, it has been received with scepticism and recently with outright opposition by the UK Treasury and several academic economists (see, in particular, Goodhart 1989). According to the 'counter-plan' published by the British Government last November, binding Community rules on the size of budget deficits are neither necessary nor desirable. They are unnecessary because 'fixed exchange rate regimes have in the past operated successfully without such rules, as do the overwhelming majority of federal states today. Market pressures and multilateral surveillance will prevent deficits becoming unsustainable or unneighbourly.' Moreover, such rules are undesirable 'because they infringe on

January 1990, Tel-Aviv. Paper presented at the conference on 'Aspects of Central Bank Policy-Making' organized by the Bank of Israel and the David Horowitz Institute. Opinions were widely divergent on the issue whether monetary union should be complemented with budgetary rules.

the principle of subsidiarity and could lead to acute political difficulties within member states' (HM Treasury 1989).

To put this debate in perspective, it is useful to recall two key features of the Delors Report. First, the project involves more than a gradual strengthening of the existing exchange rate agreements in Europe. Although the Report borrows from the 1970 Werner Plan and defines monetary union in terms of irrevocably fixed parities and complete and irreversible mobility of capital, the key feature of the proposed monetary union is the common monetary policy. Secondly, following the model of the Bundesbank statute, the primary aim of the European Central Bank (ECB) is defined as being that of ensuring price stability; and only 'subject to the foregoing' does the Report consider that 'the System should support the general economic policy set at the Community level by the competent bodies' (paragraph 32).

Both features clearly require a high degree of consensus on the conduct of monetary policy; the question, which the Committee could not avoid, is whether they also require convergence and/or the centralization of decision-making powers in other areas of economic policy. Although the Report deals with a broad range of policies (the single market, competition, regional and structural policies, wage and price formation), fiscal policy unquestionably receives the greatest attention.

The preoccupations of the Delors Report are justified, but the argument that a fiscal rule is a logical prerequisite for the viability of a monetary union is not compelling.[1] By contrast, it is of the greatest importance that a strong monetary constitution be designed, providing for a clear separation between monetary and fiscal policy; in this regard, this paper attempts to go somewhat beyond the Delors Report, in terms of both analysis and proposals.

2. PRELIMINARY REMARKS ON FISCAL DISCIPLINE

Before going into the main issue, I shall make my position clear on two points. First, much greater fiscal discipline than we have seen so far in some European countries is necessary in its own

[1] See Chapter 6.

right and would facilitate the transition towards greater exchange rate stability. Among the major countries, Italy has to take a decisive step to turn its primary deficit into a surplus and start to repay the public debt. Should the attempts to achieve this objective fail, there is a potential threat to financial stability both in Italy and in neighbouring countries. It may also become very difficult, if not impossible, to achieve and maintain the credibility required to stay within the narrow band of the European Monetary System. In spite of well-known theoretical ambiguities about the effects of the budget on the exchange rate, it is clear that a major fiscal correction in Italy would strengthen cohesion within the EMS by enhancing confidence and eliminating any residual fear of future monetization of the debt.[2]

Secondly, the experience of Italy and several other countries in the last two decades shows how difficult it is to conjugate discretion and responsibility in budgetary matters and provides strong support for proposals aimed at substantially reducing budgetary discretion.[3] This issue will not be dealt with here, apart from noting that institutional changes could be made at the national level, in much the same way as in the United States, where most states have adopted some kind of fiscal rule (typically precluding the issue of debt to cover current expenditures), but have not been required to do so by the central government. The Community could perhaps take the lead by seeking to co-ordinate and 'harmonize' member states' rules, as it does in many other fields. This is altogether different from transferring fiscal powers to the Community and making this a condition for further progress in the direction of the monetary union.

---

[2] See Galli and Masera (1991) for a demonstration of the conditions in which these effects dominate the familiar Mundell–Fleming–Dornbusch effect with short- as well as long-run capital mobility.

[3] The formation of large public debts can be seen as a case of 'government failure', which may be due to fiscal illusion (as argued by Buchanan *et al.* 1986), but may also be accounted for in models of rational agents (see e.g. Tabellini and Alesina 1988). There is hence an issue of how to correct for the resulting intertemporal inefficiency, while at the same time allowing for some degree of discretion to respond to exceptional or unexpected circumstances.

3. THE CONTROVERSY

There are several aspects to the general question of how much fiscal union is necessary for monetary union. A useful distinction can be made between issues relating to fiscal *discipline* and issues relating to fiscal *co-ordination*. Much of the controversy at the political level concerns fiscal discipline and whether a monetary union is conceivable while some countries have very large public-sector debts and may run into financing difficulties. On the other hand, co-ordination issues are predominant in the scientific literature: the focus is not on public debts, but on fiscal policy as a tool for macro-economic stabilization. Discussion of this aspect is deferred to Section 7.

Emphasis on fiscal discipline is mainly justified by two preoccupations. They concern monetary policy and distributive functions respectively, and can be formulated in the following terms:

(a) Divergent fiscal policies may lead to conflicting views about the appropriate *stance* of the union's monetary policy because the financially weak countries may advocate a permissive monetary policy in order to ease the financing of their budget deficits and/or reduce the burden of their debt.

(b) Conflicts may also arise, and perhaps more disruptively, on issues related to the *distribution* of credit and real resources among the Community countries; some may fear that the role and functions attributed to the ECB could result in its being obliged *de facto* to support or even bail out members that run into serious financial difficulties.

Although there is some overlap between these two points, it is useful to treat them separately: the first relates to the overall stance of the union (the level of interest rates, the total *amount* of the ECB's assets, etc.) while in the second the emphasis is on distributive issues (interest rate differentials between countries, the composition of the ECB's assets, etc.). Both impinge on the viability of the union in the sense that serious economic tensions could lead to political disagreement and, in the worst scenario, to the dissolution of the union itself.

Opinions appear to be divided between those who believe that discipline should be imposed through Community rules and those who stress the role of markets and the fact that, in a union, fiscal authorities are subject to a more stringent set of incentives. According to the Delors Report (paragraph 30),

market perceptions do not necessarily provide strong and compelling signals;

access to a large capital market may actually facilitate the financing of economic imbalances for some time;

rather than leading to a gradual adaptation, market views about the creditworthiness of official borrowers may change abruptly and result in the closure of access to market financing.

These arguments are rather difficult to assess. On the one hand, it is hard to draw on the past experience of sovereign nations to imagine what would happen after a major shift in regime; on the other, there is no conclusive evidence regarding the extent to which the experience of federal states is relevant to the European union.

Clearly, the amount of discipline that markets have been able to impose so far on sovereign nations has to be considered insufficient: otherwise the issue would not arise. The question is therefore whether conditions change once a monetary union is in place. Two points can be mentioned:

liberalization of capital movements and of the domestic financial system;

elimination of the possibility for individual countries to resort to devaluations and to the monetization of the budget deficit.

The first point (which is an essential part of the programme for the monetary union, but none the less only a part) is obviously important; any form of financial restriction makes it less likely that views about the creditworthiness of borrowers will be reflected in yield differentials in the markets. Governments have often resorted to financial restrictions in order to avoid the more painful (at least in the short run) route of reducing primary deficits. There is, however, at least one counter example: the USA in the 1980s.

The second point is less obvious. Inability to monetize, coupled with exchange rate fixity, implies that interest rates will have to be more responsive to market sentiment. It is not clear, however, whether high interest rates are actually more compelling than the sanctions markets inflict today, through speculative attacks in the foreign exchange markets. Governments would probably have less scope to cushion the effects of a loss of confidence; moreover, the source of the problem would be clearer in the first case than in the second. In the experience of federal states, yield differentials on the debts of different regions do show up when markets are reasonably convinced that the central government will not intervene. A good example is Canada:[4] in the provincial bond market there is a yield spread of up to 50 or 60 basis points between the (fiscally and economically) stronger provinces and the weaker provinces. It is not clear, however, how much fiscal discipline these spreads have induced. It is even more difficult to tell whether spreads of this size could induce discipline in the large, politically independent nations of Europe.

Another argument pointing in the direction of greater discipline is suggested by game-theory research on externalities. An individual country does not value the negative externality on foreign inflation stemming from an appreciation of its currency; hence there is a tendency for it to overexpand fiscal policy and appreciate the exchange rate in order to sustain the level of activity, while at the same time curbing inflation at the expense of its neighbours. This resembles the path the USA followed at the beginning of the last decade. Presumably, in the long run, the gains from this policy tend to diminish, since a depreciation is required to balance the current account, inclusive of interest payments; this, however, may not happen for some time (as the US case proves) and in the meantime large debts are accumulated. In a monetary union this source of 'fiscal indiscipline' is eliminated; there may, on the contrary, be a tendency for fiscal policy to be underexpansionary if its effect on foreign output is sufficiently large (see Ploeg 1989).

Both arguments (market mechanisms and externalities) suggest that problems of fiscal indiscipline are less likely to arise in a monetary union. It none the less cannot be concluded that they would be completely eliminated. For this reason, I share the preoccupations expressed by the Delors Report. A possible solution is to impose fiscal rules and endow the Community with the authority to control national budgets. In principle, this eliminates

[4] See Bishop *et al.* 1989.

the problem at the root, but it would encounter political opposition and clearly be extremely demanding on both member states and the Community; the former would be asked to give up a conspicuous part of their sovereignty, while the Community would be faced with the very complex problem of devising the rules and enforcing them on otherwise sovereign nations. Another solution would be to design monetary rules that would prevent fiscal problems from interfering with the conduct of monetary policy. I shall argue that there is a degree of substitutability between monetary and fiscal rules.

4. BUDGET DEFICITS AND THE UNION'S MONETARY POLICY

As mentioned at the beginning of the previous section, the first problem to be tackled concerns the stance of the union's monetary policy: will financially weak countries advocate a permissive monetary policy in order to reduce the burden of their debts? In principle, this is comparable to the general problem of the relations between monetary and fiscal authorities in a sovereign nation. The issues concern the amount of autonomy the monetary authorities should be given, the body (Ministry of Finance, the Government, the Parliament, etc.) to which they should be accountable, how their officials should be appointed, and how the final objectives and operating targets of monetary policy should be defined.

Some answers to these questions can be found in the Delors Report. As recalled above, the final objective (price stability) should be defined at the outset in the statute of the ECB. The Report also states that the Council of the ECB (composed of the governors of member states' central banks and the members of the Board appointed by the European Council) should be independent of instructions from national governments and Community authorities. To ensure independence, the Report calls for 'appropriate security of tenure' for the members of the Council. As to accountability, the Report proposes that the ECB should report to the European Parliament and to the European Council. In addition, 'supervision of the administration of the

System would be carried out independently of the Community bodies, for instance by a supervisory council or by a committee of independent auditors'.

This is clearly a very general framework, which needs to be worked out in greater detail; several problems are still open, particularly as regards accountability (e.g. does the European Parliament have sufficient powers for the proposed task?). In this respect, two points need to be made. First, in contrast with most federations, the critical issue is independence from regional (i.e. national) rather than central (i.e. Community) authorities. This has implications for the architecture of the federative structure of the ECB recommended by the Delors Report. In particular, great care will be necessary in designing the relations between the central body (the Board) and the Council, in which national central banks are represented. Voting schemes, the specification of the issues to be submitted to the Council, and the frequency of meetings etc. should be such as to give the Board the bulk of the responsibility for the final conduct of monetary policy.

The second point is that, with a correct institutional design, there is likely to be a high degree of cohesion around the basic principle of price stability, despite the divergent fiscal positions of individual countries. Europe has been vaccinated by the painful experiences of high inflation in the 1970s and disinflation in the 1980s. Even in countries with large budget deficits, central banks have found widespread support for a strong commitment to price stability. The success of the EMS is largely due to this consensus; it has shown that a significant degree of monetary convergence can be achieved and maintained for some time, even with diverging fundamentals.

In addition, the prospect of monetary union is likely to bring about greater convergence than has been seen so far. Here again there is something to learn from the EMS; in spite of the considerable margins of flexibility allowed by the System, there is evidence that it has had a powerful impact on agents' expectations about the future growth of nominal variables.[5] On this account, high inflation countries have gained a lot; low inflation countries have not lost. I would also argue, though more on the basis of judgement than hard evidence, that—unfortunately with the

[5] See Giavazzi and Giovannini 1989.

exception of my own country—the EMS has exerted a disciplinary influence on fiscal policies too. A monetary union is a much
more radical change compared with current conditions than was
the EMS compared with the unco-ordinated, but managed floats
of the 1970s, and I expect it to exert a much greater effect on the
expectations and actual behaviour of both private agents and
fiscal authorities.

5. THE DISTRIBUTIVE PROBLEM

The second preoccupation that determines a request for institutionalized fiscal discipline is essentially a distributive issue. In
short, the question is whether, in a monetary union, there would
be a tendency or even an implicit obligation for the strong members to support the fiscally weak ones, especially in the event of
acute financing difficulties or outright debt crises.

It should be noted at the outset that the issue of public debt
crises is likely to become more important once the union is in
place since, as argued in Section 3, with adjustable parities a loss
of confidence usually shows up in the foreign exchange market,
while in a union it would mainly affect the market for government paper. By advocating the exclusion of the fiscal authorities
from direct access to central-bank credit (paragraph 30), the
Delors Committee showed its awareness of the possible distributive implications of a monetary union, though it did not make
this explicit or go into certain central banking technicalities that I
will touch upon below.

It should also be noted that the relations between the monetary and distributive functions of transnational monetary
arrangements have always been an important issue and have
often generated considerable confusion. It is sufficient to recall
the Bretton Woods debate on Keynes's Bancor project, the main
aim of which was to create international liquidity. Keynes proposed that liquidity should be created by extending credit to
countries with a balance-of-payments deficit, his purpose being to
avoid the deflationary tendencies of the 1930s, which he attributed basically to the fact that adjustment was a necessity for
deficit countries and only an option for surplus countries. I agree
with the view that the Keynes plan was not only inflationary but

also unworkable[6] because its mechanism meant that surplus countries would be obliged *de facto* to finance deficit countries almost indefinitely. It is essential that traps of this sort be avoided in the design of the European monetary union. Here again, this can be done either by imposing fiscal rules or by defining a set of monetary rules that would prevent the central monetary authority from becoming involved in the problems of individual countries.

6. THE FUNCTIONS OF THE ECB

To show the relationship between the distributive issue and the operations of a European central bank, it is useful to distinguish between three of the possible functions of any transnational monetary arrangement: (i) creation of liquidity, (ii) intermediation of credit, and (iii) transfer of resources. These functions are clearly distinct in principle, though they may be hard to distinguish in practice. Often the accounting nature of a particular operation is not sufficient to classify it in one of these three categories; other information is necessary. Consider, for instance, a world composed of two identical countries, using a common fiat currency issued by a transnational institution. If an operation results in a certain amount of currency being allocated to just one of the two countries (say country A), there is clearly a transfer of resources because country A acquires purchasing power over goods and services produced by country B. If, instead, the same operation is undertaken with both country A and country B, the transfer effect vanishes and the outcome is an increase in the quantity of world money. Likewise, the purchase of a government's bonds by an international institution may be a credit, a transfer, or a creation of liquidity, depending not only on the operations undertaken with other governments but also on the criteria adopted for the redistribution of the interest income accruing on the bonds. The economic effects also depend, as explained below, on market perceptions about the substitutability between bonds issued by different governments.

While it is clear that the central European authority should

6 See Cohen 1989.

perform function (i) and not function (iii), it is less clear whether or to what extent it should perform function (ii). To gain an understanding of this problem, it is useful to go through an exercise that can be labelled 'accounting engineering': i.e. thinking, with reference to the budget of the central European institution, about the operations and the constraints which would define its activity.

Imagine a situation in which, at the end of the process foreseen by the Delors Committee and with a common currency (say, the ECU), the ECB has, on the liabilities side, the *entire* monetary base of the Community plus the initial capital conferred by member states. On the assets side, suppose, for the moment, that the ECB has essentially national government bonds. The profits (interest revenue minus operating costs) would be paid out to member states according to their share of the capital (quotas, in IMF jargon). To keep things simple, for the moment I shall ignore the relations between the central monetary authority and the national branches of the System.

Several fairly general propositions can be applied to such a simplified system:

1. Transfers of real resources between countries depend, as a first approximation, on the distribution of the quotas (and hence of the profits) of the ECB and not on the distribution of its assets. The revenues of the ECB would essentially be the Community seigniorage, defined as the ECU monetary base times a nominal interest rate. To have an idea of the order of magnitude, the monetary base in 1988 was 9.3 per cent of Community GDP (Table 9.1), while the average long-term interest rate was 9.9 per cent: multiplying these two numbers gives a value (0.92 per cent of GDP) which is fairly close to that of the Community budget.[7]

2. Neutrality in the distribution of resources mainly requires that quotas be distributed in the same proportion as holdings of ECU monetary base by residents of member countries. On the stated assumption that the entire seigniorage levied on residents of the Community accrues to the ECB, this scheme would generally result in countries neither

---

[7] The relevant number may become smaller in the future since some countries may reduce their reserve ratios. See Gros and Thygesen 1990.

losing nor gaining.[8] On the other hand, if some sort of GDP criterion were used, there would be a redistribution in favour of countries with a high income velocity of the monetary base. As things stand today, the United Kingdom, which has a high income velocity, would receive 17 per cent instead of 6 per cent of total Community seigniorage (Table 9.1). The latter is a little less than 6 per cent of British GDP, so that with this criterion the United Kingdom would receive a transfer of about 0.6 per cent of its GDP every year. Spain would lose almost 1.1 per cent. Since they are largely due to differences in reserve ratios, differences in income velocities will probably shrink in the future; they none the less might remain significant, as is often the case between regions of the same country.

3. Purchases of bonds by the ECB give rise to credit relations, in addition to creating liquidity, only if their distribution among countries differs from that of the quotas. The share of a particular country's bonds in the ECB's total assets is not relevant; what matters is the difference between this

TABLE 9.1. *Monetary base and GDP in the European Community (1988; %)*

Country	Monetary base/GDP	Share of GDP	Share of monetary base
Belgium	7.5	3.2	2.6
Denmark	3.7	2.3	0.9
France	5.8	20.0	12.5
Germany	9.9	25.3	26.9
Greece	14.9	1.1	1.8
Ireland	10.1	0.7	0.7
Italy	14.6	17.5	27.4
The Netherlands	8.1	4.8	4.2
Portugal	13.5	0.9	1.3
Spain	20.4	7.2	15.7
UK	3.3	17.0	6.0
TOTAL	9.3	100.0	100.0

[8] Minor redistributions, relative to the present situation, would occur to the extent that currencies are held outside the issuing country.

share and the country's share of the ECB's capital. This can easily be seen by noting that, if the two shares are equal, the country is effectively paying no interest on those of its bonds in the ECB's portfolio.

These points are of critical importance and their implications should be discussed at an early stage of the construction of the new system. More or less disguised redistributions are much more likely to result from wrongly designed rules for the balance sheet and profit and loss account of the ECB than from a lack of fiscal rules. On the other hand, it is not easy to establish what the correct design should be. The difficulties concern the operational implementation of distributive neutrality and the desirable limits to credit operations. As to the first, hair-splitting implementation of the monetary base criterion proposed above is almost impossible. Except for reserve currencies, we currently have a reasonably good measure of the monetary base held by residents because this aggregate has a precise counterpart in the liabilities of the central bank. But, with a common currency or with a considerable amount of currency substitution (as would occur with irrevocably fixed parities), there would no longer be such a measure and statistical approximations would have to be used. It is to be hoped that a reasonable political agreement will be found on this point. It should be noted in passing that no difficulties should be raised by those who are showing sympathy toward the British plan for a market route to the union, based on currency competition; according to this plan, the whole seigniorage of the Community would accrue every year to the single country whose currency wins the market contest.

The other issue is whether, or to what extent, the ECB should extend credit to individual countries. Some limits (maximum amount of lending, time within which a country's share should go back to its quota) should certainly be fixed, at the very least to avoid large and continuous overshoots of the quotas, which would in practice amount to transfers. The question is how tight these limits should be; an extreme proposal is to impose a rule fixing the composition of the ECB's portfolio and hence of its open market operations. If the mix is right, as discussed above, the ECB would be precluded from extending credit; its functions would be strictly limited to the creation of outside ECUs.

Though I do not have a fully worked out solution to this problem, I am inclined to favour a rather strict rule of this kind. The main advantage is that it would eliminate any scope for pressure by fiscal authorities of individual countries aimed at finding support for their debts.[9] In addition, together with a clear provision excluding the possibility of a bail-out by any Community body, such a rule would greatly reinforce market discipline. It would also be much easier to implement and enforce than budgetary rules.

There are difficulties, however. Some are basically technical and probably not very hard to solve: for instance, what should be done when the ECB incurs a loss due to a fall in the market value of the debt of an individual country? How should the loss be distributed among members? A more substantial problem is that a strict rule would prevent the ECB from doing most of the things which effectively keep central bankers busy nowadays: maintaining orderly conditions on the money markets, guaranteeing the smooth functioning of the payment system, and lending of last resort to the government and commercial banks.

Can we do without these functions? Or should they be attributed to the national authorities? If the second is the right answer, then the question becomes whether these functions can be performed through sterilized interventions, that is, operations which do not impinge on the overall monetary base of the Community. For instance, national central banks could intervene to stabilize a particular market or to provide liquidity to a bank operating in the domestic clearing system by using deposits with commercial banks or other assets in their portfolio. With the government, they could operate like an investment bank by helping it to place its debentures on the market on the most favourable terms. Quite clearly this would be a major change compared with present practices and leaves open the question of how the activities of national central banks would be financed.

There are two possible objections to the proposal of adopting rather strict rules on the composition of the ECB's assets. The first is that they are irrelevant because bonds issued by different countries are likely to be very close or even perfect substitutes. If this was the case, a shift in the composition of the ECB's assets would be completely offset by a shift in the opposite direction in

---

[9] On this point see Kenen 1969, Casella and Feinstein 1988, and Branson 1989.

the composition of private portfolios, thus leaving interest rates on each country's bonds unaffected; the ECB would still perform function (ii), credit intermediation, but it would have no real or monetary consequences. The question is how seriously one should take the assumption of perfect substitutability. Clearly distributional issues are likely to arise when a country runs into financial difficulties (i.e. when the assumption of perfect substitution is violated because markets perceive different levels of risk). More generally, if perfect substitution were really the rule, all loans extended at market rates by international organizations (or any other large institution or individual) would be irrelevant. In practice, I believe that such activities are often very important, owing to capital market segmentation, imperfect substitutability, asymmetric information, signalling effects, or whatever. My conclusion is that considering substitution effects may somewhat reduce, but certainly cannot eliminate, the concern about the distributive aspects of the ECB's activities.

The second objection is that the problem would be solved more simply by requiring the ECB to hold liabilities issued by private agents (mainly banks) rather than by national governments. This, however, is not a proposal of the Delors Report, which states in paragraph 32 that 'While complying with the provision not to lend to public-sector authorities, the System could buy and sell government securities on the market as a means of conducting monetary policy.' The idea none the less conforms with the spirit of the Delors Report because it emphasizes the distinction between monetary and fiscal authorities and therefore deserves favourable attention. It would not however eliminate the problem of the distribution of ECB credit among countries, at least until the geographical distribution of the ownership of banks came to coincide closely with national boundaries, as today. In addition, national governments would have an indirect interest in a generous ECB financing policy towards domestic banks, as long as the latter remained among the major holders of their debts.

These problems will undoubtedly lose much of their importance as Europe proceeds along the road of unification and a sense of supranational solidarity develops with national boundaries becoming little more than geographic expressions. This, however, is still rather a long way off.

7. CO-ORDINATION OF FISCAL POLICIES

The discussion has so far dealt with the issue of whether a sound common monetary policy can be pursued even if individual countries have different degrees of fiscal discipline. It has been argued that this should be feasible and that the key prerequisite is the existence not of fiscal rules but of a strong monetary constitution granting the ECB sufficient independence from national governments.

Whether and to what extent fiscal policy should be co-ordinated at the Community level is a separate issue since, even if every country was fiscally responsible and monetary authorities were completely autonomous, it could be argued that fiscal policy should not be left entirely to the discretion of national governments. Basically three arguments have been put forward in support of this view:[10]

(a) Undue appropriation of Community saving by one country. A large budget deficit in one country puts pressure on the overall level of interest rates, crowds out productive investment, and diverts some Community saving to that country.

(b) Greater externalities. Monetary union is part of a larger programme of economic integration and would contribute to the latter's implementation. As countries become more integrated, the external effects of domestic policies take on greater importance. Since individual countries do not take account of such externalities, the outcome might be significantly inferior to what could be achieved with co-ordination.

(c) Policy co-ordination with third countries. Without some fiscal powers at the Community level, the EMU would lack an important tool in negotiating with third countries and co-ordinating macro-economic policies. On this score, an excessive burden would fall on monetary policy.

Overall, argument (a) appears unconvincing, while (b) and (c) are not compelling reasons for endowing the Community with powers over national budgets.

[10] See Lamfalussy 1989 and Thygesen 1989b.

The first argument is unconvincing because there is no obligation for residents of the Community to finance the budget deficit of the expanding country. In a monetary union, individual governments, as well as firms and households, are part of a single and fundamentally competitive credit market in which lenders can choose the most appropriate destination of their savings. If the safe bonds issued by the government of country A are more attractive than, say, the productive capital of country B, residents of country B will be well advised to purchase them. This behaviour will maximize private returns; it will also generally maximize the social welfare of country B. Undue appropriation of foreign savings would only be possible if country A encountered refinancing problems and was able to tax foreign residents through implicit bail-out obligations, which, as argued before, should not be a feature of the EMU.

Nor would the inflow of saving to the expanding country necessarily be larger with a monetary union than with, say, managed exchange rates. Such inflows are the counterpart of current account deficits; budgetary expansion may well be associated with a larger current account deficit if, in addition to an increase in domestic income, it causes an appreciation of the real exchange rate.

As to argument (*b*), the issue is the increase in the relevant externalities and, more importantly, whether the resulting suboptimalities can be overcome through voluntary co-operation. As far as I know, no assessment has been made of the first point. It can, however, be argued that the mobility of goods, labour, and capital throughout Europe will not be much greater, and may even turn out to be less, than that prevailing today between Canada and the United States or among the Benelux countries; in neither of these cases has there been a request for a transnational fiscal authority. At the very least it can be affirmed that the request is no more compelling in the case of the European Community.

On the second point (voluntary co-operation), if all the member countries recognize that, as a result of unco-ordinated decisions, aggregate fiscal policy is too restrictive and unemployment too high, it should not be difficult to overcome the problem with regular consultations. A more likely and serious situation arises when countries do not share the same assessment, either because they believe in different models of the economy or because they have different macro-economic utility functions; in this case, however, there is no clear argument for co-operation based on welfare considerations.

Argument (*c*) concerning policy co-ordination with third countries probably has more validity. Clearly, without some authority on fiscal matters, the EC will be in a weaker position than otherwise in international relations. No single Community authority will be able to enter into commitments with the United States, Japan, or any other country on an important aspect of macro-economic policy, without previous consultations with national governments. While this is true, it should also be noted that Europe will remain in a weak position in many other areas (environment, defence, etc.) simply because it is not a political union; on the other hand, its authority in international relations will be enhanced because it will at least have a common monetary policy. Whatever the intrinsic merits of arguments (*b*) and (*c*), they have a common logical premiss in the belief that some fiscal activism is needed for the purpose of macro-economic stabilization and are clearly incompatible with requests for rigid forms of fiscal discipline, such as continuously balanced budgets.

If some fiscal activism is deemed necessary, the question arises as to the budgets that should be used to achieve the desired fiscal stance for the Community as a whole. The Delors Report suggests the Community should have the authority to flex national budgetary policies, because the Community budget is too small to have a macro-economic impact. Apart from being very difficult, such a route does not appear indispensable.

The budget of the Community, now around 1 per cent of Community GDP, will not exceed 3 or 4 per cent in the foreseeable future. This is small compared with most federations; clearly the *masse de manœuvre* on the expenditure side will remain very limited. However, on the revenue side, where it is probably more appropriate to intervene for stabilization purposes (in view of the greater reversibility of such action), it is certainly not impossible to envisage changes of two or more percentage points of GDP. What matters here is not so much size, but flexibility. Since changes in expenditure of this order of magnitude are out of the question, the issue is whether a tax cut could credibly be transitory: otherwise Community borrowing would quickly grow out of proportion. At present the Community budget is essentially constrained to be continuously balanced. If some activism is called for, the best route appears to be to relax this constraint somewhat, for instance by requiring that the budget be balanced on average over cycles of, say, five years. In most normal circumstances, this should enable the Community to have an impact on the overall fiscal stance in Europe. In exceptional circumstances (say, a major depression) there is no reason to exclude the possibility of concerted action by national governments.

The main conclusion of this section is that the arguments for a transfer of powers to the Community in the budgetary field are not decisive. In addition, those who advocate such a transfer as a way to improve the efficiency of macro-economic policies should recognize that allowing the Community to run temporary deficits or surpluses in its own budget is both more natural and less contentious than endowing it with authority over national budgets.

8. CONCLUSIONS

This chapter has dealt with the question of how much fiscal discipline and co-ordination are necessary for a monetary union to be viable. The basic suggestion is that there are no compelling arguments that a common monetary policy also requires a common fiscal policy or a major shift in decision-making power from national to Community authorities. It is much more important that a strong monetary constitution be adopted based on two principles, both requiring a clear separation between monetary and fiscal policy: price stability and distributive neutrality. The Delors Report is very explicit as regards the former and sets out some of the institutional consequences, in terms of the autonomy and accountability of the ECB. The principle of distributive neutrality should be made more explicit. In Section 6 above some of its implications for the functions and operations of the ECB have been indicated. In essence, they should prevent the ECB from being involved in any way in the financial position of member states; financial markets must be convinced that neither the central bank nor any other Community institution implicitly guarantees the obligations of national governments. At the technical level, the remaining challenge is to design a well-balanced system whereby the central authority controls the aggregate supply of base money, while national authorities perform the remaining central banking operations, with sterilized interventions.

To the extent that the contention concerns the co-ordination of fiscal and monetary policies rather than the monetary implications of fiscal discipline (or lack of it), the solution should and can be found in a more flexible use of the Community budget, rather than in Community control over national budgets. Last but not least, a major fiscal correction in some European countries (including Italy) is necessary to achieve greater financial and exchange rate stability in the transition towards a monetary union. To this end, and to avoid repeating past mistakes in the future, it may be appropriate to design rules which substantially reduce governments' discretion in the budgetary field. This could best be done at the national level, with the EC taking the lead by promoting the adoption of such rules and, possibly, 'harmonizing' them across countries. This, of course, is a different proposal from that of transferring fiscal powers to the Community and making the formation of a monetary union conditional on such a transfer.

10

Monetary Union and Political Union

1. THE LAWSON DECLARATION

I shall now attempt to answer the question whether a monetary union is conceivable in the absence of a political union. The question is not a new one, but in the debate on monetary union that the Community has recently revived, it was raised on the same day as the Report of the Delors Committee was made public in April 1989. The British Chancellor of the Exchequer, Nigel Lawson, declared that 'monetary unity would require political union, which is not on the agenda'. In a way he was right, though he probably had in mind a concept of political union for which his statement would not be valid. At all events, the links between the economic and political dimensions of the Community to which he was pointing are undoubtedly critical.

There are two ways to make Lawson's proposition true. The first is to say that the EC is *already* a political union; the second, that the Community's vocation is *to become* a political union and that monetary union is an important part of the process.

2. THE COMMUNITY IS ALREADY A POLITICAL UNION

Good arguments can be put forward to substantiate the contention that the EC is already a political union in many respects. It can hardly be denied, for instance, that establishing joint,

September 1991, Ann Arbor. Paper presented to the conference on 'Europe after 1992', organized by the University of Michigan. The section of that paper devoted to the relationship between monetary union and political union is reproduced here because of the importance of this theme in the public debate and because the European Council had established that the final decision on the treaties on political union and economic and monetary union would be taken jointly.

supranational management of coal and steel—the two fundamental natural resources of the nineteenth and early twentieth centuries, over which France, Germany, and the rest of Europe fought cruel wars—was a highly political project. And the protracted battles over majority voting that were fought in the preparation of the Treaty of Rome, in the De Gaulle-Hallstein crisis of 1965, and on many subsequent occasions, were eminently political. Similarly, the firm desire of Greece, Spain, and Portugal to link the restoration of democracy to participation in the EC is a clear expression of the political, not just economic, value of the Community.

'Political' is what 'affects the state or its government'.[1] The Community is already concerned with matters that deeply affect the state and its government. Abolishing barriers to trade, setting agricultural prices, deregulating the banking sector, stipulating association treaties with third countries, harmonizing indirect taxes, and combating state aid to industry are all acts of government. The fact that their content is economic does not deprive them of a strong political character. Such acts involve choices between different, often conflicting, interests.

The present EC is a political union not only because of the political character of the matters falling under its jurisdiction. Its institutional structure has many more analogies with a 'national' constitutional system than with international fora for consultation and co-operation. The Community has effective decision-making authority in the areas covered by the Treaty of Rome, an authority organized in the classic threefold division into a legislative, executive, and judicial branch. Drawing a parallel with the US institutional system, it has a House of Representatives (the European Parliament), a Senate (the Council of Ministers), an Administration (the Commission), and a Supreme Court (the Court of Justice). The supremacy of Community law over national legislation is well established. Community law can be directly invoked by firms and individuals and is applied in national courts. These considerations suggest that the British Chancellor's remarks were right, but mistimed. It was precisely because the EEC was a political union that the UK

---

[1] *Concise Oxford Dictionary.*

decided not to become a member in the 1950s, and the EC continued to be a political union in 1989.

3. MONETARY UNION AS PART OF THE PROCESS OF POLITICAL UNION

I shall now examine the second interpretation of Lawson's proposition, namely that monetary union is an important step on the road to political union. In effect, monetary policy has always been the prerogative of the state, and this explains the profound political significance of the transfer of responsibility for monetary policy from sovereign states to a supranational entity—a significance that is recognized by both the proponents and the opponents of EMU.

The political content of monetary policy varies with the type of monetary regime in force and with the role assigned to monetary policy within the general conduct of economic policy. At one extreme there are fiat money regimes with a central bank subject to political control; in this case monetary policy represents just one of the many instruments of economic policy the government can use in combination or alternation with others. At the other extreme there are metal standards with a strong central bank, in this case the supply of money is largely determined outside the direct control of policy. Monetary history shows frequent swings between these extremes, depending on the institutional setting, the intellectual and political climate, and the ability of the ruling authority to extract seigniorage from the use of money. It is interesting to note that international monetary regimes have generally been developed around metal standards, in which the political content of monetary policy is relatively low. By contrast, monetary isolationism prevailed when countries decided to use the monetary lever actively as an instrument of economic policy management.

Both recent economic research and the experience of the long inflation of the 1970s have led to a consensus that it is suboptimal to harness monetary policy to multiple objectives. With sophisticated financial markets and forward-looking economic agents, monetary policy has only a temporary effect on real economic activity, while it primarily affects the overall level of prices.[2] Attempts to use monetary policy to stimulate growth and employment are in the end unsuccessful and only lead to higher inflation. The generally accepted view among economists today is that in a fiat money system the supply of money should be regulated with the primary objective of promoting price stability.

Another element that both experience and theory show to be important is credibility. The achievement of price stability will be greatly facilitated if economic agents are convinced that the central bank will not, even temporarily, sacrifice the objective of price stability for faster economic growth.[3] This conviction can be fostered by showing the market that any such temptation will be resisted.[4] One way to bolster the credibility of this objective is to assign the responsibility for monetary policy to an institution that is not subject to political influence.[5] In countries where price stability had been lacking for many years, credibility has been re-established through membership of the EMS.[6] The independence of the central bank might not be a sufficient safeguard, however; it is no less important that public opinion should agree on the priority to be given to the objective of price stability. The experience of the last ten years suggests that such a consensus now exists in most of the Community countries.

In the light of these considerations the present historical circumstances appear propitious for taking the politically crucial decision to create a monetary union without, or before, attributing to the Community other important public functions, ranging from fiscal policy to internal and external security. For one thing public opinion is more inclined than in the past to accept an independent, stability-orientated central bank. And from the central banks' point of view the Community is the most favourable institutional environment in which to perform their function in an independent, stability-orientated fashion.

In the preparation of the treaty on economic and monetary union a consensus was reached at an early stage that the single monetary policy of the Community should be conducted by a European Central Bank, which would be independent both of the Community institutions and of national authorities. The ECB

---

[2] See Friedman 1968 and Phelps 1972. For more recent developments, see Lucas and Sargent 1981.

[3] See Barro and Gordon 1983.

[4] See Barro 1984.

[5] See Rogoff 1985.

[6] See Giavazzi and Pagano 1988.

will have as its overriding objective price stability and, without prejudice to this, support for the general economic policy of the Community. It is therefore agreed that the political dimension of Community monetary policy will be relatively small.

Another important political aspect of European monetary union is the legitimacy of the ECB. In any democracy, bodies charged with certain tasks have to be legitimated, directly or indirectly, by the elected representatives. This must also hold true for the central bank.

In the economic and monetary union, the legitimacy of the ECB will be achieved in four ways. In the first place, the EMU treaty and the Statute of the ECB, which is a protocol attached to it, are to be approved by all the governments of the Community and by the national parliaments, i.e. by the elected representatives of all the member states. The Court of Justice will be directly responsible for ensuring compliance with the law in the interpretation and implementation of the new treaty and its protocols. Secondly, the members of the ECB Council who are national central-bank governors will be appointed via national procedures, while the remaining members will be appointed by the Heads of State and Government, acting on a proposal from the EC Council of Ministers. Thirdly, provision has been made for the President of the Council of Finance Ministers to attend the meetings of the ECB Council as an observer, and for the President of the ECB Council to attend meetings of the Council of Finance Ministers when matters relating to the objectives and tasks of the European System of Central Banks are discussed. Finally, the ECB will present an annual report on the activities of the System to the European Council, the Council of Ministers, the European Parliament, and the Commission, while the members of the ECB Board may be asked to attend meetings of the economic and monetary committees of the European Parliament. By means of these provisions the ECB, though independent in the exercise of its tasks, will clearly fit into the political structure of the Community and interact directly with the other institutions.

4. THE TREATY ON POLITICAL UNION

The link between monetary and political union is also substantiated in a forward-looking perspective. Economic and monetary union is part of an evolutionary process that started in the early 1950s and has gone through many stages: the Coal and Steel Community, the common market, various enlargements from the original six member states to the present twelve, and repeated changes in procedures and institutions.

In 1988–9 when the monetary union project was relaunched and the decision taken to call an intergovernmental conference to negotiate a new treaty, the Heads of State and Government perhaps did not foresee that the initiative would soon be followed by others, outside the economic and monetary field. Instead, they themselves took such a step, partly in response to the need to define a new order in Europe following the fall of the Berlin Wall and of the regimes in central and Eastern European countries. Political union was put on the European agenda in April 1990, a few weeks after the first free elections in East Germany. The statement made by Lawson a year earlier was thus both confirmed and negated.

The Heads of State and Government have decided that the development of the Community will be based on two new treaties, to be drawn up in parallel and dealing respectively with economic and monetary union and political union. To dwell upon the content and problems of political union is beyond the scope of this paper. The only point that needs to be stressed is that the concept of political union is much less clear-cut, much more elusive, than might appear at first sight. Only for the highly centralized and tightly organized nation-states, whose cultural and constitutional identity and structure have been built up over centuries, is political union a comprehensive reality in which 'the state' tends to monopolize all the functions of government. But even in Europe very few nation-states conform to this particular model. For the others, the functions 'affecting the state or its government' are divided among many levels of government, institutions, and agencies.

To interpret political union as meaning that the Community should give itself a government structure similar to that of

France or Britain would be a mistake; the establishment of a
constitution of this type is clearly not on the agenda, nor will be
in the future. However, the single market and economic and
monetary union do not depend on there being this particular
form of political union. Subsidiarity, not the Leviathan, is the
catchword for European political union.

11

On the Eve of Maastricht

1. INTRODUCTION

In November 1989, street demonstrations in Leipzig and East Berlin were the prelude to the fall of the Berlin Wall and the unification of Germany. At the time it was far from clear that two years later we would be so close to a decisive step on the way to economic and monetary union. There was also widespread fear that the changes in Central Europe might distract German attention from the development of the Community; the outcome confirms that it is the destiny of predictions to be belied by events.

In order to consider the current state of the debate and negotiations on monetary union, it should be recalled, in a nutshell, that completing the whole process of monetary union implies overcoming three hurdles: the signing, ratification, and implementation of the treaty on economic and monetary union. The time horizons of these three tasks are less than ten weeks for the first, little more than a year for the second, and most of this decade for the third.

Each of the three steps is crucial and each involves special difficulties and dangers. There are plenty of examples in history of very important negotiations that broke down; at this moment there is a risk that the GATT talks will end in this way. The damage caused by a breakdown of negotiations may be much greater than the benefits accruing from a successful outcome, because it is not only the future that is at stake but also the past—the preservation of the inherited capital of international co-operation.

There are also examples of treaties that were signed but never

October–November 1991, Vienna. Forum of Creditanstalt-Bankverein on 11 October. The text illustrates the terms of the debate in the weeks preceding the European Council meeting at Maastricht. It is followed by an unpublished note of 8 November to Jacques Delors, aimed at clarifying the crucial points still to be settled during the negotiations.

ratified. For the Community the prime example is the Treaty for a European Defence Community. Had this Treaty been implemented, it would undoubtedly have made political union in Europe a reality in the mid-1950s, but in one country, France, that Treaty was not ratified. Finally, there are instances of treaties (and laws) that were signed and approved by Parliaments, but never implemented because they were ill-conceived or inconsistent. The need to reach consensus on the first two steps may so debase the 'quality' of the agreement that implementation turns out to be impossible; the compromises reached in order to overcome one hurdle may well make it more difficult to overcome the others.

To summarize the state of play on economic and monetary union, I shall first briefly describe the issues that in my view have already been settled in the negotiations as of October 1991, and then examine those that are still open in more detail. The former are not less important (indeed, perhaps 80 or 90 per cent of all the major issues have been settled), but success in overcoming the three hurdles mentioned above is less certain for the issues that are still outstanding.

2. THE ISSUES THAT HAVE BEEN SETTLED

Among the issues that can be considered as settled is the meaning to be attributed to the term 'economic and monetary union'. In passing, it needs to be remembered that the subject of the treaty is economic *and* monetary union, and not just monetary union. As for the latter, it is surprising to see how greatly ideas about what a monetary union really is have evolved since the negotiations started. They appear to have reached a stable conclusion only a couple of years after the Hanover European Council meeting in June 1988, when the Heads of State and Government decided to set up the Delors Committee.

It is now clear that a monetary union is not what economists call a monetary regime, nor an exchange rate regime, namely a rule that dictates how monetary policy, exchange rate policy, and central-bank actions should be conducted. Although for a long time, and still very often in common language, monetary union is taken to mean irrevocably fixed exchange rates, it is now clear that a true monetary union cannot be reduced merely to an exchange rate rule, but requires the creation of a single centre for decisions in the field of monetary policy and eventually of a single currency. Of course, if we have a single monetary policy, a single central bank, and a plurality of currencies, we still have a 'price' at which one currency is exchanged against another, but this price has no more economic significance than the exchange of a £10 note for two £5 notes. This ratio can be called a price or an exchange rate, but in reality the exchange is a purely mechanical operation performed, for example, by a cashier at the window of a bank; the price is no longer determined on the basis of supply and demand.

If monetary union is interpreted merely as a fixed rate regime, the problem arises of *who* is to decide monetary policy for the whole group of countries involved. The traditional solution to this problem has been leadership, or hegemony: one country— generally the USA in the post-war period—acts as a sort of world central bank. It is not far from the truth to say that the Bundesbank has played a similar role in the Community since the inception of the EMS. But exchange rates are not irrevocably fixed in the EMS and it is certain that the Community could never make the leadership of one national currency an institutional principle.

Just as it is not the hegemony of a national currency, a monetary union is not a regime of currency competition. For a time the British Government tried to persuade the other member states to accept a regime in which the only rule would be that each national currency could compete against the others. However, my participation in meetings and negotiations has convinced me that not even my British friends really believed their proposals could lead to monetary union.

It is now generally accepted that a monetary union is a regime in which there is one central bank, a focal point where monetary policy is decided—such as we have today within each country. And if this is the condition, it does not make much sense to keep a plurality of currencies and currency denominations for very long. It is much more efficient to move to a single currency, which would enormously facilitate all the economic comparisons on which economic life is based.

Another issue that is now settled is the institutional structure of the economic and monetary union. The monetary part will be based on a single central bank with a federal structure, in which the national central banks will play a role similar to that of the District Banks and Landeszentralbanken in the Federal Reserve System and the Bundesbank respectively. As to the economic part of the union, it is now accepted that the existing Community institutions (the Commission, the Council of Ministers, the Parliament, etc.) will retain their roles and expand their functions if new powers in the economic field are attributed to the union. It has also been agreed that the new monetary institution will have independent status, and will not be subject to instructions from the outside, that its primary objective will be to pursue price stability, and that it will report on, and be accountable for, its actions to public opinion, the European Parliament, and the Council. Accountability is the counterpart of independence.

Many other points are now also settled. The process of economic and monetary union is entirely determined by the definition and acceptance of the *final* setting of the union, with the transition designed accordingly. The union will be based on one treaty; two or three years ago there was protracted discussion over whether there should be one treaty for each step or a single treaty for the whole process; the latter solution was adopted in the end because the idea prevailed that there should be a commitment to the entire process.

More generally, it should be noted that the issues that have been settled are essentially those concerning the final phase. This is not to say that there are no open problems concerning the final phase; the press still carries debates on what budgetary rules should be written into the treaty, on who should conduct exchange rate policies, and on certain details of the institutional relationship between the central bank and the European Parliament and the Commission. However, the points remaining to be clarified are relatively minor, in the sense that they are not decisive for the signature, the ratification, or the implementation of the treaty, the three hurdles mentioned above. While the problems concerning the final phase are basically solved, finding and agreeing on the solutions was by no means easy. It took three and a half years of hard work; for each of them, diverging positions were expressed at one stage or another in the lengthy process of technical and political negotiation.

3. OPEN ISSUES: THE TRANSITION

Turning to the issues that are still open, it can be said that they essentially concern the transition to the final phase. This is not surprising; it is a natural consequence of the decision to 'start from the end', i.e. by defining the point of arrival. Obviously, without a transition there will never be a monetary union; a treaty lacking adequate provisions concerning the transition would provide a beautiful description of paradise but lack the necessary indications of how to reach it.

The debate on the transition reflects a still open, though not altogether explicit, confrontation between those who really want a monetary union and those who do not. The political commitment to proceed has been so strong and so explicit at the highest levels of EC governments that openly opposing it would not have been easy. Mental reservations, and outright opposition, have been expressed in indirect, implicit form, by proposing a transition process that would delay decisions, multiply requisites, and so on. Opposition is not confined to any particular countries; the debate on monetary union is very much a debate *within* each member state and its institutions; the pros and cons are being weighed even by individuals, because many people are genuinely perplexed, divided in their own minds on the merits and risks of such a momentous change.

There are essentially three open issues regarding the transition: the first concerns the *tasks and powers* of the monetary institution in phase two; the second involves the *conditions* that must be satisfied before passing to the final stage; and the third relates to the *procedures* for deciding the date on which the third phase is to start. I shall now comment briefly on each of these points.

4. THE EUROPEAN MONETARY INSTITUTE

The definition of the tasks and powers of the monetary institution in the second phase is difficult because it requires the reconciliation of conflicting needs. The first is to respect the universally accepted fact that monetary policy is not divisible, that responsibility for it cannot be shared between the national and the

Community levels; if sovereignty is to be transferred, it will have to be transferred *en bloc*, in order to avoid an intermediate situation in which money is managed at more than one level. A second point on which everyone now agrees is that monetary policy during the transition should remain in national hands. Finally, it is accepted that a single monetary policy with a single central bank will have to operate fully from the first day of the final phase.

These three points determine both the scope and the scale of the preparatory work that has to be done in the course of the transition. What is necessary is to create a monetary system for the Community having the same uniformity as we now observe in each country. Only in this way will the central bank be able to conduct its policy. Imagine the situation we would have in any of our countries if the central bank had to conduct monetary policy in a system in which banks were subject to completely different reserve requirements, in which several clearing and settlement systems operated simultaneously with different working hours, criteria for access, and systems of collateral, and in which the statistical and accounting returns banks submitted to their central bank were so different that any calculation of the monetary and credit aggregates would be meaningless. In such conditions an efficient monetary policy would be impossible. This is a picture of what the Community system would be like on the day a single monetary policy started if no serious preparatory work had been done. Failure to do this work would certainly result in the monetary union being doomed.

Aware of this risk, a year ago in Rome the Heads of State and Government decided that the European Central Bank would be created at the beginning of stage two. In the same way as the Commission and the Court of Justice were created in 1958 to participate actively from the start, albeit with powers that were initially limited, in the process of creating the EEC. Regrettably, the Rome decision has subsequently been changed and it is no longer envisaged that the European Central Bank will operate in stage two, but rather the European Monetary Institute, a provisional institution. The precise structure, tasks, and powers of the Institute have still to be defined and the success of the transition will largely depend on how this is done. The new institution will need to be given sufficient authority to perform this preparatory work at both the conceptual level and the practical level without violating the condition that current monetary policy decisions are to remain a national prerogative during the transition. This authority, of course, will not come of itself; it cannot be obtained by purely voluntary co-operation among central banks. What is needed is a solid legal and institutional basis, a structure with its own financial foundation.

The solution to the problem of reconciling the necessary preparations with the maintenance of national responsibility for monetary policy in stage two is to be found in a concept that exists in the German language and not in many others: it lies in entrusting *Prozesspolitik* (current policies) to national central banks and *Ordnungspolitik* (i.e. structural policies) to the common institution. In order to leave national responsibility untouched in phase two, it could be decided that the decisions and regulations adopted by the monetary institution would come into force only on the first day of the final phase.

5. CONVERGENCE CRITERIA FOR STAGE TWO

The second open issue concerns the conditions of economic convergence that have to be satisfied to start phase three. This is an old *querelle* in the Community. It used to be known as the dispute between 'economists' and 'monetarists': between those who said that economic performance (growth, stability, etc.) had to come first and that monetary arrangements should follow, and those who believed monetary arrangements could precede and themselves bring about the changes in economic performance. This *querelle* is still present in the current debate; the extreme version of the economists' argument is known as the 'crowning approach' (*Krönungstheorie*), meaning that monetary union will be the crowning of a long period of convergence to be achieved by other means. At the other extreme, the pure version of the monetarists' approach holds that, regardless of the convergence conditions, we should proceed in the monetary field and that the desired economic performance will follow. Taking a middle course, the Delors Report advocated an approach based on 'parallelism':

Parallel advancement in economic and monetary integration would be indispensable in order to avoid imbalances which would cause economic strains and loss of political support for developing the Community further into an economic and monetary union. Perfect parallelism at each and every point of time would be impossible and could even be counterproductive.[1]

The debate of the last two years has seen powerful pressures at work to deviate from the line recommended by the Delors Report in favour of a position closer to the crowning approach of the economists. It is now agreed that a degree of economic convergence, in terms of greater price stability and sounder budgetary and financial conditions, has to be achieved before the final phase of the union begins. From a strictly economic point of view, I am not sure that convergence is a *sine qua non*, that monetary union would be impossible or have an inflationary bias unless convergence had made substantial progress. Convergence is undoubtedly desirable. Italy still has to make considerable improvements as regards price stability and sound public finances and the Italian Government intends to exploit the process leading to monetary union to strengthen and stimulate the adjustment of the economy. Convergence is economically desirable *per se* rather than a necessary condition for monetary union; on the other hand, it is a *political* necessity. Indeed, it would be difficult to persuade public opinion in countries such as Germany and the Netherlands that the union is desirable if it involves drawing closer to countries with highly divergent macro-economic conditions. Referring to the description given above of the three hurdles on the road to economic and monetary union, convergence is not indispensable for the third—implementing the treaty—but it is certainly necessary for the first two (its signature and ratification).

Differences regarding the convergence conditions to be satisfied before passing to the third stage have narrowed considerably in the past weeks, but they have not completely disappeared. There is now widespread agreement that countries will have to satisfy a set of performance criteria concerning inflation, public finances, exchange rate stability, and interest rates in order to qualify for phase three. The balance between quantitative criteria and the

---

[1] Committee for the Study of Economic and Monetary Union 1989: para. 25.

overall judgement concerning a country's situation has still to be struck. Countries that do not meet these performance criteria will postpone their participation in the final stage of the union.

6. THE 'OPTING-OUT' CLAUSE

The third issue concerns the procedures for deciding the start of phase three. In the jargon of the EMU negotiations this is called the issue of the 'opting-out' clause. In reality, this is another old Community issue and basically concerns the exact nature of the commitment countries enter into when signing a treaty. We know that, by its very construction, a treaty cannot come into force unless there is unanimous acceptance by all those who sign it (and this is stated in Article 236 of the Treaty of Rome). Accordingly, the question is whether approval of the Treaty, by signing and ratifying it, is the last act for which complete unanimity is required, or whether, after signing the Treaty, countries will still be free to decide whether to implement it or not. In the latter case the provisions of the Treaty would have to be drafted so as not to be binding.

This issue is linked to the problem of a 'two-speed' Community, to the underlying reservations the United Kingdom has about EMU, and, more generally, to the development of the Community's institutions. If by two, or multiple, speeds we mean that not all the member states simultaneously introduce new agreements or arrangements approved by the Community (whether in a treaty or a directive), this practice is already firmly established in the tradition of the Community. Indeed, there are many instances of new arrangements and new directives being adopted unanimously, but not implemented by all the countries at the same time: the introduction of VAT, the creation of the EMS, and the provisions of important directives concerning banking and other sectors. In no case, however, has a treaty, directive, or law been signed that has not implied a commitment by the signatories. In other words, the legal basis for not immediately implementing a certain arrangement together with the other member states has not been a 'right not to implement', but a special derogation or concession.

Similarly, in no case has the system of Community institutions been divided, with the creation of separate institutional arrangements for those who are part of the vanguard and for those who are lagging behind. In short, delayed compliance with certain Community arrangements has always been occasional and exceptional, never part of the constitutional rules. The problem now is how to preserve the binding nature of the 'community pact'—the very essence of the Community, the feature that distinguishes it from international bodies with no powers—while enabling the UK to make its final decision some years from now, through a parliamentary vote to be taken after the Treaty has been signed and ratified.

These two positions appear irreconcilable, although the ingenuity of lawyers will probably help find a way out. One solution that, in my view, should not be accepted would make the possibility of deferring the decision a rule of the Treaty. Such an application of the so-called principle of 'no coercion' would be destructive for the Community; it would mean that having signed the Treaty a country could still decide whether to apply it or not. If a general 'opting-out clause' were written into the Treaty, even with only the UK in mind, how can we be sure that no other country would invoke the clause? A clause of this kind would imply abandoning the very concept of a legal instrument on which to found a common commitment among sovereign nations. After all, the rule of law *is* based on coercion: 'the high contracting parties' stipulate a rule (a treaty) and then the rule applies, and there is coercion. The rule has to be freely accepted, it has to be based on the popular will, on the democratic tradition of our countries, but democracy and the people's will do not contemplate the freedom not to obey the law. The third open issue is whether or not the Treaty will be consistent with this fundamental principle on which the Community has so far been based.

7. CONCLUSIONS

The three fundamental issues briefly summarized above are still under debate in these last weeks of negotiations before Maastricht. It is still hard to predict how they will be solved.

Behind each issue there is one country. Behind the opting-out issue there is the UK, which is not ready to forgo monetary sovereignty, but is also unwilling to break with the Community or to be left out of the mainstream of European history. Behind the issue of the convergence conditions there is Italy, a founding member of the Community, a large country, and one with a divergent economy. No other country presents these three features simultaneously. Behind the issue of the tasks and functions of the European Monetary Institute there is the Federal Republic of Germany, where there are strong supporters of a weak EMI, one in which nothing more than voluntary co-operation would be possible, a Committee of Governors with a new name. If the reluctance to transfer any decision-making capacity to a common institution were to prevail, there would be no bridge linking phase one to phase three; no matter how great the solemnity with which the commitment to the final phase were written in the treaty, the final phase would never be reached.

Note sent to Jacques Delors on 8 November 1991: 'The EMU Treaty: The Two Essential Questions'

1. For 42 years the method used for constructing the European Community has been based on two principles: commitment to a precise objective and the creation of the legal and institutional instruments to achieve it. This method is associated with the names of Monnet, Adenauer, Schuman, De Gasperi, and Spaak. In October 1990 eleven countries signed a detailed agreement in Rome to establish economic and monetary union by this method. Today, despite appearances, there is a danger that the correct path will be abandoned.

2. Of the points still to be resolved in the EMU Treaty, there are only two that will determine whether all the efforts undertaken since Hanover culminate in success or failure:

(*a*) the wording of the 'opting-out' clause;

(*b*) the preparations for stage 3.

3. In the Presidency's draft (text of 28 October) the proposed solution to questions (*a*) and (*b*) is completely unacceptable, for the following reasons:

(*a*) '*Opting-out*': the formula for Article 109G, paragraph 2, emasculates the Treaty: its signature and ratification would commit signatories to nothing. No national Parliament will fail to invoke this clause. Public opinion, political circles, and the markets will understand that in practice the real decision on EMU has been postponed until 1996;

(b) *Preparations for stage 3*: the solution proposed for the European Monetary Institute (Article 109D, paragraph 3, and the EMI Statute, Articles 4.3, 10.4, and 15.3) provides for neither a commitment to stage 3 nor the necessary powers to prepare for it; it is as though one had wanted to prepare for the single market without a timetable and on the basis of purely voluntary co-operation, without Community legislation, without a Commission, without majority voting.

Taken together, the Presidency's proposed solutions to points (a) and (b) strip the Treaty of its two essential elements, namely a commitment to the final objective and the means to achieve it. The Treaty is downgraded to the level of a simple declaration.

4. All efforts must therefore be concentrated on strengthening the Treaty in these two essential respects. The factors favouring and impeding a satisfactory solution are considerable in both cases. In particular:

(a) *'Opting-out'*: the favourable factors are the will expressed by eleven countries at the European Council in Rome and the Community approach that has always rejected an 'à la carte Europe'. The obstacles are British opposition and the desire the Presidency's draft has aroused in national Parliaments to maintain the ultimate power of decision until 1996;

(b) *Preparations for stage 3*: here too the favourable factor is the Community approach, which has always been to base the attainment of common objectives on effective Community institutions and procedures. The obstacle is the opposition of those who, on the pretext of maintaining full monetary sovereignty during stage 2, are actually against EMU.

5. On each of these two points there is a solution that satisfies the legitimate demands of those creating the obstacles but at the same time saves the Treaty. The two solutions are formulated as follows:

(a) *'Opting-out'*: separate the question of 'British reservations' from that of 'democratic legitimacy'. To cover the British question a declaration (or even a protocol) would be appended to the Treaty along the lines of the German declaration on Berlin that accompanied the signing of the Treaty of Rome. As to the question of 'democratic legitimacy', the role of the European Parliament provided for in Article 109F, paragraph 2, and the control that each national Parliament normally exercises over major government decisions appear sufficient; naturally, the Treaty does not refer explicitly to this control function. Nevertheless, if additional safeguards had to be provided in order to reach agreement, a declaration could be added to the Treaty (or a formula inserted in the Treaty itself) recalling the countries' domestic institutional procedures;

(*b*) *Preparations for stage 3*: separate the assignment of a specific task and real powers to the EMI from the full protection of monetary sovereignty in stage 2. The first part can be achieved by giving full force of law to the acts and procedures of the EMI for the preparation of stage 3: majority voting, binding decisions, own funds, strong Presidency (i.e. a full-time external President, etc.). National monetary sovereignty is preserved by ensuring that decisions will not come into effect until the first day of stage 3 (and the European Central Bank will, of course, always be able to amend decisions taken by the EMI). In principle, the decisions would never come into effect if stage 3 never materialized.

6. A possible wording of the amendments that appear indispensable has been formulated at the technical level; other formulations can doubtless be found.

12
Agenda for Stage Two

1. INTRODUCTION

The Maastricht European Council is expected to approve a constitution for monetary union in the form of an amendment to the Treaty of Rome; this will subsequently be submitted for ratification by the Parliaments of the member states. A number of aspects of the new Treaty still have to be defined. Some, not of secondary importance, are of a legal and institutional nature and are beyond the scope of this chapter, which focuses rather on the functional and operational issues that will have to be tackled in order to prepare the final stage of monetary union. We are thus taking a 'post-Treaty' view, even though the solutions the Treaty supplies to these outstanding legal and institutional aspects of transition will either facilitate or hinder the resolution of the functional and operational problems under discussion.

The building of Europe does not consist only of actions; it is also an intellectual exercise. It is not just a question of applying an existing model of political, economic, or monetary order. For economists, the creation first of the single market and then of economic and monetary union implies having to rethink the very foundations of economic management, the relations between the market economy and market institutions, the allocation to different levels of government of responsibility for economic policy, and the aims and distribution of central banking functions.

Implementation of the Treaty involves the creation of a European Central Bank, just as implementation of the Treaty of Rome and of the Single European Act subtends the creation of a single European market. The Treaty will embody a concept of central banking; but the task of defining the functions and

November 1991, Rome. Paper written with F. Saccomanni and presented at the meeting to commemorate Stefano Vona. The chapter is written to give substance to the point that the transaction to the final phase of EMU required substantive preparatory work.

instruments of the European Central Bank will not end there. During the implementation phase the elaboration and discussion of ideas will continue, within the confines agreed in the texts, and will reach a much deeper level of analysis than is possible in a constitutional document. Our starting-point must therefore be a detailed conceptual view of the functions and instruments of the central bank.

2. THE FINAL OBJECTIVE

The basic methodological approach adopted in the negotiations on economic and monetary union consisted in first determining the final objective of unification: an institutional arrangement based on a single currency and managed by a single central bank. The issue of monetary union was thus immediately defined in the same terms as in the past when individual states drafted legislation on their national currency and central bank. The functions performed by central banks vary in detail from one country to another according to traditions and concepts that have developed over many years. More important than the differences, however, is the body of tasks, instruments, and *modi operandi* that is common to the central banks of the industrial nations.

On one basic paradigm there is consensus: a central bank is an institution entrusted by law with public functions in three fields: the payment system, monetary policy, and supervision of the banking system. The three functions are deliberately listed here in this order, although it does not reflect their relative importance. In the beginning money was a means of payment. Modern central banks grew out of the revolution that occurred in the payment system when paper replaced metal, that is, when fiat money replaced commodity money. That revolution also generated the basic elements of the monetary systems that have gradually evolved since the middle of the last century: the need for a final issuer whose liabilities are universally accepted and legally recognized; the possibility of varying the stock of money in circulation at will, regardless of the amount of gold reserves; the scope for part of the money stock to be created by market operators such as banks; and the need for these operators to be supervised. The very close links between the three functions are reflected in the relations between the central bank and commercial banks.

Within the payment system, the primary function of central banks has shifted away from the, albeit important, production and distribution of banknotes to the management and regulation of the interbank payment system. To a large extent, monetary policy is conducted through dealings between the central bank and ordinary banks: the money stock is a multiple of the central-bank money held by banks, which depends on the volume of interbank transactions that banks must settle in monetary base. Even compulsory reserves are more of a constraint on commercial banks' demand for central-bank money for their transactions than a portfolio requirement. Finally, even in countries where the central bank has no responsibility for banking supervision, it retains a direct interest in and responsibility for the health of the commercial banks, since they multiply the money that is originally the monopoly of the central bank; the money they create must be perceived as the perfect equivalent of central-bank money. A central bank can function properly only if the public has complete confidence in 'all' money. This threefold concept of the central bank's role clearly pervades the Treaty, even though, as we shall see, pride of place is assigned to the monetary function.

Generally speaking, a monetary system has a unitary structure: a single central bank and a single currency. The latter implies the certainty of being able, in any circumstances, to change a deposit held in a commercial bank for an equivalent amount in central bank notes. The currency is single not merely in name, but because the central bank guarantees and maintains the unitary character of the system by means of the functions it performs in the three fields mentioned above.

The central bank has a dual nature, one public and one private. It is a public institution, in so far as it applies regulations and performs functions characteristic of command and control, and a bank, that is a financial institution that operates in the markets using the same, typically private-law contractual instruments as other banking and financial institutions. This dualism, the public and private nature typical of all central banks, is also reflected in the Treaty. The European Central Bank will have regulatory powers as well as an operational capacity. The Treaty differs in two respects from the existing central-bank and currency legislation of the member states. The European monetary constitution is both more rigid and more decentralized than the legal systems of the member states, including those with a federal structure.

The rigidity stems from the fact that much of the legislation regulating monetary union is in the form of a treaty: in other words it can be modified only through the same procedure of intergovernmental negotiation and parliamentary ratification that applies to the Treaty of Rome as a whole. This rigidity is intended to guarantee the member states that there will not be an excessive transfer of powers to supranational institutions. In the specific context of monetary union, it also meets the requirement that the European Central Bank should have a high degree of independence. It is as if the statute of a national central bank were written into the Constitution rather than contained in ordinary legislation.

The other feature of the European System of Central Banks (ESCB), its decentralization, is also linked to the laborious negotiating process. The debate has not always distinguished clearly between the issue of nationality versus supranationality and that of centralization versus decentralization within a supranational framework. Prior to the Single European Act, the Community had a highly centralized structure in which supranationality was synonymous with 'centralization in Brussels'. With the Single European Act and the transition to a different method for integrating the market, there arose a combination of supranationality and decentralization, of which the principle of mutual recognition is the most significant expression. In the monetary field the Treaty implies moving the legislation on central banking out of the national sphere and placing it at the Community level, no matter how decentralized the Community system may eventually be.

As a result of the acceptance of a decentralized structure for the central bank in the final stage of the union, the peripheral structure of the ESCB, consisting of the national central banks, will be called upon to take part not only in the formulation of the System's policies but also in their implementation. This is a fundamental prescription; it will perhaps be reconsidered in the future, but it would appear to be the only realistic proposal to adopt at the start.

3. THE TRANSITION

The decision to base the project for monetary union on the definition of the final goal resulted in the difficulties to be overcome in the negotiations being concentrated in the issue of transition. The technical problems involved in conceiving an orderly passage of functions were supplemented by those of a political nature stemming from the unresolved confrontation between supporters and opposers of the actual achievement of monetary union.

In the debate on the procedures and stages of the transition, which took place within countries as much as between them, it was possible yet again to distinguish the three methodological approaches that have marked debates between the European nations since just after the Second World War. They can be labelled as individual virtue, voluntary co-ordination, and institutionalized supranationality.

The method of individual virtue reflects the conviction that the achievement of common goals can only be the fruit of virtuous conduct by each country; unity is obtained if everybody moves towards the same objective. If a goal is truly desired, this should be demonstrated by everybody working towards it; if they do not, it is proof that supranational institutions are an unnatural and unrealistic solution. According to this view, institutions are merely ornamental; they cannot and must not take the place of responsible actions by individual nations. This concept, which has its roots in the political thinking of the anarchists, has always been present in international economic relations and boasts illustrious advocates, such as Ludwig Erhard and Beryl Sprinkel.

The method of voluntary co-ordination recognizes the need for countries to co-operate in order to achieve a common goal and admits that the building of a polis requires more than merely 'keeping one's house in order'. The contribution of this method to co-operation is limited, however, to fora for consultation and voluntary instruments; it offers neither the legal force of signed agreements nor majority voting nor truly common institutions. This concept, too, has a distinguished history, including the Polish Diet, the League of Nations, and the Western European Union.

Finally, there is the institutional method; this consists in the creation of legal and institutional instruments with just the supranationality that is needed to enable a common goal to be achieved. It considers the institutions not as mere fora for consultation but as the powers that provide the motive force of the process leading to the common goal. It was this method, which owes its twentieth-century invention to Jean Monnet, that was followed in building the European Community, starting with the early Coal and Steel Treaty.

Throughout the negotiations that are about to be concluded, these three approaches confronted each other as the articles covering the legal and institutional aspects of the transition were prepared. Even though the functional and operational aspects were not central to the negotiations, what follows shows that the problems to be addressed during the transition are so complex that any method other than the one we have labelled institutional would be unrealistic. From the start of the debate on the transition there was agreement on two key points that fixed the limits within which ideas were then discussed. The first point is that the responsibility for the conduct of monetary policy during the transition must remain in the hands of national monetary authorities. All ideas of joint, national and Community, responsibility have to be discarded, while the principle that monetary policy is indivisible is firmly asserted. The second point is that from day one of stage three there must be just one monetary policy, decided and implemented by the European Central Bank. If these limits are not exceeded, the agenda for the transition is clearly not the anticipation of parts of stage three; it is the preparation, following the institutional method, of the instruments necessary for union; it is not a question of premarital relations, but of building a home.

In every country the central banking functions are performed with instruments and methods that have been honed over the decades. The unity and consistency of the monetary system, which provides the basis for the central bank's operations, are not in doubt. Within each country the homogeneity of this 'platform' does not only serve the needs of the central bank; it is the end product of a body of legislation that has been built up gradually, of a market structure developed over many years, and of a common economic and linguistic heritage.

The construction of a platform for monetary union is a task

that has some analogies with the preparation of the single market. It was decided in 1985 that, from 1 January 1993 on, all goods, services, persons, and capital should be able to circulate freely within a single market, without technical, regulatory, tariff, or fiscal frontiers. The six years that the Community set itself to attain this goal were not conceived simply as a period of 'standing and waiting', nor as one during which each country was expected to get on with its own preparations at home, in accordance with the method of individual virtue; nor was it thought that the regulatory framework of the single market would emerge spontaneously as a result of a purely voluntary co-ordination of national laws. These six years represented the time necessary for the Community institutions to conceive, discuss, and approve the directives creating the single market and for economic operators to conform to them. The platform was built according to a method that was defined right from the start: mutual recognition, minimum harmonization of national regulations, and a programme of three hundred directives.

The steps needed to prepare the transition to economic and monetary union are: a thorough and systematic examination of the existing national platforms; their assessment in the light of the tasks of the European Central Bank; the identification of the minimum content of the common platform; and the construction of that platform by means of legislative acts and operational actions. The following pages offer a methodological contribution on the first two stages of this preparation. Obviously our investigation and assessment of the national platforms are not sufficient to identify the minimum contents of the common platform; we none the less felt it impossible to move towards the common platform without an attempt at reconnaissance, which has so far been carried out only in very general terms.

The reconnaissance should not be based on the assumption that everything has to be harmonized. The Community abandoned this approach in the 1980s when it put aside the impossible dream of total harmonization and adopted the method of minimum harmonization and mutual recognition, based on the principle of subsidiarity. But it is equally important to avoid the risk that structural weaknesses or shortcomings in the platform will be revealed too late, when a common monetary policy is already in operation. The risk of a false start needs to be kept to an absolute minimum. The aim should be to prepare a soft landing on the first day of the final stage, by meeting all the minimum conditions necessary to ensure that the single monetary policy can operate efficiently and credibly from the very start. If necessary, improvements can be made subsequently, as events unfold.

4. THE STARTING-POINT

The starting-point for the process of creating the platform is the identification of the essential features of the functions and instruments of each member country's central bank. This is necessary both to exclude the purely formal differences that are inevitable in any group of institutions with different histories and to permit the principle of subsidiarity to be applied—in other words to exclude from the process of unification all the matters that can be left to the discretionary powers of the national central banks.

This exercise has been carried out with reference to the functions and instruments envisaged in the draft Statute of the ESCB for the final stage. Article 3 of the Statute explicitly mentions the functions associated with the payment system, the conduct of monetary policy, and the supervision of the banking and financial system. However, the ESCB is assigned a prominent role only for the first two functions: in the matter of prudential supervision its role will be to 'contribute to the smooth conduct of policies pursued by the competent authorities'. Table 12.1 gives a summary of the principal central bank instruments and their importance in the exercise of the various functions, together with an indication of the relevant articles of the ESCB Statute.[1]

It can be seen from the table that all the principal powers necessary to perform central-bank functions are explicitly covered in the Statute. No specific provision is made for powers to carry out inspections of banks. This is an important instrument of banking supervision and, potentially, for the oversight of the payment system—particularly in countries where prudential supervision is not the responsibility of the central bank. Powers of sanction are specifically provided for in Article 19 for non-compliance with

---

[1] The Statute of the ESCB is included in the Appendix of Documents.

reserve requirements. Sanctions may also be necessary to enforce provisions concerning the payment system. On the other hand, Article 20 of the Statute gives the ESCB power to use such other operational methods of monetary control as it sees fit.

Table 12.1 also shows which central bank instruments are relevant to more than one function. For example, the availability of adequate statistical information is essential for all three functions. Advances, which are important for monetary policy and for their

TABLE 12.1. *Instruments of central banking and performance of institutional tasks*

Instruments	Powers of the ESCB	Importance for the performance of institutional tasks		
		Payment system	Monetary policy	Stability-orientated supervision
PRODUCTION AND DISTRIBUTION OF NOTES	R, E (art. 16)	***	*	—
OPERATIONS:				
Discounting (rate and quantity)	E (art. 18.1)	—	**	**
Advances (rate and quantity)	E (art. 18.1)	***	**	**
Open market operations	E (art. 18.1)	*	***	—
Foreign exchange market operations	E (art. 18.1)	—	***	—
REGULATORY:				
Compulsory reserves	R, E (art. 19.1)	**	**	**
Liquidity ratios	C (art. 25.1)	**	—	***
Solvency ratios	S (art. 25.2)	**	—	***
On-site controls		*	—	**
Sanctions	R (arts. 19.1, 22)	**	**	**
Access to clearing and settlement system	E (art. 22)	***	*	**
STATISTICS:				
General	E (art. 5)	**	***	***
Central credit register	E (art. 5)	—	—	**

Type of power: R = regulatory, E = executive, S = specific executive, C = consultative. Importance for task performance: *** = essential, ** = important, * = limited.

contribution to the stability of the banking system, are essential to ensure the day-to-day functioning of interbank settlement systems. All these links between instruments will need to be kept in mind when drawing up the agenda for phase two of monetary union.

Starting from Table 12.1, it is possible to compare and analyse the situation of each function in the EC countries, using summary tables to highlight the principal aspects of the three central banking functions in each country. One or more 'blow-ups' were then added to compare the operational procedures actually in force.[2]

In interpreting these tables, it should be borne in mind that the importance attributed to each of the three functions, and the degree to which they have been harmonized, have been very different during the process of Community integration. In the case of the prudential function, a start had already been made on co-ordinating supervisory activities and achieving minimum harmonization under the provisions of the Treaty of Rome. Following the adoption of the First Directive on Banking Co-ordination in 1977, of the Directive on Supervision on a Consolidated Basis in 1983, and of the Directive on Annual and Consolidated Accounts in 1986, the basic regulations for implementing the single market for banking services were completed in 1989 with the approval of the Second Directive on Banking Co-ordination and Directives on Own Funds and Solvency Ratios. Most of this Community legislation has already been or is in the process of being transposed into national legislation.

The functions relevant to the payment system have been under study by the Group of Ten since the 1970s, following a number of bank crises; however, consideration has only recently been given to the basic principles of co-operation between countries. Even more recent is the launching of initiatives within the Community, where the volume of cross-border operations and the imminent creation of a single market for banking services lend urgency to this issue. The sources of regulations in the dif-

---

[2] The sources used in preparing the tables are the central banks' bulletins and annual reports, together with other documents available. Where the importance of a particular aspect is rated, this reflects our own judgement, based on our understanding of the available information.

ferent countries (civil law, bankruptcy laws, agreements between operators) are numerous and not necessarily consistent.

On the monetary front, co-operation between the EC central banks, which was formally sanctioned in 1964 with the creation of the Committee of Governors, has hinged since 1979 on the exchange rate mechanism of the EMS. National decisions in matters of monetary policy are not co-ordinated, though they are usually notified in advance. The study and comparison of the intermediate objectives of monetary policy have acquired a certain importance at the Community level, but no significant progress has been made towards harmonizing instruments and procedures. It should be noted, however, that financial innovation, deregulation in the money and financial markets, and exchange liberalization have brought considerable changes to the procedures for conducting monetary policy in all the leading industrial countries, thereby blurring many of the differences and bringing *de facto* convergence. Central banks have increasingly tended to intervene through open market operations rather than administrative instruments.

5. THE PAYMENT SYSTEM

The reconnaissance of the payment system, the results of which are given in Table 12.2, consisted in classifying the basic functions of each country's system and identifying the authorities responsible for their performance. While all the EC countries recognize the central bank's key role in the payment system, it is explicitly defined by law only in a few. The tasks assigned to the central bank range from a general mandate to ensure the smooth running and security of the financial system (France), or to facilitate the operation of the mechanisms for transmitting money (Spain), to specific responsibilities at the operational level such as the exclusive management of the clearing system (Italy). In some countries a number of not unimportant functions are performed by institutions other than the central bank.

In all the countries considered, the central bank issues banknotes and performs Treasury services on behalf of the state, international organizations, and other central banks (Table 12.2, rows A and B). It also supervises the payment system, even in

TABLE 12.2. *Payment system: activities and competent bodies*

	B	DK	D	GR	E	F	IRL	I	L	NL	P	UK
A. NOTE ISSUE	CB	CB	CB	CB	CB	CB	CB	CB	CB	CB	CB	CB
B. TREASURY SERVICES:												
For the government	CB	CB	CB	CB	CB	CB	CB	CB	CB	CB	CB	CB
For international entities and other central banks	CB	CB	CB	CB	CB	CB	CB	CB	P	CB	CB	CB
C. SUPERVISION AND REGULATION:												
Issue of general rules	IB	IB	CB	IB	IB	CB	IB	CB	P	B	CB	IB
Enforcement of rules	CB	P	CB	CB	CB	CB	CB	CB	P	B	CB	IB
D. INTERBANK PAYMENT SYSTEMS:												
Oversight	CB	CB	CB	CB	CB	CB	CB	CB	CB	CB	CB	CB
Management of clearing	IB	CB	B/CB	CB	IB	CB	B	CB	B	B	CB	IB
Settlement services	CB	CB	CB	CB	CB	CB	CB	CB	P	CB	CB	CB
Liquidity facilities	CB	CB	CB	CB	CB	CB	CB	CB	CB	CB	CB	CB
E. SECURITIES TRANSACTIONS:												
Centralized depositary systems:												
government securities	CB	CB	CB	CB	CB	CB	B	CB	B	CB	CB	IB
other securities	B	B	B	B	B	B	B	P	B	B	B	B
Clearing systems:												
government securities	B	CB	CB	B	B	CB	B	CB	B	CB	CB	B
other securities	B	B	B	B	B	B	B	B	B	B	B	B

CB = central bank, P = public body or owned by the central bank, IB = interbank body, B = banks or private bodies countries, such as Belgium, Germany, and Denmark, where it has no formal responsibility for prudential supervision. In every country except the Netherlands the central bank is responsible for drawing up the general rules and ensuring that they are complied with (rows in *C*). Regulatory functions are handled in different ways: in some countries they are performed *directly*, as laid down in general legislation in France and in specific provisions concerning the payment system in Italy and Germany; in other countries they are performed *indirectly* through participation in interbank organizations in which, as a rule, the central bank acts as chairman.

The exercise of regulatory functions is usually associated with involvement on the operational side. The countries in which the central bank has the most extensive regulatory powers are also those in which it provides the broadest range of services: a significant example of this is Italy, where the Bank of Italy operates the securities clearing and settlement system, a service that in other countries is provided by interbank and/or private agencies.

The central bank supplies settlement services to interbank payment systems in all the member states; this is the very essence of the role of central-bank money today. The provision of settlement services means that the banking system, and hence the entire economy, have access to a means of final settlement, that is one that is immediately valid as full discharge. It is in the interbank payments sector that 'systemic risk' may arise: the inability of one bank to settle its debit position in central-bank money could set off a chain reaction and lead to the collapse of the whole system. Central banks thus acquire additional responsibility, not only because the increased use of their money enhances the safety and efficiency of the system, but also because it is up to them to ensure that the organization and rules of the interbank payment system keep systemic risk to a minimum. The supply of settlement services always involves the central bank in the provision of liquidity facilities to permit the orderly closure of the systems (last in D).

On the whole, Table 12.2 offers a relatively homogeneous picture, at least as regards the degree of central bank involvement. However, this impression is attenuated when the payment systems are examined in more detail. This has been done for the operational features of interbank payment circuits, which are at

Table 12.2(D). *Interbank payment systems*

	B	DK	D	GR	E	F	IRL	I	L	NL	P	UK
CLEARING												
Clearing systems:												
large-value	No	No	Yes	No	No	Yes	Yes	Yes	No	Yes	No	Yes
retail	No	No	Yes	No	No	Yes	No	Yes	No	Yes	No	Yes
unspecialized	Yes	Yes	No	Yes	Yes	No	Yes	Yes	Yes	No	Yes	No
Public Management	No	No	Yes	Yes	Yes	Yes	No	Yes	No	No	Yes	No
Access reserved to banks	Yes	Yes	Yes	Yes	Yes	Yes	Yes	Yes	Yes	Yes	Yes	Yes
Risk-control measures:												
limits on exposure	No	No	No	No	No	Yes	No	No	No	Yes	No	Yes
'unwinding' of balances possible	Yes	Yes	Yes	Yes	Yes	Yes	Yes	Yes	Yes	Yes	Yes	No
CENTRAL BANK LIQUIDITY FACILITIES												
Intraday facilities (for gross settlement systems)	No	Yes	Yes	No	No	Yes	Yes	Yes	No	No	No	No
Collateralized	No	Yes	Yes	No	No	No	No	Yes	No	No	No	No
Caps	No	No	No	No	No	Yes	Yes	Yes	No	Yes	No	No
Granted discretionally	No	Yes	No	No	No	No	No	No	No	No	No	No
Explicit	No	Yes	Yes	No	No	Yes	No	No	No	No	No	No
End-of-day facilities (for clearing systems)	Yes	Yes	Yes	Yes	Yes	Yes	Yes	Yes	Yes	Yes	Yes	Yes

F = full cost, R = running cost, N = free of charge

[a] In operation from 1 January 1993.

[b] Different charges for continuous and clearing settlement.

the heart of every system. The blow-up of row D of Table 12.2 shows that the only element common to all countries is that access to the clearing system is limited to banks. The degree of specialization varies: in some countries there are specialized systems for handling wholesale and retail operations, in others all transactions are channelled into a single procedure. Other important differences are found in the hours of business and, more particularly, in the times at which settlement of the final clearing balances is made: twelve countries have nine different closing times, with a maximum difference of six hours between Luxemburg and France. These differences could pose a serious risk for international payments linked to foreign currency operations, since they enable operations in one currency to be irrevocably settled in one market with no certainty regarding the outcome of the corresponding operations in the other.

The aspect of clearing systems for which the disparities between countries are greatest appears to be that of risk control. This is due both to a lack of comprehensive risk reduction policies among market participants and to the existence of varying approaches to the problem among central banks. The provision of intraday credit, which is an important instrument for the management of liquidity risk, is another field in which there are significant differences (see final section of Table 12.2(D)). No more than six of the twelve central banks actually provide such facilities (the Bank of France will start to do so on 1 January 1993), but they manage them in different ways and only three (the Bank of France, the Bundesbank, and the Danish Nationalbank) grant them explicitly. Every country grants facilities at the close of business, and they are more uniform.

On the whole, the differences between the various national approaches to the central banking issues involved in payment systems are considerable. Studies have been started within the Committee of Governors to identify the areas where harmonization may be needed. It should none the less be borne in mind that the agenda for payment systems will have to go beyond achieving a minimum level of harmonization; extensive operational links will also have to be established between national systems as the prerequisite for real monetary union.

6. MONETARY POLICY

Monetary policy naturally being the province of the central bank in all the Community countries, the reconnaissance of the national platforms is directed at determining how much, and how, the various instruments are used rather than the institutions competent to use them. Like Table 12.2, Table 12.3 has the primary purpose of ordering the instruments of monetary policy in a framework that is comprehensive and systematic enough to cover all the central banks of the Community. Operations are classed by the four major categories of counterparty (banks, the Treasury, the domestic market, and the foreign exchange market), and the general features of the *modus operandi* of each type are shown. Compulsory reserves are classed as an instrument apart, and the table classifies the countries according to whether they actively adjust the volume of reserves and their remuneration.

The table shows that domestic market operations are widely used as a means of monetary control (row B). As to the other instruments, the extent to which they are used varies significantly. The most marked disparities concern operations with the Treasury and the handling of compulsory reserves (rows D and E). When these items are blown up, the differences are even sharper.

Treasury current account overdrafts (in Table 12.3(D)) range from a low of 0.06 per cent of GDP in Belgium to a high of 6 per cent in Italy, with values lying between 0.5 per cent and 1.0 per cent in the Netherlands and France. Interest rates on the overdraft range from respectively zero and 1 per cent in France and Italy, to the lombard rate in Germany and market rates in the United Kingdom. There are also substantial differences in the central banks' government securities operations, both at issue and in the open market.

The most significant differences in compulsory reserves (Table 12.3(E)) concern the size of the requirement (which ranges from zero in Belgium, the Netherlands, and Denmark to 22.5 per cent of deposits in Italy), the rate of return, and the treatment of foreign currency deposits. There is greater uniformity as regards the possibility of mobilizing reserves, though closer examination

TABLE 12.3. *Monetary policy: instruments and their utilization*

	B	DK	D	GR	E	F	IRL	I	NL	P	UK
OPERATIONS											
A. Individual intermediaries	*	***	***	*	*	—	*	*	**	*	*
B. In the domestic market	***	*	***	*	***	***	***	***	**	***	***
C. In the foreign exchange market:											
use of forward operations	—	*	*	—	*	**	*	—	*	—	***
degree of sterilization	*	*	***	*	**	**	***	**	*	**	**
D. With the Treasury:											
volume	*	—	*	***	**	*	*	***	*	**	—
interest rate	***	—	***	*	—	—	***	*	***	—	—
REGULATIONS											
E. Compulsory reserves:											
volume	—	—	*	**	*	*	**	***	—	***	*
interest rate	—	—	—	**	—	—	**	**	—	**	—
F. Quantitative controls	—	—	—	—	—	—	**	—	—	—	—

*** = high or extensive, ** = intermediate, * = low or limited.

Note: Luxemburg is not included in this table because the creation of money by the Luxemburg Monetary Institute is governed by the agreement signed with the National Bank of Belgium in 1977.

would reveal considerable differences in the proportion that can be drawn and the reference period for compliance with the requirement, etc.

It should be noted that the disparities highlighted by these two tables are likely to be attenuated over the next few years independently of the action required to construct the operational platform for a single monetary policy. Operations with the Treasury will have to comply with the ban on the monetary financing of deficits envisaged in the Treaty and the Statute. As regards compulsory reserves, it is not a question of a Community-wide reform but of intervention by the one country that is significantly out of line, namely Italy. This will be needed more to put Italian banks on an equal competitive footing than to promote the monetary policy of the European Central Bank. However, if the latter were to adopt compulsory reserves as an instrument of monetary policy, it would be necessary to standardize features and procedures that are still far from homogeneous.

The main areas in which action is required to prepare the common monetary policy platform are thus operations with the market and individual intermediaries.[3] These are examined in the blow-up of rows A and B of Table 12.3. This shows that there is substantial uniformity as regards open market operations, thanks to the international integration of markets and the increasingly widespread use of the same operational techniques. All central banks make extensive use of open market operations, with repurchase agreements the instrument generally preferred. Consequently, the central bank normally has considerable discretion in setting both the volume and the cost of the liquidity it provides. Moreover, open market operations generally have a strong impact on market interest rates. Nevertheless, there remain important differences in the way in which the central banks operate, and these will have to be tackled if a single monetary policy is to be achieved. The differences concern the type and quality of the securities used in outright and temporary open

[3] This distinction may seem an arbitrary one, in that market operations are necessarily conducted through intermediaries. But for the purposes of this chapter, regardless of the technical nature of the instrument, it is useful to distinguish between operations aimed at affecting the liquidity conditions of the market, and hence interest rates, and those intended to supply liquidity to a particular bank that is unable to obtain it on the market.

market operations, auction techniques, timing, settlement terms, and so on.

Harmonizing operations with individual banks appear to be even more complicated. In this field there are no forces fostering integration independently of monetary union. Moreover, central banks do not use their operations with individual banks exclusively for the purpose of monetary control but also with the aim of supporting the payment system and safeguarding bank stability, and their approaches differ substantially as regards methods and even principles. The debate on lending of last resort that marked the drafting of the Statute of the European System of Central Banks highlighted these differences.

In the operational sphere, the conditions on which central-bank credit is granted would have to be made more uniform, especially as regards access to the discount window, assets eligible as collateral, penalty rates, and the settlement of debtor positions. More generally, the survey revealed numerous differences between countries. Table 12.3(a–b) shows, for instance, that the high utilization rate of central-bank credit and its impact on market interest rates makes it a complementary instrument of monetary policy in Germany, Denmark, and Italy. In Germany considerable recourse is made to the discount and lombard facilities, but the effect on market rates is attenuated by the fact that the discount facility is always fully drawn. This instrument is used less in Italy, but the linkage with market rates is stronger, owing chiefly to the mechanism of fixed-term advances. In France, central-bank credit to individual intermediaries is inoperative in practice. In the United Kingdom and Spain its link with market rates is feeble or nil, as the instrument is used for lending of last resort rather than for monetary control.

7. BANKING SUPERVISION

Analysis of the agenda in the field of banking supervision is complicated by the fact that neither the organization of the sub-functions (regulation, authorization, inspections, etc.) nor the institutions mandated to exercise them can be readily fitted into a conceptual framework common to all the Community countries and derived from an accepted economic theory. Table 12.4

TABLE 12.3(D). *Treasury financing by the central bank*

	B	DK	D	GR	E	F	IRL	I	L	NL	P	UK.
OVERDRAFT:												
Automatic access[a]	Yes	No	No	Yes	Yes	Yes	Yes	Yes	Yes[b]	No	Yes	No
Limit (stock)[c]	0.1	0	0.4	4.8	2.3	0.6	0	6.0	n.a.	0.9	2.5	0
Limit (flow)[c]	0	0	0	1.6	0	0.2	0	0.6	n.a.	0.3	0.5	0
Limit:												
permanent	Fixed	0	Fixed	No	No	Fixed[d]	Fixed	n.a.	n.a.	3% budget revenues	10% budget revenues	0[e]
periodic	n.a.	n.a.	n.a.	Month end: 10% budget expenditure	Year end: fixed[f]	n.a.	Year end: 0	Month end: 14% budget expenditure	n.a.	n.a.	n.a.	n.a.
Interest rate	Advances	0 or dis-count[g]	Lombard	1.5%	0	0	Prime	1%	n.a.	Discount	0	Market

OPERATIONS IN
GOVERNMENT
SECURITIES:

At issue	No	No	No	Yes	Yes	Yes	No	Yes	Yes	Yes	n.a.	Yes	Yes
Open market	Yes	Yes	No	Yes	Yes	Yes	Yes	Yes	Yes	No	n.a.	Yes	Yes
Financing of intermediaries	Yes	No	No	No	No	No	No	Yes	Yes	No	n.a.	Yes	No

n.a. = not applicable

[a] 'Yes' if no formal act by the central bank is required for the Treasury to draw on its overdraft.

[b] Not utilized in practice.

[c] Limit on utilization expressed as % of GDP/GNP in most recent year for which data are available (as a rule 1990).

[d] Limit revised twice a year with reference to the revaluation of official reserves.

[e] Overdrafts not permitted on Treasury current account; to ensure this the Bank of England grants short-term advances at market rates.

[f] Limit is level recorded at 31 December 1989.

[g] No interest paid on deposits of less than 3 million DKR; amounts above this limit earn interest at the discount rate less two % points.

Table 12.3(E). *Monetary policy: compulsory reserves*

	B[a]	DK[b]	D	GR	E	F	IRL	I	L	NL[c]	P	UK[d]
RATIOS:												
Sight deposits	0	n.a.	6.6/9.9/12.1[e]	8	5	4.1	8	22.5[f]	0	n.a.	17	n.a.
Term deposits	0	n.a.	4.95	8	5	2.0	8	22.5	0	n.a.	17	n.a.
Savings account deposits and CDs	0	n.a.	4.15	8	5	0.5	8	22.5	0	n.a.	17	n.a.
INTEREST	n.a.	n.a.	No	Yes[g]	No	No	Yes	Yes	n.a.	n.a.	Yes[h]	n.a.
FOREIGN DEPOSITS												
Non-residents	n.a.	n.a.	Yes[i]	Yes	Yes	No	Yes[j]	No[k]	n.a.	n.a.	Yes	n.a.
Foreign exchange	n.a.	n.a.	Yes	No	No	Yes[l]	Yes	Yes	n.a.	n.a.	No	n.a.
DEDUCTIONS:												
Capital and reserves	n.a.	n.a.	No	No	No	No	No	Yes	n.a.	n.a.	No	n.a.
Vault cash	n.a.	n.a.	Yes	No	No	Yes	Yes	No	n.a.	n.a.	No	n.a.
AVERAGE LAG (DAYS)	n.a.	n.a.	15	10	12	15	20	45	n.a.	n.a.	3	n.a.
COMPUTATION AS AVERAGE OF DAILY BALANCES	n.a.	n.a.	Yes	No	Yes	Yes	No	Yes	n.a.	n.a.	Yes	n.a.

n.a. = not applicable

a The law provides for its introduction, on the basis of agreements between the central bank and the banks, with maximum ratios of 8% for sight deposits, 4.5% for term deposits, and 2% for savings deposits.

b Reserve requirements were formally abolished in March 1991.

c The aggregate amount of monetary base to be absorbed by means of the compulsory reserves is set every 3 months and divided among the banks in relation to their liabilities.

d The cash ratio is negligible and not used as a monetary policy instrument.

e Ratios applicable respectively to the following brackets: up to DM10m., from DM10m. to DM100m., and more than DM100m.

f Maximum ratio for stocks; for flows the ratio is 25% for increases and 22.5% for decreases.

g About 60% earns interest at the rate of 12.5%, the rest is non-interest-bearing.

h At the margin, the rate is close to the market rate; the average rate, calculated at the end of 1990 was around 7.5%.

i Non-residents' sight deposits are subject to a reserve requirement of 12.1%; those in foreign currencies are calculated on the basis of net flows.

j Net positions.

k Except for the lira deposits of non-resident non-bank customers.

l The rate is currently 0.

TABLE 12.3(A–B). *Monetary policy: instruments and their utilization (operations by individuals and in domestic market)*

	B	DK	D	GR	E	F	IRL	I	NL	P	UK
INDIVIDUAL INTERMEDIARIES:											
Extent of use	*	***	***	*	*	—	*	*	**	*	*
Central-bank discretion in determining quantity of liquidity supplied	*	**	**	—	**	—	*	**	**	***	***
Central-bank discretion in determining cost of liquidity supplied	***	***	***	—	***	—	***	**	**	***	***
Ability to influence market rates	**	***	**	—	*	—	**	***	*	—	—
IN THE DOMESTIC MARKET:											
Extent of use	***	*	***	*	***	***	***	***	**	***	***
Use of repurchase agreements	***	*	***	*	***	***	***	***	***	*	*
Central-bank discretion in determining quantity of liquidity supplied	**	***	***	***	***	***	***	***	*	—	—
Central-bank discretion in determining cost of liquidity supplied	***	***	***	***	***	***	***	—	***	***	***
Ability to influence market rates	***	*	***	***	***	***	**	***	***	***	***

*** = high or extensive, ** = intermediate, * = low or limited.

Note: Luxemburg is not included in this table because the creation of money by the Luxemburg Monetary Institute is governed by the agreement signed with the National Bank of Belgium in 1977.

Table 12.4. *Banking supervision: functions and competent authorities*

	B	DK	D	GR	E	F	IRL	I	L	NL	P	UK
A. REGULATION	P/CB	P	P/CB	CB	CB	P/CB	CB	CB	CB	CB	CB	CB
B. AUTHORIZATION	P	P	P	CB	CB	P/CB	CB	CB	CB	CB	CB	CB
C. STATISTICS	P/CB	P	P/CB	CB	CB	CB/P	CB	CB	CB	CB	CB	CB
Central credit register	CB	—	CB	—	CB	CB	—	CB	—	O	CB	—
D. PRUDENTIAL SUPERVISION:												
Liquidity ratios	P	P	P/CB	CB	CB	P/CB	CB	CB	CB	CB	CB	CB
Solvency ratios	P	P	P/CB	CB	CB	P/CB	CB	CB	CB	CB	CB	CB
Risk concentration	P	P	P/CB	CB	CB	P/CB	CB	CB	CB	CB	CB	CB
E. ON-SITE CONTROLS	O/CB/P	P	CB	P/CB	CB	CB	O/CB	CB	CB	O/CB		
F. SANCTIONS/REVOCATION OF AUTHORIZATION	P	P	P	CB	CB	P/CB	CB	CB	CB	CB	CB	CB
G. DEPOSIT PROTECTION	S/CB	S	S	—	CB/S	S	CB	S/CB	S/CB	CB	—	S/CB
Memorandum item												
NON-BANK SUPERVISION	P	P	P/CB	CB/P	CB	P/CB	CB	CB/P	CB	CB	CB	P

CB = central bank (LMI in Luxemburg), P = public agency separate from central bank, with general supervisory responsibilities, S = other autonomous bodies with specific tasks, O = other persons appointed by the supervisory authority (e.g. auditors) should thus be considered no more than a preliminary reconnaissance report, subject to possibly far-reaching revision.

The banking surpervision function is divided into seven major sub-functions (excluding the supervision of non-bank entities); the authorities empowered to carry out these activities are grouped in turn into four distinct categories. Some sub-functions are performed in the Community by as many as three different types of institution. Bank inspections (row E), for instance, are conducted by central banks, public agencies with supervisory powers, and outside auditors, and more than one authority may be involved even within a single country. However, careful examination of the involvement of the central banks in the various sub-functions (Table 12.5) shows that it is substantial or intermediate in most of the member states. And even where the central bank is not institutionally responsible for banking supervision, as in Belgium and Germany, it still plays a major role in the areas of regulation and statistical analysis (Table 12.4, rows A and C). In fact, close co-operation between monetary policy and banking

TABLE 12.5. *Banking supervision: involvement of the central bank*

	B	DK	D	GR	E	F	IRL	I	L	NL	P	UK
REGULATION	*	—	**	***	***	**	***	***	***	***	***	***
AUTHORIZATION	—	—	—	***	***	**	***	***	***	***	***	***
STATISTICS	**	—	***	***	***	***	***	***	***	***	***	***
Central credit register	***	—	***	—	***	***	—	***	—	—	***	—
PRUDENTIAL SUPERVISION:												
Liquidity ratios	—	—	**	***	***	***	***	***	***	***	***	***
Solvency ratios	—	—	**	***	***	***	***	***	***	***	***	***
Risk concentration	—	—	**	***	***	***	***	***	***	***	***	***
ON-SITE CONTROLS	*	—	*	***	***	***	***	***	**	***	***	**
SANCTIONS/REVOCATION OF AUTHORIZATION	—	—	—	***	***	***	***	***	***	***	***	***
DEPOSIT PROTECTION	**	—	—	—	***	—	***	**	**	***	—	**
Memorandum item												
NON-BANK SUPERVISION	—	—	**	**	***	***	***	***	***	***	***	—

*** = extensive, ** = intermediate, * = limited.

supervision is needed in both these areas to avoid subjecting the banks to conflicting or excessively burdensome requirements. In Germany in particular, the central bank plays an important part in the analysis of prudential returns.

From the foregoing, and given that the banking supervision function has undergone far-reaching 'minimal harmonization' since the 1970s with a view to the common market and later the single market, one might expect uniformity to be already sufficient for the final stage of economic and monetary union. This is not the case, however. The Community's action in preparing for the single market involved the legislative and regulatory framework, not the executive stage, the moment in which supervision is actually exercised. Only a few general principles of co-operation have been laid down for this stage, whereas it is legitimate to hold that the formation of a 'single' banking system will have to be accompanied by a more unified organization of practical supervisory activity. Everywhere, banking legislation grants broad discretionary powers to the executive organs of prudential supervision. Executive decentralization is an efficient organizing principle (and one that is followed even within national systems such as Italy's), because familiarity with the national economy and shared historical and juridical origins unquestionably confer a substantial comparative advantage on the individual member states in exercising prudential supervision over credit institutions rooted in the reality of their home countries. However, to avoid inconsistencies and conflicts that would be detrimental to the stability which supervision is intended to guarantee, a common set of guidelines is indispensable. And this can only be provided by a common body with the authority to issue instructions, resolve doubts, and settle conflicts of interpretation.

Assuming that in the near future the Community's banking system remains essentially one formed by banks with a definite national base and ramifications abroad, certain differences in supervisory practices can be considered acceptable under the principle of subsidiarity. But the elimination of all internal barriers to banking activity and the transition to a single currency are likely to lead gradually to an increasing number of truly supranational banks. National approaches and disparities in supervisory practices would become increasingly serious impediments to effective prudential supervision, and even greater difficulties could arise in handling failures involving such institutions, especially as regards lending of last resort and liquidation.

A platform must therefore also be envisaged for banking supervision, especially as more detailed analysis brings out significant differences between national approaches to supervisory functions, instruments, and procedures. Tables 12.4(B) and (E) highlight, by way of example, the differences between Italy and the United Kingdom in both the regulations and the operating procedures governing the two supervisory sub-functions examined in the preceding tables, namely authorization and inspection. The salient features of the Italian authorization procedure are a large initial capital requirement, the statutory definition of fit-and-proper-person criteria, and rigid separation between banking and commerce. In the United Kingdom the initial capital requirement is much lower, the supervisory authorities have broad discretionary powers in determining fit-and-proper-person criteria, and there is no rule concerning separation between banking and commerce. In the area of inspections, the United Kingdom makes extensive use of external auditors and lengthy on-site general inspections are unusual, whereas in Italy they are the rule. Finally, Table 12.4(G) compares some of the key features of the deposit protection schemes of ten member states (as can be seen in Table 12.4, Portugal and Greece do not yet have them). The main disparities concern the level of protection and point to a difference in objectives: simple protection for small savers in many countries, but also defence of systemic stability in others, notably Germany and Italy.

A major difficulty stems from the fact that the Treaty and the Statute of the ESCB do not attribute clear, let alone exclusive, powers to the central institution in this sphere, as they do for payment system and monetary policy matters. As was noted in Section 2 above, decentralization within the ESCB has sometimes been confused with the retention of strong national jurisdiction in banking supervision. It may not always be clear whether, in carrying out its supervisory responsibilities, the central bank is acting under national powers and legislation or under those of the ESCB. Consequently, more than in the other functions, the preparation of the platform in the area of banking supervision will have to rely on voluntary co-operation.

TABLE 12.4(B). *Banking supervision: authorization procedures in the United Kingdom and Italy*

	United Kingdom	Italy
MINIMUM INITIAL CAPITAL: (millions of ECUs)		
Domestic Commercial Banks	1.4	16.3
Other domestic banks	Building societies: 0.14	Co-operative banks: 6.5; rural and artisans' banks: 1 or 2
Branches of foreign banks	No endowment fund	8.15
REQUIREMENTS:		
Professional Competence	Yes	Yes
Definition	Discretional	Rigidly specified by law
Scope:		
shareholders	Owners and other persons who exercise a significant influence	No
administrators	Administrators and managers (all officials with managerial and accounting responsibilities)	Chairman, managing director, general manager, and members of the governing bodies with powers to grant credit
Integrity	Yes	Yes
Definition	Discretional	Rigidly specified by law
Scope:		
shareholders	Owners and other persons who exercise a significant influence	Persons holding (directly or indirectly) more than 2% of the capital
administrators	Administrators and managers (all officials with managerial and accounting responsibilities)	Chairman, managing director, general manager, and members of the governing bodies with powers to grant credit
SEPARATION OF BANKING AND COMMERCE	No	Yes Non-financial enterprises may not own more than 15% of the capital

TABLE 12.4(E). *Banking supervision: on-site controls in the United Kingdom and Italy*

	United Kingdom	Italy
INDEPENDENT AUDITORS	Yes	No
SUPERVISORY INSPECTORS	Yes: own staff and persons seconded from major banks	
Scope of controls	Particularly organizational aspects, internal controls, and loan portfolios	Normally comprehensive
Duration	2–10 days	From 6 weeks to 10 months (depending on size)
Frequency	Every 4–5 years	Every 5–6 years

8. CONCLUSIONS

The examination of the national platforms of central bank functions and instruments has revealed large disparities in many areas. The inventory drawn up provides the basis for determining, through the joint application of the principles of central banking and subsidiarity, the cases in which differences should be eliminated during stage two of EMU to avoid the danger of stage three proving unworkable for lack of preparation. It seems reasonable to conclude that a degree of minimal harmonization will be necessary.

This conclusion follows from our assumption that the ESCB will have a decentralized operational structure, at least during the running-in period. But even if this assumption were abandoned, the agenda for the harmonization of national platforms would have to be even larger. If it were judged to be more efficient in phase three to entrust the execution of central banking functions to a single national central bank (as in the United States, where the Federal Reserve Bank of New York is the operational centre of the entire System), it would be necessary to make the payment systems of all the Community countries virtually identical. Only in this way could the monetary policy measures adopted by the central body be transmitted uniformly throughout the

Table 12.4(G). *Banking supervision: deposit protection schemes*

	B	DK	D	E	F	IRL	I	L	NL	UK
SOURCE OF FINANCING:										
Public	No	No	No	Yes	No	No	No	No	No	No
Private	Yes	Yes	Yes	Yes	Yes	Yes	Yes	Yes	Yes	Yes
AMOUNT GUARANTEED:										
(000s ECUs)	11.8	31.9	30% bank's capital	11.7	57.3	19.5	651.7	11.8	17.3	28.5
Total compensation	Yes	Yes	Yes	Yes	Yes	No	up to 130.3	Yes	Yes	No
Partial compensation	No	No	No	No	No	max 13	75% of remaining 521.4	No	No	75%
Protection extended to foreign currency deposits	No	Yes	Yes	Yes	No	No	Yes	Yes	Yes	No
SCOPE OF INTERVENTION:										
In case of winding up	Yes	Yes	Yes	Yes	Yes	Yes	Yes	Yes	Yes	Yes
Independently of winding up	Yes	No	Yes	Yes	Yes	No	Yes	No	No	No

Note: Deposit protection schemes have not yet been introduced in Portugal or Greece.

Community. Moreover, the centralization of functions and instruments would in itself imply a high degree of harmonization. Finally, it is easy to foresee that the delegation of tasks to a single national central bank would only be practicable for what we have called market-orientated instruments, since otherwise the executive central bank would have to be equipped to operate with every commercial bank doing business in the Community. On the other hand, centralizing market instruments while decentralizing operations with individual banks would require co-ordination and consistency between centre and periphery in the delicate border area between monetary stability and the stability of the banking and payment systems. In economic terms the risk of inconsistencies and conflicts is all too obvious. At the institutional level, the principle of the indivisibility of monetary policy would be violated. It follows that decentralization is the only practicable approach for stage three.

A more general conclusion can be drawn. It appears that, even before measures to harmonize instruments and procedures are considered, the agenda for stage two will require a more general, but also more arduous, analysis of the principles on which central banking is based. The issues involved are those addressed here and can be summarized in a series of dilemmas: centralization or decentralization, market operations or operations with individual banks, and monetary stability or systemic stability.

It was awareness of the importance of these issues that underlay Italy's vigorous advocacy, right up to the very end, of the view that the European Central Bank needed to be created at the outset of stage two. It therefore appears all the more necessary that the European Monetary Institute, which is to precede the ECB, be endowed with the structures and powers needed to prepare for stage three in all the complex aspects this paper has sought to elucidate. On the eve of the Maastricht European Council, we are profoundly aware that the ultimate proof of the new Treaty will be in its implementation.

APPENDIX 1

Sources of the Chapters

Chapter 1. Rules and Institutions in Multi-Country Economies: 'Rules and Institutions in the Government of Multicountry Economies', in L. Tsoukalis (ed.), *The Political Economy of International Money* (London, Royal Institute of International Affairs, Chatham House, 1985; Beverly Hills, Calif., Sage Publications, 1985).

Chapter 2. Capital Mobility: Why is the Treaty not Implemented?: 'I mercati europei dei capitali fra liberalizzazione e restrizioni', *Bancaria*, 6 (June 1982).

Chapter 3. Lessons from the European Monetary System: 'Lessons from the European Monetary System', Banca d'Italia, *Economic Bulletin*, 2 (Feb. 1986).

Chapter 4. The ECU's Coming of Age: 'The ECU's Coming of Age', in W. Eizenga, E. F. Limburg, and J. J. Polo (eds.), *The Quest for National and Global Economic Stability*, 'Liber Amicorum' in honour of James Hendrikus Johannes Witteveen (Dordrecht, Kluwer Academic Publishers, 1988).

Chapter 5. After the Single European Act: Efficiency, Stability, and Equity: 'Stratégies internationales et intégration européenne', Paris 1987.

Chapter 6. The EMS is not Enough: The Need for Monetary Union: 'The EMS: A Long-Term View', in F. Giavazzi, S. Micossi, and M. Miller (eds.), *The European Monetary System* (Cambridge, CUP 1989).

Chapter 7. The Delors Report: From Intentions to Action: 'Recent Developments and Perspectives in Monetary and Financial Integration in the Community', mimeo Kronberg, Nov. 1989.

Chapter 8. Monetary Union and Competition: 'Unione e concorrenza monetaria: note per un dibattito', *Politica Economica*, 3 (1990).

Chapter 9. Fiscal Compatibility and Monetary Constitution: 'Towards a European Central Bank: Fiscal Compatibility and Monetary Constitution; in Z. Eckstein (ed.), *Aspects of Central Bank Policy-Making* (Berlin, Springer-Verlag, 1991).

Chapter 10. Monetary Union and Political Union: 'Key Questions on Economic and Monetary Union', in W. J. Adams (ed.), *Singular Europe: Economy and Polity of the European Community after 1992* (Ann Arbor, Mich., University of Michigan Press, 1992).

Chapter 11. On the Eve of Maastricht: 'Monetary Union: Proof of European Integration', mimeo, Vienna, 11 Oct. 1991.

Chapter 12. Agenda for Stage Two: 'Agenda for Stage Two: Preparing the Monetary Platform', written with F. Saccomanni, *CEPR Occasional Paper*, 7 (1992).

APPENDIX 2

Chronology

GENERAL CHRONOLOGY

1950

May The French Foreign Minister, Robert Schuman, announced a proposal, drafted largely by Jean Monnet, 'to pool the coal and steel resources of France and Germany in an organization open to all European countries'.

July Establishment of the European Payments Union (EPU), a multilateral payment agreement among the leading European countries.

1951

Apr. Signature of the Treaty of Paris establishing the European Coal and Steel Community.

1952

May Signature of the Treaty establishing the European Defence Community.

1954

Aug. The French National Assembly failed to ratify the European Defence Community Treaty.

1955

June The Messina Resolution, in which the Heads of State of the countries participating in the ECSC announced the objective of creating a common market, developing common institutions, and harmonizing their social policies.

Oct. Jean Monnet set up the Action Committee for the United States of Europe (the Monnet Committee).

1957

Mar. Signature of the Treaty of Rome establishing the European Economic Community and of the Treaty establishing the European Atomic Energy Community (Euratom).

1958

Mar. Establishment of the Monetary Committee pursuant to Article 105 of the Treaty of Rome 'to keep under review the monetary and financial situation of the Member States and of the Community'.

Dec. Return to convertibility for current transactions of the currencies of the leading European countries.

1959

May First meeting of the Council of Economics and Finance Ministers (ECOFIN).

1960

May First Directive on the liberalization of capital movements.

1961

Mar. First revaluation of the Deutschmark and the Dutch guilder (4.75%).

July The Monnet Committee proposes the creation of a European Union of Monetary Reserves as a first step towards a European currency.

1962

Dec. Second Directive on the liberalization of capital movements.

1964

May Creation of the Committee of Governors of the Central Banks of the EEC Member States (Council Decision).

Oct. Proposal for a Third Directive on the liberalization of capital movements (never approved).

1965

Apr. Signature in Brussels of the Treaty merging the Executives of the EEC, the ECSC, and Euratom, thereby establishing a single Council and a single Commission of the European Communities.

1966

Nov. Segrè Report on the development of a European capital market.

1968

May France introduced comprehensive controls on capital movements.

1969

July Creation of the Special Drawing Right (SDR).

Aug. Devaluation of the French franc (12.5%).

Sept. Suspension of the parity of the Deutschmark, re-established a month later with a 9.3% revaluation.

Dec. The Heads of State and Government of the member states meeting at The Hague agreed on the objective of economic and monetary union and on the proposal to create a European Reserve Fund.

1970

Feb. Agreement signed by the Governors of the Central Banks of the EEC member states establishing a system of short-term monetary support.

Oct. Werner Report on the attainment by stages of economic and monetary union.

1971

Mar. Mechanism set up for medium-term financial assistance (Council Decision).

Aug. Declaration of the inconvertibility of the US dollar, which marked the end of the Bretton Woods system. Introduction of a 10% surtax on US imports.

Dec. Meeting of the Group of Ten at the Smithsonian Institute in Washington. New parities were agreed for the leading currencies; the dollar was devalued against gold from 35 to 38 dollars per ounce.

1972

Mar. Council Directive on regulating international capital flows and neutralizing their undesirable effects on domestic liquidity.

Introduction of the currency 'Snake', the exchange rate agreement between Belgium, France, Germany, Italy, and the Netherlands. Norway joined in May, together with Denmark and the UK, but the two latter countries dropped out again in June. Denmark rejoined in October (the realignments that occurred during the life of the Snake are listed at the end of this Appendix).

Oct. European Council in Paris. The meeting confirmed the objective of economic and monetary union adopted at The Hague, recognized the need for a Community Regional Development Fund and decided that a European Monetary Cooperation Fund (EMCF) should be set up by April 1973.

1973

Jan. The UK, Ireland, and Denmark became members of the European Communities.

Feb. Devaluation of the US dollar; the official price of gold was raised to 42.22 dollars per ounce.
Italy withdrew from the Snake.

Mar. The Smithsonian parities were abandoned and replaced by a floating rate regime.

July Italy introduced a 50% non-interest-bearing deposit against investments abroad.

1974

Jan. France withdrew from the Snake.

Sept. Germany completely liberalized capital movements.

1975

Mar. Creation of the European Unit of Account (EUA) as a basket comprising fixed quantities of the currencies of the nine member states. The EUA replaced the gold-based unit used since the creation of the Community to compute the amounts involved in the common agricultural policy and the budget.

July France rejoined the Snake.

Nov. All Saints Day manifesto on European monetary union signed by nine economists and published in *The Economist*. The manifesto proposed the creation of a parallel currency.

Dec. Tindemans Report on political union.

1976

Jan. Meeting of the IMF countries at Kingston (Jamaica). Formal recognition was given to the floating rates of the leading currencies. The Fund's Articles of Agreement were amended, with special reference to the demonetization of gold, the official price of which was abolished, and a new method for valuing the SDR introduced, based on a basket of currencies.

Mar. France definitively abandoned the Snake.

Apr. Italy introduced strict exchange controls and made infractions a penal offence (Law no. 159).

1977

Apr. MacDougall Report on the role of federal finance in overcoming regional disequilibria in the Community.

Oct. Speech by Roy Jenkins, President of the Commission, in Florence. Jenkins proposed reviving the project for monetary unification with the creation of a single currency and a single European monetary authority.

1978

Apr. European Council in Copenhagen. At the meeting Valéry Giscard d'Estaing and Helmut Schmidt proposed the creation of a European Monetary System.

July European Council in Bremen. The meeting approved the guidelines for a European Monetary System.

Dec. European Council in Brussels. The meeting decided to set up the European Monetary System.

1979

Mar. The European Monetary System started operations with the participation of Belgium, Denmark, France, Germany, Ireland, Italy, and the Netherlands. The ECU was created; its value was initially made equal to that of the EUA, which it replaced in Community computations in January 1981. The fluctuation margins were fixed at 6% for the Italian lira and at 2.25% for all the other currencies (the realignments within the EMS are listed at the end of this chronology).

May Margaret Thatcher was elected Prime Minister in the UK.

June First elections to the European Parliament by direct universal suffrage.

Oct. The UK completely liberalized capital movements.

1981

Jan. Greece became a member of the European Communities.

May François Mitterrand was elected President of the French Republic.

1982

Feb. Fifth realignment within the EMS, accompanied by a change in Belgium's economic policy.

Feb. Meeting at the EC Commission in Brussels of the banks active in the ECU market, to initiate the study of a clearing system for the settlement of ECU balances.

Oct. Helmut Kohl became Chancellor of the Federal German Republic.

1983

Mar. The Committee of Governors of the Central Banks of the EEC Member States adopted directives on an outline agreement between banks and the BIS for an ECU clearing system.

Seventh realignment within the EMS, accompanied by changes in the economic policies of France and Denmark.

1984

Feb. The European Parliament approved the preliminary draft Treaty establishing the European Union prepared by the Spinelli Commission. Among other things, the text revived the proposal for an economic and monetary union.

May Speech by François Mitterrand to the European Parliament in Strasbourg, in which the French President backed the idea of a Treaty on European Union.

June European Council in Fontainebleau. The meeting set up an *ad hoc* committee on institutional problems (Dooge Committee) and appointed Jacques Delors President of the EC Commission.

Sept. First revision of the ECU weights and inclusion of the Greek drachma.

1985

Mar. Mikhail Gorbachev became First Secretary of the Communist Party of the Soviet Union.

June European Council in Milan. At the proposal of Italy the meeting agreed to convene an intergovernmental conference to negotiate a revision of the Treaty of Rome.

Sept. Plaza Agreement between the USA, Japan, Germany, France, and the UK on concerted intervention to correct the overvaluation of the dollar.

Creation of the ECU Bankers' Association (EBA) for banks active in the ECU market as well as the European Investment Bank.

1986

Jan. Spain and Portugal became members of the European Communities.

Feb. Signature of the Single European Act, which provided for the completion of the internal market by 1992. The Act inserted the EMS in the Treaty of Rome and laid down that 'In so far as further development in the field of economic and monetary policy necessitates institutional changes, the provisions of Article 236 shall be applicable'.

May Commission proposal (Delors document) to bring forward the deadline for the complete liberalization of capital movements.

Oct. The ECU clearing system came into operation.

Nov. Council Directive amending the First Council Directive for the implementation of Article 67 of the Treaty on the liberalization of capital movements.

Dec. Foundation of the Giscard d'Estaing–Schmidt Committee for the Monetary Union of Europe.

1987

Jan. Eleventh realignment within the EMS, caused primarily by financial pressures. This was the last realignment prior to the signing of the Maastricht Treaty.

Feb. Louvre Accord among the G7 countries to stabilize the US dollar.

May Italy adopted measures to liberalize capital movements and abolished the non-interest-bearing deposit against investments abroad.

June The right to settle ECU clearing balances in currencies making up the basket was abolished.

Sept. Informal ECOFIN Council in Nyborg. The meeting adopted the changes to the Exchange Rate Mechanism decided by the Governors of the Central Banks of the EEC Member States in Basle on 8 September and strengthened the very-short-term credit facility and the procedure for monitoring monetary conditions in the Community.

1988

Feb. Special European Council in Brussels. The meeting decided to double the Community's structural funds by 1992.

Mar. Presentation of the Giscard d'Estaing–Schmidt Committee's proposal for monetary union.

June Approval of the last Council Directive on the liberalization of capital movements. This fixed 1 July 1990 as the date by which the liberalization of capital movements within the Community was to be completed, apart from the derogations granted to Spain, Ireland, Greece, and Portugal.

European Council in Hanover. The meeting agreed to set up a Committee, chaired by Jacques Delors, with the task of studying and proposing concrete stages leading towards economic and monetary union (see Appendix 3).

1989

Apr. Presentation of the Delors Report.

June Spain became a member of the EMS with a 6% fluctuation margin.

European Council in Madrid. The meeting fixed 1 July 1990 as the date for the start of the first stage of the realization of Economic and Monetary Union in accordance with the guidelines established by the Delors Committee and asked the competent EC bodies to carry out the preparatory work for the organization of an inter-governmental conference to lay down the subsequent stages (see Appendix 3).

Sept. Second revision of the ECU weights and inclusion of the Spanish peseta and the Portuguese escudo.

Oct. Report of the Guigou Group identifying the main issues to be settled with a view to a Treaty on Economic and Monetary Union.

Nov. Fall of the Berlin Wall.

Dec. European Council in Strasbourg. The meeting agreed to convene an Intergovernmental Conference on Economic and Monetary Union charged with preparing an amendment of the Treaty with a view to the final stages of EMU and agreed that the first meeting of the Conference would be held before the end of 1990 (see Appendix 3).

1990

Jan. The Italian lira adhered to the narrow fluctuation band.

Mar. Free elections were held in the German Democratic Republic.
Revision of the co-ordination procedures for the attainment of progressive convergence of economic policies and performance during stage one of economic and monetary union (EC Council Decision).

Letter written jointly by Chancellor Kohl and President Mitterrand to the other Heads of State and Government of the member states proposing to accelerate the process of European unification by fixing a timetable for the Intergovernmental Conference on Monetary Union and holding a parallel conference on political union.

Apr. Special European Council in Dublin. The meeting discussed the proposal of President Mitterrand and Chancellor Kohl (see Appendix 3).

Italy completely liberalized capital movements.

June European Council in Dublin. The meeting agreed to convene an Intergovernmental Conference on Political Union to work in parallel with that on Economic and Monetary Union.

July The Treaty on the Economic, Monetary, and Social Union between the Federal and Democratic Republics of Germany came into effect. The East German mark was replaced by the Deutschmark.

Oct. Unification of Germany.

The UK became a member of the ERM with a 6% fluctuation margin.

European Council in Rome. The meeting agreed (with the exception of the UK) on the main aspects of the Economic and Monetary Union.

Nov. Draft Statute of the European System of Central Banks and of the European Central Bank prepared by the Committee of Governors of the Central Banks of the EEC Member States.

Margaret Thatcher resigned as Prime Minister.

Conference of National MPs of the member states and of Members of the European Parliament (European Assembly).

Dec. Draft Treaty prepared by the EC Commission for the Intergovernmental Conference.

Opening in Rome of the Intergovernmental Conferences on Political Union and Economic and Monetary Union.

1991

June European Council in Luxemburg. The meeting agreed that the final decision on the texts of the Treaties on Political Union and Economic and Monetary Union would be taken at the European Council in Maastricht at the end of 1991 (see Appendix 3).

Sept. Informal ECOFIN Council in Apeldorn. The meeting modified the decision of the Rome European Council and agreed that a

European Monetary Institute would operate in the second phase of monetary union instead of the European Central Bank.

Nov. Resolution adopted by the Giscard d'Estaing–Schmidt Committee criticizing the draft Treaty prepared by the Dutch Presidency and calling for a date to be fixed for the passage to the third phase of monetary union.

Dec. Conclusion of the Intergovernmental Conferences on Political Union and Economic and Monetary Union.

European Council in Maastricht and final agreement on the texts of the draft Treaties on Political Union and Economic and Monetary Union. It was decided that the passage to the third phase of monetary union, in which the single currency would be adopted, should take place at the latest by 1 January 1999 and that the UK would benefit from a special opting-out clause that would not apply to the other member states (see Appendix 4).

1992

Feb. Signature of the Maastricht Treaty on European Union.

Apr. Portugal became a member of the EMS Exchange Rate Mechanism, with a 6% fluctuation margin.

June First Danish referendum: the Danes voted by a narrow margin to reject the Maastricht Treaty, thereby putting its implementation in doubt.

Sept. Intense speculative pressures developed in European exchange markets, involving several EMS currencies. Even after a devaluation of the lira, the pressures did not abate, forcing the UK and Italian authorities to suspend participation in the ERM, and Spain to devalue the peseta.

Referendum in France: the French approved the ratification of the Maastricht Treaty.

Dec. The European Council decided that negotiations on EC membership would start with Austria, Finland, and Sweden in January 1993; negotiations with Norway were to start later in the year.

Referendum in Switzerland: the Swiss rejected participation in the European Economic Area.

1993

Jan. Inauguration of the Single European Market, providing for the free movement of persons, goods, services, and capital in an area without internal frontiers.

May Second Danish referendum: the Danes approved the ratification of the Maastricht Treaty, after an agreement had been reached allowing Denmark to opt out of participation in the final stage of EMU and a common defence policy.

Meeting in Kolding of EC finance ministers and central-bank governors to review the functioning of the EMS in the light of the earlier currency turmoil. Although the EMS was considered to be basically sound, it was found that closer confidential monitoring of EMS currencies was required, to assess the need for timely policy corrections or, if necessary, parity realignments before market pressures developed.

Aug. Following renewed speculative pressure on several EMS currencies, it was decided temporarily to widen the ERM fluctuation margins to $\pm 15\%$.

Oct. The European Council chose Frankfurt as the seat of the future European Central Bank, as well as of the European Monetary Institute to be established at the start of Stage Two of EMU.

Nov. The Maastricht Treaty came into force, following its ratification by all the member states.

Dec. Alexander Lamfalussy appointed as Chairman of the European Monetary Institute.

CHRONOLOGY OF THE SNAKE

1972

Apr. Birth of the 'Snake', the exchange rate agreement between Belgium, France, Germany, Italy, Luxemburg, and the Netherlands.

May Denmark, the UK and Norway joined.

June The UK and Denmark withdrew.

Oct. Denmark rejoined.

1973

Feb. Italy withdrew.

Mar. Sweden joined.

June Revaluation of the Deutschmark.

Sept. Revaluation of the Dutch guilder.

Nov. Revaluation of the Danish krone.

1974

Jan. France withdrew.

1975

July France rejoined.

1976

Mar. France dropped out definitively.

Oct. The Frankfurt realignment: the Deutschmark was revalued and the Scandinavian currencies were devalued.

1977

Apr. The Scandinavian currencies were devalued.

Aug. Sweden withdrew and the other Scandinavian currencies were devalued.

1978

Feb. Devaluation of the Norwegian krone.

Oct. Revaluation against the Danish krone of the Deutschmark (4%), the Dutch guilder, and the Belgian franc (2%).

Dec. Norway withdrew.

1979

Mar. End of the Snake and start of the European Monetary System.

REALIGNMENTS IN THE EUROPEAN MONETARY SYSTEM

1979

Mar. The European Monetary System started operations with the participation of Belgium, Denmark, France, Germany, Ireland, Italy, and the Netherlands.

Sept. Revaluation of the Deutschmark (2%) and devaluation of the Danish krone (3%).

Nov. Devaluation of the Danish krone (5%).

1981

Mar. Devaluation of the Italian lira (6%).

Oct. Revaluation of the Deutschmark and the Dutch guilder (5.5%) and devaluation of the French franc and the Italian lira (3%).

1982

Feb. Devaluation of the Belgian franc (8.5%) and the Danish krone (3%).

June Revaluation of the Deutschmark and the Dutch guilder (4.25%) and devaluation of the French franc (5.75%) and the Italian lira (2.75%).

1983

Mar. Revaluation of the Deutschmark (5.5%), the Dutch guilder (3.35%), the Danish krone (2.5%) and the Belgian franc (1.5%); devaluation of the Italian lira (2.5%) and the Irish punt (3.5%).

1985

July Devaluation of the Italian lira (6%) and revaluation of all the other currencies.

1986

Apr. Revaluation of the Deutschmark and the Dutch guilder (3%), the Danish krone and the Belgian franc (1%); devaluation of the French franc (3%).

Aug. Devaluation of the Irish punt (8%).

1987

Jan. Revaluation of the Deutschmark and the Dutch guilder (3%), devaluation of the Belgian franc (2%).

1992

Sept. Devaluation of the Italian lira (3.5%) and revaluation of all the other ERM currencies (3.5%).
Devaluation of the Spanish peseta (5%).

Nov. Devaluation of the Spanish peseta and Portuguese escudo (6%).

1993

Feb. Devaluation of the Irish punt (10%).

May Devaluation of the Spanish peseta (8%) and the Portuguese escudo (6.5%).

Aug. The ERM fluctuation margins were widened to ± 15%.

APPENDIX 3

Conclusions of the European Council: 1988–1991

HANOVER, 27 AND 28 JUNE 1988

The European Council recalls that, in adopting the Single Act, the Member States confirmed the objective of progressive realization of economic and monetary union.

They therefore decided to examine at the European Council meeting in Madrid in June 1989 the means of achieving this union.

To that end they decided to entrust to a Committee the task of studying and proposing concrete stages leading towards this union.

The Committee will be chaired by Mr Jacques Delors, President of the European Commission.

The Heads of State or Government agreed to invite the President or Governor of their central banks to take part in a personal capacity in the proceedings of the Committee, which will also include one other member of the Commission and three personalities designated by common agreement by the Heads of State or Government. They have agreed to invite:

- Mr Niels Thygesen, Professor of Economics, Copenhagen;
- Mr Lamfalussy, General Manager of the Bank for International Settlements in Basle, Professor of Monetary Economics at the Catholic University of Louvain-la-Neuve;
- Mr Miguel Boyer, President of Banco Exterior de Espana.

The Committee should have completed its proceedings in good time to enable the Ministers for Economic Affairs and for Finance to examine its results before the European Council meeting in Madrid.

MADRID, 26 AND 27 JUNE 1989

1. The European Council restated its determination progressively to achieve Economic and Monetary Union as provided for in the Single Act and confirmed at the European Council meeting in Hanover. Economic and Monetary Union must be seen in the perspective of the

completion of the Internal Market and in the context of economic and social cohesion.

2. The European Council considered that the report by the committee chaired by Jacques Delors, which defines a process designed to lead by stages to Economic and Monetary Union, fulfilled the mandate given in Hanover. The European Council felt that its realization would have to take account of the parallelism between economic and monetary aspects, respect the principle of 'subsidiarity' and allow for the diversity of specific situations.

3. The European Council decided that the first stage of the realization of Economic and Monetary Union would begin on 1 July 1990.

4. The European Council asked the competent bodies (the ECOFIN and General Affairs Councils, the Commission, the Committee of Central Bank Governors and the Monetary Committee):

(a) to adopt the provisions necessary for the launch of the first stage on 1 July 1990;

(b) to carry out the preparatory work for the organization of an intergovernmental conference to lay down the subsequent stages; that conference would meet once the first stage had begun and would be preceded by full and adequate preparation.

STRASBOURG, 8 AND 9 DECEMBER 1989

1. The European Council examined the work carried out since the European Council meeting in Madrid with a view to a meeting of the Intergovernmental Conference.

It noted the agreement reached in the ECOFIN Council and the initiatives of the Governors of the Central Banks with a view to strengthening the co-ordination of economic policies and improving collaboration between Central banks. It notes that these decisions will enable the first stage of EMU as defined in the report from the Delors Committee to begin on 1 July 1990.

2. It took note of the report from the High Level Working Party, which identified the main technical, institutional and political issues to be discussed with a view to a Treaty on Economic and Monetary Union.

On this basis, and following a discussion on the calling of an Intergovernmental Conference charged with preparing an amendment of the Treaty with a view to the final stages of EMU, the President of the European Council noted that the necessary majority existed for convening such a conference under Article 236 of the Treaty. That conference will meet, under the auspices of the Italian authorities, before the end of

1990. It will draw up its own agenda and set the timetable for its proceedings.

3. The European Council emphasized, in this context, the need to ensure the proper observance of democratic control in each of the Member States.

With a view to the new term of the European Parliament which will begin in 1994, it calls for Economic and Monetary Union to comply fully with this democratic requirement.

4. The European Council also took note of the Commission's intention to submit before 1 April a composite paper on all aspects of the achievement of Economic and Monetary Union which will take into account all available analyses and contributions.

The European Council emphasized the need for the Council (General Affairs) and the ECOFIN Council to use the period prior to the opening of the Conference to ensure the best possible preparation.

The proceedings as a whole will be examined by the Council (General Affairs) in preparation for the European Council meeting in Dublin.

DUBLIN, 28 APRIL 1990

The Community will establish in stages an Economic and Monetary Union in accordance with the principles of economic and social cohesion and in accordance with the conclusions of the European Councils in Madrid and Strasbourg. The preparations for the Intergovernmental Conference on EMU which are already well advanced will be further intensified with a view to permitting that Conference, which will open in December 1990, to conclude its work rapidly with the objective of ratification by Member States before the end of 1992.

DUBLIN, 25 AND 26 JUNE 1990

The first stage of Economic and Monetary Union will come into effect on 1 July 1990. The European Council considered that this new stage should be used to ensure convergence in the economic performance of Member States, to advance cohesion and to further the use of the ECU, all of which are of importance for the further progress towards EMU.

The European Council reviewed the preparation of the forthcoming Intergovernmental Conference. It noted that all the relevant issues are now being fully and thoroughly clarified, with the constructive contribution of all Member States, and that common ground is emerging in a number of fields. In these circumstances the European Council decided that the Intergovernmental Conference will open on 13 December 1990 with a view to establishing the final stages of Economic and Monetary Union in the perspective of the completion of the Internal Market and in the context of economic and social cohesion. The Conference should conclude its work rapidly with the objective of ratification of the results by Member States before the end of 1992.

The European Council asked the ECOFIN Council and the General Affairs Council assisted by the competent bodies to carry out their work in such a way that negotiations on a concrete basis can be entered into as soon as the Conference opens.

ROME, 27 AND 28 OCTOBER 1990

The European Council in Madrid fixed the date for the start of the first phase of Economic and Monetary Union; in Strasbourg and Dublin it set the timetable for the Intergovernmental Conference and the ratification of its results. It now notes with satisfaction the important developments that have occurred in the wake of these decisions.

The European Council takes note of the results of the preparatory work that constitutes the basis for the Intergovernmental Conference.

For the final phase of Economic and Monetary Union *eleven Member States* consider that the work on the amendment of the Treaty will be directed to the following points:

- for Economic Union, an open market system, that combines price stability with growth, employment and environmental protection; and is dedicated to sound and sustainable financial and budgetary conditions and to economic and social cohesion. To this end, the ability to act of the Community institutions will be strengthened;
- for Monetary Union, the creation of a new monetary institution comprising Member States' central banks and a central organ, exercising full responsibility for monetary policy.

The monetary institution's prime task will be to maintain price stability; without prejudice to this objective, it will support the general economic policy of the Community. The institution as such, as well as the members of its Council, will be independent of instructions. It will report to the institutions which are politically responsible.

With the achievement of the final phase of Economic and Monetary Union, exchange rates will be irrevocably fixed. The Community will have a single currency—a strong and stable ECU—which will be an expression of its identity and unity. During the transitional phase, the ECU will be further strengthened and developed.

The second phase will start on 1 January 1994 after:

- the single market programme has been achieved;
- the Treaty has been ratified; and, by its provisions;
- a process has been set in train designed to ensure the independence of the members of the new monetary institution at the latest when monetary powers have been transferred;
- the monetary financing of budget deficits has been prohibited and any responsibility on the part of the Community or its Member States for one Member State's debt precluded;
- the greatest possible number of Member States have adhered to the exchange rate mechanism.

The European Council recalls that, in order to move on to the second phase, further satisfactory and lasting progress towards real and monetary convergence will have to be achieved, especially as regards price stability and the restoration of sound public finances.

At the start of the second phase, the new Community institution will be established. This will make it possible, in particular:

- to strengthen the co-ordination of monetary policies;
- to develop the instruments and procedures needed for the future conduct of a single monetary policy;
- to oversee the development of the ECU.

At the latest within three years from the start of the second phase, the Commission and the Council of the monetary institution will report to the ECOFIN Council and to the General Affairs Council on the functioning of the second phase and in particular on the progress made in real convergence, in order to prepare the decision concerning the passage to the third phase, which will occur within a reasonable time. The General Affairs Council will submit the dossier to the European Council.

The Treaty may lay down transitional provisions for the successive stages of economic and monetary union according to the circumstances of the different countries.

The United Kingdom is unable to accept the approach set out above. But it agrees that the overriding objective of monetary policy should be price stability, that the Community's development should be based on an open market system, that excessive budget deficits should be avoided, and that there should be no monetary financing of deficits nor the assumption of responsibility on the part of the Community or its Member States for one Member State's debts. The United Kingdom, while ready to move beyond stage one through the creation of a new monetary institution and a common Community currency, believes that decisions on the substance of that move should precede decisions on its timing. But it would be ready to see the approach it advocates come into effect as soon as possible after ratification on the necessary Treaty provision.

LUXEMBURG, 28 AND 29 JUNE 1991

The Intergovernmental Conference has revealed, with its draft Treaty and the draft statute of the ESCB annexed thereto, that there are broad areas of agreement on the basic components of EMU. At the next European Council these draft texts should be finalized according to the guidelines worked out there and in keeping with the European Council's conclusions of 27 and 28 October 1990, recalling the United Kingdom reserve attached thereto.

The European Council emphasizes the need to make satisfactory and lasting progress with economic and monetary convergence as of now, and as part of the first stage of Economic and Monetary Union, with particular reference to price stability and sound public finance.

In this context, the European Council notes that in the near future several Governments intend to submit specific multi-annual programmes designed to secure the requisite progress on convergence, which will quantify the objectives and the means of securing them. The European Council would encourage other Governments to submit such programmes and calls upon the Commission and the ECOFIN Council to report regularly on the implementation of these programmes and on progress with convergence.

MAASTRICHT, 9 AND 10 DECEMBER 1991

The Intergovernmental Conferences on Political Union and Economic and Monetary Union, meeting at the level of Heads of State and Government, reached agreement on the Draft Treaty on European Union based on the texts (doc. SN 252/1/91) concerning Political Union and on the Draft Treaty text concerning Economic and Monetary Union. The necessary final legal editing and harmonization of the texts will be completed with a view to signature of the Treaty at the beginning of February 1992.

With particular reference to social policy the European Council confirms that the present provisions of the Treaty can be considered an 'acquis communautaire'.

The European Council notes that eleven Member States desire to continue on the path laid down by the Social Charter in 1989. To this end it has been agreed to annex to the Treaty a Protocol concerning social policy which will commit the Institutions of the Community to take and implement the necessary decisions while adapting the decision-making procedures for application by eleven Member States.

APPENDIX 4

Economic and Monetary Union in the Treaty of Maastricht

TREATY PROVISIONS

Article 3a

1. . . . the activities of the Member States and the Community shall include, as provided in this Treaty and in accordance with the timetable set out therein, the adoption of an economic policy which is based on the close coordination of Member States' economic policies, on the internal market and on the definition of common objectives, and conducted in accordance with the principle of an open market economy with free competition.

2. Concurrently with the foregoing, and as provided in this Treaty and in accordance with the timetable and the procedures set out therein, these activities shall include the irrevocable fixing of exchange rates leading to the introduction of a single currency, the ECU, and the definition and conduct of a single monetary policy and exchange rate policy the primary objective of both of which shall be to maintain price stability and, without prejudice to this objective, to support the general economic policies in the Community, in accordance with the principle of an open market economy with free competition.

3. These activities of the Member States and the Community shall entail compliance with the following guiding principles; stable prices, sound public finances and monetary conditions and a sustainable balance of payments.

Article 4a

A European System of Central Banks (hereinafter referred to as 'ESCB') and a European Central Bank (hereinafter referred to as 'ECB') shall be established in accordance with the procedures laid down in this Treaty; they shall act within the limits of the powers conferred upon them by this Treaty and by the Statute of the ESCB and of the ECB (hereinafter referred to as 'Statute of the ESCB') annexed thereto.

TITLE VI
ECONOMIC AND MONETARY POLICY

Chapter 1 Economic Policy

Article 104

1. Overdraft facilities or any other type of credit facility with the ECB or with the central banks of the Member States (hereinafter referred to as 'national central banks') in favour of Community institutions or bodies, central governments, regional, local or other public authorities, other bodies governed by public law, or public undertakings of Member States shall be prohibited, as shall the purchase directly from them by the ECB or national central banks of debt instruments. . . .

Article 104a

1. Any measure, not based on prudential considerations, establishing privileged access by Community institutions or bodies, central governments, regional, local or other public authorities, other bodies governed by public law, or public undertakings of Member States to financial institutions shall be prohibited. . . .

Article 104b

1. The Community shall not be liable for or assume the commitments of central governments, regional, local or other public authorities, other bodies governed by public law, or public undertakings of any Member State, without prejudice to mutual financial guarantees for the joint execution of a specific project. A Member State shall not be liable for or assume the commitments of central governments, regional, local or other public authorities, other bodies governed by public law or public undertakings of another Member State, without prejudice to mutual financial guarantees for the joint execution of a specific project. . . .

Article 104c

1. Member States shall avoid excessive government deficits.
2. The Commission shall monitor the development of the budgetary situation and of the stock of government debt in the Member States with a

view to identifying gross errors. In particular it shall examine compliance with budgetary discipline on the basis of the following two criteria:

(*a*) whether the ratio of the planned or actual government deficit to gross domestic product exceeds a reference value, unless
- either the ratio has declined substantially and continuously and reached a level that comes close to the reference value;
- or, alternatively, the excess over the reference value is only exceptional and temporary and the ratio remains close to the reference value;

(*b*) whether the ratio of government debt to gross domestic product exceeds a reference value, unless the ratio is sufficiently diminishing and approaching the reference value at a satisfactory pace.

The reference values are specified in the Protocol on the excessive deficit procedure annexed to this Treaty.

3. If a Member State does not fulfil the requirements under one or both of these criteria, the Commission shall prepare a report. The report of the Commission shall also take into account whether the government deficit exceeds government investment expenditure and take into account all other relevant factors, including the medium term economic and budgetary position of the Member State.

The Commission may also prepare a report if, notwithstanding the fulfilment of the requirements under the criteria, it is of the opinion that there is a risk of an excessive deficit in a Member State. . . .

Chapter 2 Monetary Policy

Article 105

1. The primary objective of the ESCB shall be to maintain price stability. Without prejudice to the objective of price stability, the ESCB shall support the general economic policies in the Community with a view to contributing to the achievement of the objectives of the Community as laid down in Article 2. The ESCB shall act in accordance with the principle of an open market economy with free competition, favouring an efficient allocation of resources, and in compliance with the principles laid down in Article 3*a*.

2. The basic tasks to be carried out through the ESCB shall be:

- to define and implement the monetary policy of the Community;
- to conduct foreign exchange operations consistent with the provisions of Article 109;
- to hold and manage the official foreign reserves of the Member States;
- to promote the smooth operation of payment systems.

3. The third indent of paragraph 2 shall be without prejudice to the holding and management by the governments of Member States of foreign exchange working balances.

4. The ECB shall be consulted:

• on any proposed Community act in its fields of competence;
• by national authorities regarding any draft legislative provision in its fields of competence, but within the limits and under the conditions set out by the Council in accordance with the procedure laid down in Article 106(6).

The ECB may submit opinions to the appropriate Community institutions or bodies or to national authorities on matters in its fields of competence.

5. The ESCB shall contribute to the smooth conduct of policies pursued by the competent authorities relating to the prudential supervision of credit institutions and the stability of the financial system.

6. The Council may, acting unanimously on a proposal from the Commission and after consulting the ECB and after receiving the assent of the European Parliament, confer upon the ECB specific tasks concerning policies relating to the prudential supervision of credit institutions and other financial institutions with the exception of insurance undertakings.

Article 105a

1. The ECB shall have the exclusive right to authorize the issue of bank notes within the Community. The ECB and the national central banks may issue such notes. The bank notes issued by the ECB and the national central banks shall be the only such notes to have the status of legal tender within the Community.

2. Member States may issue coins subject to approval by the ECB of the volume of the issue. The Council may, acting in accordance with the procedure referred to in Article 189c and after consulting the ECB, adopt measures to harmonize the denominations and technical specifications of all coins intended for circulation to the extent necessary to permit their smooth circulation within the Community.

Article 107

When exercising the powers and carrying out the tasks and duties conferred upon them by this Treaty and the Statute of the ESCB, neither the ECB, nor a national central bank, nor any member of their decision-making bodies shall seek or take instructions from Community institutions or bodies, from any government of a Member State or from any other body. The Community institutions and bodies and the governments of the Member States undertake to respect this principle and not to seek to influence the members of the decision-making bodies of the ECB or of the national central banks in the performance of their tasks.

Chapter 4 Transitional Provisions

Article 109e

1. The second stage for achieving economic and monetary union shall begin on 1 January 1994.

2. Before the date:

(*a*) each Member State shall:

- adopt, where necessary, appropriate measures to comply with the prohibitions laid down in Article 73b, without prejudice to Article 73e, and in Articles 104 and 104*a*(1);
- adopt, if necessary, with a view to permitting the assessment provided for in subparagraph (*b*), multiannual programmes intended to ensure the lasting convergence necessary for the achievement of economic and monetary union, in particular with regard to price stability and sound public finances;

(*b*) the Council shall, on the basis of a report from the Commission, assess the progress made with regard to economic and monetary convergence, in particular with regard to price stability and sound public finances, and the progress made with the implementation of Community law concerning the internal market. . . .

4. In the second stage, Member States shall endeavour to avoid excessive government deficits.

5. During the second stage, each Member State shall, as appropriate, start the process leading to the independence of its central bank, in accordance with Article 108.

Article 109f

1. At the start of the second stage, a European Monetary Institute (hereinafter referred to as 'EMI') shall be established and take up its duties; it shall have legal personality and be directed and managed by a Council, consisting of a President and the Governors of the national central banks, one of whom shall be Vice-President. . . .

2. The EMI shall:

- strengthen cooperation between the national central banks;

- strengthen the coordination of the monetary policies of the Member States, with the aim of ensuring price stability;
- monitor the functioning of the European Monetary System;
- hold consultations concerning issues falling within the competence of the national central banks and affecting the stability of financial institutions and markets;
- take over the tasks of the European Monetary Cooperation Fund, which shall be dissolved; the modalities of dissolution are laid down in the Statute of the EMI;
- facilitate the use of the ECU and oversee its development, including the smooth functioning of the ECU clearing system.

3. For the preparation of the third stage, the EMI shall:

- prepare the instruments and the procedures necessary for carrying out a single monetary policy in the third stage;
- promote the harmonization, where necessary, of the rules and practices governing the collection, compilation and distribution of statistics in the areas within its field of competence;
- prepare the rules for operations to be undertaken by the national central banks within the framework of the ESCB;
- promote the efficiency of cross-border payments;
- supervise the technical preparation of ECU bank notes.

At the latest by 31 December 1996, the EMI shall specify the regulatory, organizational and logistical framework necessary for the ESCB to perform its tasks in the third stage. This framework shall be submitted for decision to the ECB at the date of its establishment. . . .

Article 109g

The currency composition of the ECU basket shall not be changed.

From the start of the third stage, the value of the ECU shall be irrevocably fixed in accordance with Article 109l(4).

Article 109j

The Commission and the EMI shall report to the Council on the progress made in the fulfilment by the Member States of their obligations regarding the achievement of economic and monetary union. These reports shall include an examination of the compatibility between each Member State's national legislation, including the statutes of its national central bank, and Articles 107 and 108 of this Treaty and the Statute of the ESCB. The reports shall also examine the achievement of a high degree of sustainable convergence by reference to the fulfilment by each

Member State of the following criteria:

- the achievement of a high degree of price stability; this will be apparent from a rate of inflation which is close to that of, at most, the three best performing Member States in terms of price stability;
- the sustainability of the government financial position; this will be apparent from having achieved a government budgetary position without a deficit that is excessive as determined in accordance with Article 104c(6);
- the observance of the normal fluctuation margins provided for by the Exchange Rate Mechanism of the European Monetary System, for at least two years, without devaluing against the currency of any other Member State;
- the durability of convergence achieved by the Member State and of its participation in the Exchange Rate Mechanism of the European Monetary System being reflected in the long-term interest rate levels.

The four criteria mentioned in this paragraph and the relevant periods over which they are to be respected are developed further in a Protocol annexed to this Treaty. The reports of the Commission and the EMI shall also take account of the development of the ECU, the results of the integration of markets, the situation and development of the balances of payments on current account and an examination of the development of unit labour costs and other price indices.

2. On the basis of these reports, the Council, acting by a qualified majority on a recommendation from the Commission, shall assess:

- for each Member State, whether it fulfils the necessary conditions for the adoption of a single currency;
- whether a majority of the Member States fulfil the necessary conditions for the adoption of a single currency,

and recommend its findings to the Council, meeting in the composition of the Heads of State or of Government. The European Parliament shall be consulted and forward its opinion to the Council, meeting in the composition of the Heads of State or of Government.

3. Taking due account of the reports referred to in paragraph 1 and the opinion of the European Parliament referred to in paragraph 2, the Council, meeting in the composition of the Heads of State or of Government, shall, acting by a qualified majority, not later than 31 December 1996:

- decide, on the basis of the recommendations of the Council referred to in paragraph 2, whether a majority of the Member States fulfil the necessary conditions for the adoption of a single currency;
- decide whether it is appropriate for the Community to enter the third stage,

and if so

• set the date for the beginning of the third stage.

4. If by the end of 1997 the date for the beginning of the third stage has not been set, the third stage shall start on 1 January 1999. . . .

Article 109l

1. Immediately after the decision on the date for the beginning of the third stage has been taken in accordance with Article 109j(3), or, as the case may be, immediately after 1 July 1998: . . .

• the governments of the Member States without a derogation shall appoint, in accordance with the procedure set out in Article 50 of the Statute of the ESCB, the President, the Vice-President and the other members of the Executive Board of the ECB. . . .

As soon as the Executive Board is appointed, the ESCB and the ECB shall be established and shall prepare for their full operation as described in this Treaty and the Statute of the ESCB. The full exercise of their powers shall start from the first day of the third stage.

2. As soon as the ECB is established, it shall, if necessary, take over tasks of the EMI. The EMI shall go into liquidation upon the establishment of the ECB; the modalities of liquidation are laid down in the Statute of the EMI. . . .

4. At the starting date of the third stage, the Council shall, acting with the unanimity of the Member States without a derogation, on a proposal from the Commission and after consulting the ECB, adopt the conversion rates at which their currencies shall be irrevocably fixed and at which irrevocably fixed rate the ECU shall be substituted for these currencies, and the ECU will become a currency in its own right. This measure shall by itself not modify the external value of the ECU. The Council shall, acting according to the same procedure, also take the other measures necessary for the rapid introduction of the ECU as the single currency of those Member States. . . .

APPENDIX 5

Protocol on the Statute of the European System of Central Banks and of the European Central Bank

Chapter II Objectives and Tasks of the ESCB

Article 3, Tasks

3.1. In accordance with Article 105(2) of this Treaty, the basic tasks to be carried out through the ESCB shall be:

- to define and implement the monetary policy of the Community;
- to conduct foreign exchange operations consistent with the provisions of Article 109 of this Treaty;
- to hold and manage the official foreign reserves of the Member States;
- to promote the smooth operation of payment systems.

3.2. In accordance with Article 105(3) of this Treaty, the third indent of Article 3.1 shall be without prejudice to the holding and management by the governments of the Member States of foreign exchange working balances.

3.3. In accordance with Article 105(5) of this Treaty, the ESCB shall contribute to the smooth conduct of policies pursued by the competent authorities relating to the prudential supervision of credit institutions and the stability of the financial system. . . .

Article 5, Collection of statistical information

5.1. In order to undertake the tasks of the ESCB, the ECB assisted by the national central banks, shall collect the necessary statistical information either from the competent national authorities or directly from economic agents. For these purposes it shall cooperate with the Community institutions or bodies and with the competent authorities of the Member States or third countries and with international organizations.

5.2. The national central banks shall carry out, to the extent possible, the tasks described in Article 5.1.

5.3. The ECB shall contribute to the harmonization, where necessary, of the rules and practices governing the collection, compilation and distribution of statistics in the areas within its fields of competence.

5.4. The Council, in accordance with the procedure laid down in

Article 42, shall define the natural and legal persons subject to reporting requirements, the confidentiality regime and the appropriate provisions for enforcement.

Chapter III Organization of the ESCB

Article 16, Bank notes

In accordance with Article 105a(1) of this Treaty, the Governing Council shall have the exclusive right to authorize the issue of bank notes within the Community. The ECB and the national central banks may issue such notes. The bank notes issued by the ECB and the national central banks shall be the only such notes to have the status of legal tender within the Community.

The ECB shall respect as far as possible existing practices regarding the issue and design of bank notes.

Chapter IV Monetary Functions and Operations of the ESCB

Article 18, Open market and credit operations

18.1. In order to achieve the objectives of the ESCB and to carry out its tasks, the ECB and the national central banks may:

- operate in the financial markets by buying and selling outright (spot and forward) or under repurchase agreement and by lending or borrowing claims and marketable instruments, whether in Community or in non-Community currencies, as well as precious metals;
- conduct credit operations with credit institutions and other market participants, with lending being based on adequate collateral.

18.2. The ECB shall establish general principles for open market and credit operations carried out by itself or the national central banks, including for the announcement of conditions under which they stand ready to enter into such transactions.

Article 19, Minimum reserves

19.1. Subject to Article 2, the ECB may require credit institutions established in Member States to hold minimum reserves on accounts with the ECB and national central banks in pursuance of monetary policy objectives. Regulations concerning the calculation and determination of the required minimum reserves may be established by the Governing Council. In cases of non-compliance the ECB shall be entitled to levy penalty interest and to impose other sanctions with comparable effect.

19.2. For the application of this Article, the Council shall, in accordance with the procedure laid down in Article 42, define the basis for minimum reserves and the maximum permissible ratios between those reserves and their basis, as well as the appropriate sanctions in cases of non-compliance.

Article 20, Other instruments of monetary control

The Governing Council may, by a majority of two thirds of the votes cast, decide upon the use of such other operational methods of monetary control as it sees fit, respecting Article 2.

The Council shall, in accordance with the procedure laid down in Article 42, . . .

Article 22, Clearing and payment systems

The ECB and national central banks may provide facilities, and the ECB may make regulations, to ensure efficient and sound clearing and payment systems within the Community and with other countries.

Chapter V Prudential Supervision

Article 25, Prudential supervision

25.1. The ECB may offer advice to and be consulted by the Council, the Commission and the competent authorities of the Member States on the scope and implementation of Community legislation relating to the prudential supervision of credit institutions and to the stability of the financial system.

25.2. In accordance with any decision of the Council under Article 105(6) of this Treaty, the ECB may perform specific tasks concerning policies relating to the prudential supervision of credit institutions and other financial institutions with the exception of insurance undertakings.

PROTOCOL ON THE EXCESSIVE DEFICIT PROCEDURE

Article 1

The reference values referred to in Article 104c(2) of this Treaty are:
- 3% for the ratio of the planned or actual government deficit to gross domestic product at market prices;
- 60% for the ratio of government debt to gross domestic product at market prices.

Article 2

In Article 104c of this Treaty and in this Protocol:
- government means general government, that is central government, regional or local government and social security funds, to the exclusion of commercial operations, as defined in the European System of Integrated Economic Accounts;
- deficit means net borrowing as defined in the European System of Integrated Economic Accounts;
- investment means gross fixed capital formation as defined in the European System of Integrated Economic Accounts;
- debt means total gross debt at nominal value outstanding at the end of the year and consolidated between and within the sectors of general government as defined in the first indent.

Article 3

In order to ensure the effectiveness of the excessive deficit procedure, the governments of the Member States shall be responsible under this procedure for the deficits of general government as defined in the first indent of Article 2. The Member States shall ensure that national procedures in the budgetary area enable them to meet their obligations in this area deriving from this Treaty. The Member States shall report their planned and actual deficits and the levels of their debt promptly and regularly to the Commission.

PROTOCOL ON THE CONVERGENCE CRITERIA REFERRED TO IN ARTICLE 109J OF THE TREATY ESTABLISHING THE EUROPEAN COMMUNITY

Article 1

The criterion on price stability referred to in the first indent of Article 109*j*(1) of this Treaty shall mean that a Member State has a price performance that is sustainable and an average rate of inflation, observed over a period of one year before the examination, that does not exceed by more than 1½ percentage points that of, at most, the three best performing Member States in terms of price stability. Inflation shall be measured by means of the consumer price index on a comparable basis, taking into account differences in national definitions.

Article 2

The criterion on the government budgetary position referred to in the second indent of Article 109*j*(1) of this Treaty shall mean that at the time of the examination the Member State is not the subject of a Council decision under Article 104*c*(6) of this Treaty that an excessive deficit exists.

Article 3

The criterion on participation in the Exchange Rate Mechanism of the European Monetary System referred to in the third indent of Article 109*j*(1) of this Treaty shall mean that a Member State has respected the normal fluctuation margins provided for by the Exchange Rate Mechanism of the European Monetary System without severe tensions for at least the last two years before the examination. In particular, the Member State shall not have devalued its currency's bilateral central rate against any other Member State's currency on its own initiative for the same period.

Article 4

The criterion on the convergence of interest rates referred to in the fourth indent of Article 109*j*(1) of this Treaty shall mean that, observed over a period of one year before the examination, a Member State has had an average nominal long-term interest rate that does not exceed by more than 2 percentage points that of, at most, the three best performing Member States in terms of price stability. Interest rates shall be measured on the basis of long term government bonds or comparable securities, taking into account differences in national definitions. . . .

Article 6

The Council shall, acting unanimously on a proposal from the Commission and after consulting the European Parliament, the EMI or the ECB as the case may be, and the Committee referred to in Article 109c, adopt appropriate provisions to lay down the details of the convergence criteria referred to in Article 109j of this Treaty, which shall then replace this Protocol.

PROTOCOL ON CERTAIN PROVISIONS RELATING TO THE UNITED KINGDOM OF GREAT BRITAIN AND NORTHERN IRELAND

THE HIGH CONTRACTING PARTIES,

RECOGNIZING that the United Kingdom shall not be obliged or committed to move to the third stage of Economic and Monetary Union without a separate decision to do so by its government and Parliament,

NOTING the practice of the government of the United Kingdom to fund its borrowing requirement by the sale of debt to the private sector,

HAVE AGREED the following provisions, which shall be annexed to the Treaty establishing the European Community:

1. The United Kingdom shall notify the Council whether it intends to move to the third stage before the Council makes its assessment under Article 109j(2) of this Treaty.

Unless the United Kingdom notifies the Council that it intends to move to the third stage, it shall be under no obligation to do so. . . .

4. The United Kingdom shall retain its powers in the field of monetary policy according to national law. . . .

10. If the United Kingdom does not move to the third stage, it may change its notification at any time after the beginning of that stage. . . .

11. Notwithstanding Articles 104 and 109e(3) of this Treaty and Article 21.1 of the Statute, the government of the United Kingdom may maintain its Ways and Means facility with the Bank of England if and so long as the United Kingdom does not move to the third stage.

REFERENCES

ALLEN, P. R. (1986), 'The Ecu: Birth of a New Currency?' *Group of Thirty Occasional Papers*, 20 (New York).

—— (1988), 'The Ecu and Monetary Management in Europe', in P. de Grauwe and T. Peeters (eds.), *The Ecu and European Monetary Integration* (London, Macmillan).

Associazione Bancaria Italiana (1991), *Indagine conoscitiva sui sistemi creditizi nell'ambito della Comunità Europea* (Bancaria Editrice, Rome).

Association for the Monetary Union of Europe (1988), *Un programme pour l'action* (Paris).

—— (1990), *La Monnaie européenne, monnaie optionelle* (Paris).

BAER, G. and PADOA-SCHIOPPA, T. (1989a), 'The Werner Report Revisited', *Report on Economic and Monetary Union in the European Community* [Delors Report] (Luxemburg, Office for Official Publications of the European Communities).

—— (1989b), 'The ECU, the Common Currency and the Monetary Union', *Report on Economic and Monetary Union in the European Community* [Delors Report] (Luxemburg, Office for Official Publications of the European Communities).

Banca d'Italia (1992), *Proceedings of the Workshop on Payment System Issues in the Perspective of European Monetary Unification: Perugia, 22–3 November 1990* (Rome, Banca d'Italia).

Bank of England (1990), 'EMU Beyond Stage One: The Hard Ecu', mimeo.

Bank for International Settlements (1989), *Payment Systems in Eleven Developed Countries* (Basle).

—— (1990), *Report of the Committee on Interbank Netting Schemes of the Central Banks of the Group of Ten Countries* (Basle).

BARRO, R. (1984), 'Rules vs Discretion', *NBER Working Papers*, 1473.

—— and GORDON, R. (1983), 'Rules, Discretion and Reputation in a Model of Monetary Policy', *Journal of Monetary Economics*, 1 (July).

BASEVI, G., *et al.* (1975), 'The All Saints' Day Manifesto for European Monetary Union', *The Economist* (1 November).

BATTEN, D. S., *et al.* (1990), 'The Conduct of Monetary Policy in the Major Industrial Countries; Instruments and Operating Procedures', *IMF Occasional Papers*, 70.

BERGSTRAND, J. (1983), 'Is Exchange Rate Variability "Excessive"?' *New England Economic Review* (Sept./Oct.).

BINI SMAGHI, L. (1990), 'Progressing towards European Monetary Unification: Selected Issues and Proposals', *Temi di discussione*, 133 (Banca d'Italia).

Bini Smaghi, L. and Vori, S. (1990), 'Concorrenza, egemonia e unificazione monetaria', *Politica economica* (Dec.).

Bishop, G., *et al.* (1989), *1992 and Beyond: Market Discipline Can Work in the EC Monetary Union* (New York, Salomon Brothers).

Black, S. (1985), 'International Money and International Monetary Arrangements', in R. W. Jones and P. B. Kenen (eds.) *Handbook of International Economics*, ii (Amsterdam, North Holland).

Bordo, M. D., and Schwartz, A. (1987), 'The ECU. An Imaginary or Embrionic Form of Money: What Can We Learn from History?' in P. de Grauwe and T. Peeters (eds.), *The Ecu and European Monetary Integration* (London, Macmillan).

Branson, W. (1989), 'Trade Balances, Capital Mobility, and Fiscal Policy in the EC', *The EMS in Transition*, Report of a Conference organized by the Centre for Economic Policy Research and the Secretaria General de Comercio of the Ministero de Hacienda in Madrid, on 11 and 12 May 1989 (London, CEPR).

Brillembourg, A., and Schadler, S. M. (1979), 'A Model of Currency Substitution in Exchange Rate Determination, 1973–78', *IMF Staff Papers*, 3 (Sept.).

Buchanan, J. M., Rowley, C. K., and Tollison, R. D. (1986), *Deficits* (Oxford, Blackwell).

Casella, A., and Feinstein, J. (1988), 'Management of a Common Currency', *NBER Working Papers*, 2740.

Ciampi, C. A. (1989), 'An Operational Framework for an Integrated Monetary Policy in Europe', *Report on Economic and Monetary Union in the European Community* [Delors Report] (Luxemburg, Office for Official Publications of the European Communities).

Cohen, D. (1989), 'The Costs and Benefits of a European Currency', in M. De Cecco and A. Giovannini (eds.), *A European Central Bank? Perspectives on Monetary Unification after Ten Years of the EMS* (Cambridge, CUP).

Commission of the European Communities (1966), *The Development of a European Capital Market* [Segré Report] (Brussels).

—— (1977), *Inflation and Exchange Rates: Evidence and Policy Guidelines for the European Community* [Optica Report 1976] (Brussels).

—— (1981), *European Economy*, 10 (Nov.).

—— (1982a), 'Exchange Rate Variability and Interventions within the European Monetary System', mimeo.

—— (1982b), *Economic Forecasts 1982–1983* (May–June).

—— (1984), *Five Years of Monetary Cooperation in Europe* (doc. COM(84)125 def.).

—— (1985), *Completing the Internal Market* (White paper from the Commission to the European Council, Luxemburg).

—— (1990*a*), 'Economic and Monetary Union: The Economic Rationale and Design of the System', *Report from Brussels*, 185 (Mar.).

—— (1990*b*), 'One Market, One Money: An Evolution of the Potential Benefits and Costs of Forming an Economic and Monetary Union', *European Economy*, 44 (Oct.).

Committee of Governors of the Central Banks of the EEC Member States (1985), *Questions Relating to the Use of the Private Ecu*, Report of the Group of Experts chaired by Dalgaard, 55 (Oct.).

Committee for the Study of Economic and Monetary Union (1989), *Report on Economic and Monetary Union in the European Community* [Delors Report] (Luxemburg, Office for Official Publications of the European Communities).

COOPER, R. N. (1969), 'Macroeconomic Policy Adjustment in Interdependent Economies', *Quarterly Journal of Economics*, 1 (Feb.).

COTTO, M. (1987) 'L'ampliamento del Clearing dell'Ecu', *Bancaria*, 3 (Mar.).

DAM, D. W. (1976), *The Role of Rules in the International Monetary System* (Law and Economics Center Monograph, Miami).

Delegazione Italiana presso la Conferenza Intergovernativa sull'UEM (1991), 'La Banca Centrale Europea nella "seconda fase"', *Bollettino economico*, 17 (Banca d'Italia).

Deutsche Bundesbank (1982), *Report of the Deutsche Bundesbank for the Year 1981* (Frankfurt).

Ecu Newsletter (1983), By the Istituto Bancario San Paolo di Torino (Feb.).

—— (1987), By the Istituto Bancario San Paolo di Torino (Jan.).

Ernst & Young Management Consultants (1990), ed., *A Strategy for the Ecu*, Report prepared for the Association for the Monetary Union of Europe (London, Kogan Page).

FRANKEL, A. B., and MARQUARDT, J. C. (1983), 'Payment Systems: Theory and Policy', *Federal Reserve Board, International Finance Discussion Papers*, 216.

FRATIANNI, M., and PEETERS, T. (1978), eds., *One Money for Europe* (London, Macmillan).

FRENKEL, J. A. (1981), 'Flexible Exchange Rates, Prices and the Role of News, Lessons from the 1970s', *Journal of Political Economy*, 4 (Aug.).

—— and MUSSA, M. L. (1980), 'The Efficiency of the Foreign Exchange Market and Measures of Turbulence', *American Economic Review, Papers and Proceedings*, 2 (May).

FRIEDMAN, M. (1951), 'Commodity-Reserve Currency', *Journal of Political Economy*, 3 (June).

—— (1968), 'The Role of Monetary Policies', *American Economic Review*, 1 (Mar.).

GALLI, G., and MASERA, R. S. (1991), 'Fiscal Responsibility, Monetary Policy and the Exchange Rate', in L. McKenzie and S. Zamagni (eds.), *Value and Capital: Fifty Years Later* (London, Macmillan).

GIAVAZZI, F., and GIOVANNINI, A. (1989), *Limiting Exchange Rates Flexibility: The European Monetary System* (Cambridge, Mass., MIT Press).

—— and PAGANO, M. (1988), 'The Advantage of Tying One's Hands: EMS Discipline and Central Bank Credibility', *European Economic Review*, 5 (June).

GOLD, J. (1977), 'International Capital Movements under the Law of the International Monetary Fund', *IMF Pamphlet Series*, 21.

GOMEL, G., SACCOMANNI, F., and VONA, S. (1990), 'The Experience with Economic Policy Coordination: The Tripolar and the European Dimensions', *Temi di discussione*, 140 (Banca d'Italia).

GOODHART, C. (1986), 'Why do we Need a Central Bank', *Temi di discussione*, 57 (Banca d'Italia).

—— (1989), 'The Delors Report: Was Lawson's Reaction Justifiable?' *LSE Financial Markets Group, Special Papers*, 15.

GROS, D. (1988), 'The EMS and the Determination of the European Price Level', *CEPS Working Documents*, 34.

—— and THYGESEN, N. (1990), 'Concrete Steps Towards Monetary Union', in 'Governing Europe: The Single Market and Economic and Monetary Union', *CEPS Papers*, 44.

HAYEK, F. (1976), *The Denationalisation of Money* (Hobart papers—special, 70; London, Inst. of Economic Affairs).

HM Treasury (1943), *Proposals for an International Clearing Union* (London, HMSO).

—— (1989), *An Evolutionary Approach to Economic and Monetary Union* (London, HMSO).

—— (1990), 'Beyond Stage One', speech by the Chancellor, John Major, to the German Industry Forum, London, 20 June.

HOLTFRERICH, C. L. (1989), 'The Monetary Unification Process in Nineteenth-Century Germany: Relevance and Lessons for Europe Today', in M. De Cecco and A. Giovannini (eds.), *A European Central Bank? Perspectives on Monetary Unification after Ten Years of the EMS* (Cambridge, CUP).

HOOPER, P., and KOHLHAGEN, S. W. (1978), 'The Effect of Exchange Rate Uncertainty on the Prices and Volume of International Trade', *Journal of International Economics*, 4 (Nov.).

JOHNSON, H. G., and SWOBODA, A. K., (1973), eds., *The Economics of Common Currencies* (London, Allen & Unwin).

KENEN, P. B. (1969), 'The Theory of Optimal Currency Areas: An Eclectic View', in R. A. Mundell and A. K. Swoboda (eds.), *Monetary Problems of the International Economy* (Chicago, Univ. of Chicago Press).

References 277

—— (1979), 'Exchange Rate Instability: Measurement and Implications', Princeton University, International Finance Section, Research Memorandum.

—— (1983), 'A Note on the Volatility of Floating Exchange Rates', mimeo, Princeton University.

KNEESHAW, J. T., and VAN DEN BERGH, P. (1989), 'Changes in Central Bank Money Market Operating Procedures in the 1980s', *BIS Economic Papers*, 23.

LAIDLER, D. E. W. (1978), 'Difficulties with European Monetary Union', in M. Fratianni and T. Peeters (eds.), *One Money for Europe* (London, Macmillan).

LAMFALUSSY, A. (1989), 'Macro-coordination of Fiscal Policies in an Economic and Monetary Union in Europe', *Report on Economic and Monetary Union in the European Community* [Delors Report] (Luxemburg, Office for Official Publications of the European Communities).

LANYI, A., and SUSS, E. C. (1982), 'Exchange Rate Variability: Alternative Measures and Interpretation', *IMF Staff Papers*, 4 (Dec.).

LAROSIÈRE, J. DE (1989), 'First Stage towards the Creation of a European Reserve Bank: The Creation of a European Reserve Fund', *Report on Economic and Monetary Union in the European Community* [Delors Report] (Luxemburg, Office for Official Publications of the European Communities).

LEVICH, R. M. (1981), 'Overshooting in the Foreign Exchange Market', *Group of Thirty Occasional Papers*, 5 (New York).

—— (1987), 'The Primary Market for Ecu Bonds', in R. M. Levich (ed.), *European Currency Unit: Ecu* (London, Euromoney Publications).

LÉZARDIÈRE, A. DE (1987), 'The Ecu Swap Market', in R. M. Levich (ed.), *European Currency Unit: Ecu* (London, Euromoney Publications).

LINDBECK, A. (1976), ed., 'Flexible Exchange Rates and Stabilization Policy', Proceedings of a Conference at Saltsjöbaden, Stockholm, 26–7 Aug. 1975, *The Scandinavian Journal of Economics*, 2.

—— (1977), 'International Coordination of National Economic Policies', in S. I. Katz (ed.), *US–European Monetary Relations* (Washington, DC, American Enterprise Institute for Public Policy Research).

LOUIS, J.-V. (1989), ed., *Vers un système européen de banques centrales* (Brussels, Éditions de l'Université Libre de Bruxelles).

LUCAS, R., and SARGENT, T. (1981), *Rational Expectations and Econometric Practice* (Minneapolis, Univ. of Minnesota Press).

MASCIANDARO, D., and RISTUCCIA, S. (1988), eds., *L'autonomia delle banche centrali* (Milan, Edizioni Comunità).

MASERA, R. S. (1986), 'An Increasing Role for the Ecu', *Temi di discussione*, 65 (Banca d'Italia).

MENGER, K. (1892), 'On the Origin of Money', *Economic Journal*, 2 (June).

MICOSSI, S., and PADOA-SCHIOPPA, T. (1984), 'Short-Term Interest Rates Linkages between the United States and Europe', *Temi di discussione*, 33 (Banca d'Italia).

MONNET, J. (1976), *Mémoires* (Paris, Fayard).

MUSGRAVE, R. (1958), *The Theory of Public Finance* (New York, McGraw Hill).

ORTIZ, G., and SOLIS, L. (1982), 'Currency Substitution and Monetary Independence: The Case of Mexico', in R. Cooper *et al.* (eds.), *The International Monetary System under Flexible Exchange Rates: Global, Regional and National* (Cambridge, Mass., Ballinger).

—— (1983), 'The Ecu: Exploring the Map', *Ecu Newsletter* (Feb.).

—— (1985a), 'Policy Cooperation and the EMS Experience', in W. H. Buiter and R. C. Marston (eds.), *International Economic Policy Cooperation* (Cambridge, CUP).

—— (1985b), 'Squaring the Circle, or the Conundrum of International Monetary Reform', *Catalyst*, 1.

PADOA-SCHIOPPA, T., *et al.* (1987), *Efficiency, Stability and Equity* (Oxford, OUP).

—— (1989), 'International Payment System: The Function Begets the Organ', International Symposium on Banking and Payment Services, Washington, 9 June, *Economic Bulletin*, 9 (Banca d'Italia).

—— (1990a), 'Verso quale banca centrale?', address to the Conference held to mark the start of the public activities of the Bresciani Turroni Foundation, Milan, 29 Jan. in *Matecon*, 2 (Feb.), 46–55.

—— (1990b), 'Financial and Monetary Integration in Europe: 1990, 1992 and Beyond', *Group of Thirty Occasional Paper*, 28 (New York).

—— (1991), 'Central Banks, Payment Systems and the Single Market', address to the Conference on the Consequences for Banking and Insurance of the Liberalization of Capital Movements, Brussels, October, *Economic Bulletin*, 12 (Banca d'Italia).

—— and PAPADIA, F. (1984), 'Competing Currencies and Monetary Stability', in R. S. Masera and R. Triffin (eds.), *Europe's Money* (Oxford, Clarendon Press).

PAPADIA, F. (1989), 'Une approche à l'unification monétaire européenne', *Revue d'Economie Financière*, 8–9 (Mar.–June).

PHELPS, E. (1972), *Inflation Policy and Unemployment Theory: The Cost Benefit Approach to Monetary Planning* (New York, Norton).

PLOEG, F. VAN DER (1989), 'Fiscal Aspects of Monetary Integration in Europe', *CEPR Discussion Papers*, 340.

POLAK, J. J. (1981), 'Coordination of National Economic Policies', *Group of Thirty Occasional Papers*, 7 (New York).

REBECCHINI, S., ROMA, A., TEODORI, G., and ZAUTZIK, E. A. (1991), 'I mercati monetari dei principali paesi europei e gli interventi delle banche centrali', *Rivista Bancaria*, 4 (July–Aug.).

ROGOFF, K. (1985), 'The Optimal Degree of Commitment to an Intermediate Monetary Target', *Quarterly Journal of Economics*, 403 (Nov.).

SACCOMANNI, F. (1990), 'Response to Daniel Gros and Niels Thygesen, "Concrete Steps towards Monetary Union"', in *Governing Europe: The Single Market and Economic and Monetary Union*, CEPS Papers, 44.

SCHNEIDER, H., HELLWIG, H. J., and KINGSMAN, D. J. (1986), *The German Banking System* (Frankfurt, Fritz Knapp).

STEINHERR, A. (1988) *Concrete Steps for Developing the ECU*, Report prepared by the ECU Banking Association Macrofinancial Group (Paris).

TABELLINI, G., and ALESINA, A. (1988), 'Voting on the Budget Deficit', *UCLA Working Papers*, 539.

THYGESEN, N. (1989a), 'A European Central Banking System: Some Analytical and Operational Considerations', in *Report on Economic and Monetary Union in the European Community* [Delors Report] (Luxemburg, Office for Official Publications of the European Communities).

—— (1989b), 'Have We Come Closer to Economic and Monetary Union?' speech given at the Royal Institute of International Affairs, Chatham House, 5 July.

TOBIN, J., and BRAGA DE MACEDO, J. (1980), 'The Short-Run Macroeconomics of Floating Exchange Rates: An Exposition', in J. S. Chipman and C. P. Kindleberger (eds.), *Flexible Exchange Rates and the Balance of Payments* (Amsterdam, North Holland).

TRIFFIN, R. (1960), *Gold and the Dollar Crisis* (New Haven, Conn., Yale UP).

TULLIO, G., and CONTESSO, F. (1986), 'The Determinants and Term Structure of Short-Term Ecu Interest Rates: October 1982–September 1985', *Economic Papers* (Commission of the European Communities).

UNGERER, H., EVANS, O., and NYBERG, P. (1983), 'The European Monetary System: The Experience 1979–1982', *IMF Occasional Papers*, 19.

—— et al. (1990), 'The European Monetary System: Developments and Perspectives', *IMF Occasional Papers*, 73.

WALLICH, H. C. (1972), *The Monetary Crisis of 1971: The Lessons to be Learned* (Washington, DC, The Per Jacobsson Foundation).

WALTER, N. (1976), 'Capital Controls and the Autonomy of National Demand Management: The German Case', in A. K. Swoboda (ed.), *Capital Movements and their Control* (Leiden, Sijthoff).

WERNER, P. (1970), *Report to the Council and the Commission on the Realization by Stages of Economic and Monetary Union* (Luxemburg, Office for Official Publications of the European Communities, Oct.).

YPERSELE, J. VAN, and KOEUNE, J. (1985), *Il sistema monetario europeo: origini, funzionamento e prospettive* (Luxemburg, Office for Official Publications of the European Communities).

INDEX